THE BALLERINAS

*From the Court of Louis XIV
to Pavlova*

ALSO BY PARMENIA MIGEL:

TITANIA: *The Biography of Isak Dinesen*

THE BALLERINAS

From the Court of Louis XIV

to Pavlova

Parmenia Migel

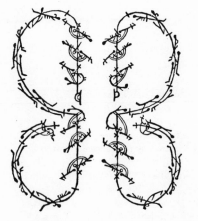

A DA CAPO PAPERBACK

Library of Congress Cataloging in Publication Data

Migel, Parmenia.
  The ballerinas, from the court of Louis XIV to
Pavlova.

  Reprint of the ed. published by Macmillan, New York.
  Bibliography: p.
  1. Dancers—Biography. 2. Ballet—History.
I. Title.
[GV1785.A1M47 1980]   792.8′2′0922 [B]   79-27155
ISBN 0-306-80115-9

This Da Capo Press paperback edition of
The Ballerinas: From the Court of Louis XIV to Pavlova
is an unabridged republication of the first edition
published in New York in 1972. It is reprinted
by arrangement with Macmillan Publishing Co., Inc.

Published by Da Capo Press, Inc.
A Subsidiary of Plenum Publishing Corporation
227 West 17th Street, New York, N.Y. 10011

For Francesco Menegatti

Contents

Illustrations

with titles as they appear on the original prints

---

*All illustrations are from the collection of the author,
except No. 6,* Barbara Campanini *by Antoine Pesne, courtesy of
Staatlichen Schlösser und Garten, Berlin.*

1   *Mademoiselle Subligny dansant a l'Opera*
Engraving by Jean Mariette (1660–1742).

2   *Isaac de Bensserade* Engraving by Gérard Edelinck (1640–1707).

3   *Jean-Baptiste Lulli*
Engraving by Dominique Sornique (1708–1756).

4   *Les Champs Elysees, c'est une Decoration du troisieme Acte de
l'Opera de VENUS IALOUSE*
Engraving by Aveline, Paris, from the design by
Giacomo Torelli (1604 or 1608–1678).

5   *Mademoiselle Prévost dansant à l'Opéra*
Engraving from the portrait by Jean Raoux, Musée des Beaux
Arts, Tours.

6   *Barbara Campanini*
Portrait by Antoine Pesne. Verwaltung der Staatlichen Schlösser
und Garten, Berlin.

7   *Choreography and Air for Menuet Dauphin and
Menuet d'Exaudet*
From M. Magny, *Principes de Chorégraphie*, Paris, 1765.

8   *Marie Sallé* Oil portrait, Ecole de Boucher, circa 1745.

9   *Mlle M^rie Sallé La Terpsichore Françoise*
Engraving by Petit from the painting by Jean-César Fenouil.

10   *Mlle Sallé*
Engraving by Nicolas de Larmessin from the painting by
Nicolas Lancret (1690–1743).

PHOTOGRAPHS BY NIKI EKSTROM

Preface

Until the comparatively recent invention of the cinema and more effective methods of dance notation, the Dance was an ephemeral art, and it was usually the fate of even the greatest ballerinas of the past to be forgotten as soon as they withdrew from the stage. When I began to write the history of the ballerinas, I had already been pursuing them for more than twenty years. For the most part they were elusive but this only made the chase more tantalizing. The trails meandered through capital cities, towns and villages, all over Europe, behind the Iron Curtain, and in America. Often enough the most promising clues led nowhere. On the other hand, it was sometimes an exciting reward to discover lost portraits and letters of dancers or, for instance, to locate the death certificate of the American Augusta Maywood in the basement of a church in Budapest (no one had ever been able to prove when or where she died) and to find and sentimentally place red roses on the grave of Lola Montez in Brooklyn.

What, one may ask, is a ballerina? For most people the word evokes a dancer in the romantic tulle costume known as a *tutu*, performing on the points of her toes, while to others it may suggest a svelte creature in skin tights, dashing off the acrobatics of the modern repertoire. For professionals of the dance world the word has only one meaning: it is, apart from the rarely bestowed title of *prima ballerina assoluta*, the highest rank to which a dancer can attain, after years of exhausting study and performance, and after working her way up through an established sequence of lesser grades. However, as derived from the Italian *ballare*, "to dance," ballerina is literally and simply a female dancer; this is the current use and the one we have observed in this book.

It is obviously impossible, in a single volume that covers more than two hundred years, to list every performance of every ballerina. For minutiae relating to the eighteenth century the reader is referred to *The London Stage, 1660–1800*, and the four great works of Emile Campardon (though even in this mine of official documents such milestones as Mlle Sallé's Paris Opéra appearances have been omitted) and also Pompeo Cambiasi's *La Scala, 1778–1889*. On the nineteenth century, a dozen books by the meticulous Ivor Guest offer a vast store of perfectly organized particulars.

Great variations in dates occur in most of the books about dancing. This is because the writers seldom were professional historians and were more interested in picturesque tales than in facts. Many actually were dancers, and the Dance, so the critics like to tell us, is an illiterate art. Newspapers are often an equally unreliable source, since reporters and critics have been known to record performances that never took place; nor can playbills and programs be wholly trusted because of last-minute cancellations and reassignments of roles. To resolve the problem of divergent dates I have attempted to coordinate the available information and opt for what seemed most logical and substantiated.

I should like to express my gratitude to Dr. Hans Horak of Vienna, Louis Jaffard of Paris, Dr. Elemèr Hankiss of Budapest, and Lucien Mars for their endless patience in the quest for Augusta Maywood; to Miss Helen Willard, Curator of the Harvard Theatre Collection, who even anticipates one's needs; Ivor Guest for permission to quote from his books; Norman Crider for his generous help in obtaining documentation; and Arthur Gregor, formerly of The Macmillan Company, for encouraging me to write this book. I am especially grateful to my husband Arne and son Niki for preserving their sense of humor while the work was in progress; and I cannot forget my indebtedness to the late Dr. William van Lennep and Ifan Kyrle Fletcher for the help and inspiration they gave me.

Part I
THE AGE OF LOUIS XIV

CHAPTER 1

The Beginnings

O<small>N THE UPPER WALLS</small> of the Foyer de la Danse at the Opéra de Paris there is a series of medallions painted by Gustave Boulanger which depict twenty of the famous ballerinas who appeared there from 1681 until the year 1860, when plans were drawn up for the present opera house. These are the Immortals of the Dance, not only of France but of Europe, since it was the ambition of every foreign ballerina in those days to perform in Paris. Among the twenty we find Camargo who was born in Brussels of Roman-Spanish descent, the German Anna Heinel, the Austrian Fanny Elssler, and half a dozen Italians. Wistful or proud, coquettish or demure, they gaze down upon their successors, as they have done for over a hundred years, and it is a commentary on the ephemeral nature of fame that many of them should be quite unknown today except to the most scholarly balletomanes.

No one can say with certainty who made up the list of ballerinas for Boulanger.[1] Vaillat, in his *Histoire de la Danse*, suggests that it may have been Arthur Saint-Léon, the Opéra's ballet master at that time. Whoever chose them was either prejudiced or careless, for he left out the Danish Lucile Grahn, soloist at the Opéra from 1839 to 1840 and a star of the renowned *Pas de Quatre;* nor did he include Pauline Leroux, Sofia Fuoco, and others, all of them more outstanding than Mlle Julia, for instance, or Thérèse Vestris, whose success was due to her influential lovers and the prestige of her brother Gaëtan. Nowadays such a list would present far greater difficulties. Considering Diaghilev's dancers and the many extraordinary performers in Europe and North and South America who emerged during the ensuing forty years, it is merely possible to indicate those who have brought some new or unique quality to the art of ballet.

The story of the great ballerinas begins with a glance at the background of the Opéra de Paris, because that institution soon became the world center and remained so until Russia took the lead at the end of the nineteenth century. Although elaborate dance productions were a feature at the courts of the Italian City States, and manuals to develop their form and technique were written in the early fifteenth century, the starting point of ballet history is usually set, quite arbitrarily, in France in 1581, when Beaujoyeulx staged the *Balet Comique de la Royne* for Catherine de' Medici.

However, the supremacy of French ballet dates from the time of Louis XIV. Throughout his long reign (1643–1715), the King commissioned entertainments known as court ballets, appearing in them personally from the age of twelve, when he had his first solo role in *Cassandre,* until he was thirty-one and became stout and self-conscious. Staged wherever the King was holding court—at the Louvre or the Palais Royal in Paris, at Saint-Germain-en-Laye, Versailles, or Fontainebleau—these spectacles still bore a general resemblance to the *Balet Comique de la Royne,* though they were less dramatic in concept. They combined *récits* (sung monologues), choruses, and dancing. The ballet interludes began with pageantlike *entrées,* and the dancers, who were mainly courtiers, were then deployed according to floor patterns or went through the evolutions of stately sarabandes, allemandes, or minuets. Professionals, who had long been respected figures in Italy, were first seen at the French court about 1630 and only in comic roles. Not until 1659 were some of the favored ones allowed to join the nobles in the *grand ballet,* which was the finale of every presentation, and even then it gave them little scope for a serious career.

A few details concerning the *Ballet de la Nuit,* performed several times during February and March 1653, will give a notion of the scale of Louis XIV's entertainments. At least eight composers collaborated with the poets and designers; the machinists, with only oil lamps at their disposal, produced realistic sunset, night or day effects, as well as rain, clouds that moved, air-borne goddesses, and even a house on fire; the cast, in addition to the courtiers and musicians, included seventy-two professionals; and fifty-three *entrées,* lasting thirteen hours, from six o'clock until dawn, did not deter people from sitting through the whole thing more than once.

In 1663 Parliament established the Académie Royale de Danse, an august body of thirteen who dealt mostly with theoretical problems. Finally, in 1669, the King founded the Académie Royale de Musique et de Danse, popularly known as the Opéra. The Abbé Pierre Perrin, first of a long line of sorely tried Opéra directors, made a start two years later with *Pomone* in the Jeu de Paume de la Bouteille, a building formerly used for court tennis, but before the season ended he was replaced by Jean-Baptiste Lully, who inaugurated a similarly improvised theatre the following autumn. Meanwhile, the unfortunate Abbé, swindled by his partners, spent fifteen of the intervening twenty months in jail for nonpayment of debts. He did, however, leave Lully a heritage of gifted singers and dancers, particularly the ballet master Beauchamps. For two decades this great performer and teacher choreographed most of the court ballets, and he is also credited with defining the basic five positions of the feet which are the foundation of all ballet technique.

Lully, though he is remembered principally for his music, was also a competent and ambitious administrator, skilled in every aspect of stagecraft. Working with Beauchamps, the designer Berain, and the witty topical librettist Benserade, he composed all the scores and assisted in the production of thirty court ballets and danced in them besides, meanwhile doing just as much to help Molière put on his comedies at the Palais Royal. When Molière died in 1673, he had enjoyed exclusive use of this stage for twelve years, and his beautiful young widow expected to continue there when she took over the responsibility of directing his troupe. Lully, however, thought otherwise. Having once coveted the Abbé Perrin's position, he now cast his eye on what seemed a far better opera house than his own, and Mme Molière was forced to move to the tiny Théâtre Guénégaud.

At the Palais Royal Lully effected a great forward step for professional dancing. Ignoring all complaints about his tyrannical methods, he imposed regular classes and rehearsals and obtained a royal edict forbidding dancers to appear anywhere in France without his permission. He reserved for himself, too, the right to compose all the opera-ballets, and since they were livelier than the sedate music which prevailed at court, the dancers were able to display their technical progress. First to star was Louis Pécourt, who also wrote one of the earliest tracts on dance notation [2]; he was followed in 1691 by Beauchamps' nephew Blondy, famous for his elevation and character roles, and Jean Balon, who was so esteemed for his abilities and good looks that he was permitted to shake hands with Louis XIV and keep his hat on in the royal presence, privileges shared only by Le Nôtre, the inspired landscape gardener of Versailles.

Oddy enough, the Opéra existed for twelve years before the first professional ballerinas were allowed on the stage. During all that time women's roles were taken by boys, which was all the more extraordinary because both Lully and Beauchamps took part in court ballets (*Alcidiane*, 1658; *La Raillerie*, 1659; *L'Impatience*, 1661; and others), when professional women appeared together with the ladies of the court and the usual young men—Saint-André, La Pierre, and Favier—made up as nymphs and shepherdesses.

The novelty of having ballerinas at the Opéra was prompted by the success of *Le Triomphe de l'Amour*, produced for Louis XIV at Saint-Germain-en-Laye in January 1681. For the occasion Lully, of course, composed the music, Berain designed costumes more sumptuous than ever, and the old poet and roué Benserade was dragged out of retirement to write the lyrics. Nevertheless, it was the ladies who triumphed. The critics gave special praise to the Dauphine and to the eight-year-old daughter of the King and Madame de Montespan, little Mademoiselle de Nantes, who not only danced but also played the castanets, an art, handed down from the Egyptians via Rome and Spain, then very popular in Paris. The following May a shortened version of the same ballet was shown at the Opéra, and Lully, not to be outdone, presented four professionals with the lead taken by:

Mlle de la Fontaine
1655–1738

NOT MUCH INFORMATION has come to light about "*la première des premières danseuses.*" [3] When she made her debut she was hailed immediately as "Queen of the Dance." "Who else, since she was the first?" remarked one critic. Others described her as prodigious, or noble—probably the apter adjective since her voluminous velvet and damask robes must have lent a dignified rather than sprightly quality to her dancing.

As for the three dancers who came on the scene with her, ballet historians disagree as to who they were and proffer their own lists. Claims are variously made for Mlles Pesant, Carré, Leclerc, Lepeintre, and Fernon, for Mlle de Subligny, who actually did not make her debut until 1688, for Mlle Roland who married the Marquis de Saint-Geniès, and for the lovely Mlle Des Mastins, who began as a dishwasher in a restaurant, became an accomplished singer when she grew too fat to dance, and died of overeating. Today little remains of these enchantresses except their names, some poems that they inspired, and a few portrait engravings.

✗ The public, first admitted to court ballets in 1630, became the Opéra's faithful patrons during the reign of Mlle de la Fontaine. Discriminating and demanding, they were also very rowdy. Spectators brought dogs into the hall, were often drunk, joined loudly in the singing, and shouted criticism or approval of the performers. Duels, although forbidden by law, were not unusual. An undesirable seat or imagined slight to a favorite actress was pretext enough for swords to be drawn in the theatre; arguments were then settled on the pavement outside, and the survivors, if any, were jailed or banished from the city. Tempers, no doubt, were sharpened by an opera house that was uncomfortable, cold, and badly lighted. The brackets of wax candles, proudly introduced by Molière in 1663, were so inadequate that individuals sat clutching candles of their own and sometimes started fires.

Indignation rose over poor fare on the stage, and the wits circulated a steady stream of verses and street songs, occasionally praising singers and dancers but mostly deriding them for their incompetence, for getting old or fat, or for their loose morals. The poems, preserved in manuscript at the Bibliothèque Nationale, are a main source of information about the appearance of the performers, their comings and goings, and especially their love affairs.

No scandal seems to have attached to the name of Mlle de la Fontaine. We are told, in fact, that she relinquished her career for the gentler customs of the Church. Though she lived on until the fourth decade of the eighteenth century, in 1690 the "Queen of the Dance" passed her sceptre to:

Marie-Thérèse Perdou de Subligny
1666–1736

MLLE DE SUBLIGNY was the daughter of a man who neglected her education, though he himself held a law degree, was an actor and the author of several plays, and also the person to whom some scholars attribute the much contested honor of editing (if not actually writing) the *Letters of a Portuguese Nun*. For seventeen years she was the Opéra's mainstay, dancing in nearly all the important productions with Balon and Blondy as her partners. Much admired for her expressive eyes and pretty figure and for remaining modest in spite of her success, she nevertheless was criticized for not having her knees and feet sufficiently turned out. Considering the long costumes worn at the time, it is a wonder that this defect was noticeable. Perhaps, like Mlle Des Mastins, she dared to shorten her skirts now and then, or perhaps, like another of her contemporaries, Mlle Maupin, she sometimes enjoyed appearing in male attire. Mlle de Subligny was also one of the first French Opéra dancers to conquer London. She crossed the Channel bearing letters of introduction to the philosopher John Locke from two of the most distinguished personalities in France, the Abbé Dubos and Fontenelle.[4] Locke was then in his sixties, in ill health and living in semiretirement in Essex, but he must have succumbed to Mlle de Subligny's charms because, as Fontenelle later reported, he offered to manage her business affairs. We hear of her last in 1735, when she was no longer the gentle creature she had been but a short-tempered old lady. She emptied a chamber pot onto the head of the violinist Francoeur and then brought suit against him but was not able to sign the plea. In spite of her learned father and literary friends, she could neither read nor write.

On this rather grotesque note Mlle de Subligny makes her exit, and it can be said that with her the first phase of opera-ballet came to an end. Her partner Balon was by then an old man, past eighty. Beauchamps had died long ago. Lully had been dead for forty-eight years, but the old tyrant had so entrenched himself that one of his sons became director of the Opéra, and after him another son, and finally his son-in-law Francine. The public, too, had grown so accustomed to the music of Lully that for half a century after his death they cared for nothing else. When Campra took office, the poets jeered: "Accept some sound advice from your friends, Campra; leave the conduct of the Opéra to others and let them try to replace Lully." Of the bygone days only the buoyant Blondy was still active. His career as dancer was ending, but he became an outstanding teacher, and many of his pupils were the celebrated performers of the future. First of these was the *première danseuse* who succeeded Mlle de Subligny:

Françoise Prévost

1680–1741

If Françoise Prévost belongs to the early period because of her dates and because of her training with Blondy, she is also quite at home among the innovators of the eighteenth century. She had the good luck to make her initial appearance in a 1699 revival of Lully's *Atys*. Louis XIV once asked Madame de Maintenon which she liked best of all the operas, and she replied that *Atys* was her favorite. "Ah," sighed the enamored King, "*Atys* is too fortunate!" For twenty-three years this opera-ballet had been equally popular with the public, and every time it was performed an eager crowd packed the theatre. So the new ballerina came in on a wave of enthusiasm, and it was obvious from the start that she too would become a favorite. Noble . . . elegant . . . graceful . . . ethereal, reported the journalists. They had said much the same about her predecessors, but Mlle Prévost had a new quality besides. She had the gift of eloquent expression and could move an audience to tears. Though she was chosen to replace Mlle de Subligny in 1705, her great moment came in 1714 at a private performance in the Duchesse du Maine's little theatre at the Château de Sceaux, when she and the aging but still agile Balon danced a mime interpretation of the final scene of Corneille's *Horace* to music especially composed by Mouret. "The effect produced was tremendous. The actors on the stage, the distinguished spectators, were all of them weeping." The event was a personal triumph for the ballerina, and as an attempt to express "the manners and passions of mankind" in dance it was also a landmark in the development of French ballet.

Françoise Prévost added further to her laurels in 1720 when she created *Les Caractères de la danse*, a solo *divertissement* designed to display all the aspects and moods of dancing. Not long after, it became a sort of showpiece for both Camargo and Sallé, and two centuries later a book devoted to this one ballet was published with a portrait of the dancer who created it and the original score by Jean-Ferry Rebel. However, no attempt to reconstruct or revive it on the stage has been made in modern times.

To grow old is sad; for dancers it is often a tragedy. Long before she retired Mlle Prévost began to teach at the Opéra's School of the Dance.[5] She taught so well, and her pupils were so apt, that they soon outstripped their instructress. They had, besides, the allure and the daring of youth and a fresh approach to their art. To the fading *première danseuse* it was evident that the time had come to abdicate, but she did not accept the fact with the grace which had been so characteristic of her dancing. Bitterness led her into acts of petty jealousy. But that is part of a later tale. . . . Meanwhile, the new era had arrived when ballerinas would compete with men in technical virtuosity and would set the trends for ballet as we know it today.

Part II
THE EIGHTEENTH CENTURY

CHAPTER 2

Marie Sallé

1707–1756

W E KNOW THE NAMES of her friends and the men who were in love with her; we know in which houses she lived, and a precise list has survived of all the possessions large and small that she accumulated; the performances of her adult career are all on record—and yet she remains a mysterious and elusive figure. Even during her lifetime legends about her flourished: that she had been a child prodigy; that she was a paragon of virtue, a "vestal virgin" who scorned men and the fortunes they laid at her feet; that she was the inventor of a completely new style of dancing. . . . But many of the tales were false or grossly exaggerated. She sat for famous painters; celebrated writers composed poems in praise of her and mentioned her in their books and correspondence; and like Mlle de Subligny she spent much time in the company of intellectuals, but not one of her remarks was ever directly quoted, and her only remaining letter, written when she was thirty-five, is a pathetic jumble of non-grammar and naive spelling. Was she unhappy? Whom, if anyone, did she love? We shall probably never know, and perhaps that is just as well. "There are some half-tone portraits," said her biographer Emile Dacier, "portraits which do not gain by having too strong a light focused upon them."

The child prodigy story was true enough. On October 18, 1716, the Lincoln's Inn Fields theatre in London announced a play, *The Unhappy Favorite*, followed by "Dancing. Serious and comic, by two children, Scholars of M. Balon, lately arrived from the Opera at Paris (M and Mlle Salle), particularly *Two Punchanellos, Two Harlequins* and a *Dame Ragonde*, the Harlequins to be perform'd by the two children." The manager John Rich was carrying on the theatre's policy of presenting French dancers, a tradition begun some thirty years earlier when his predecessor Betterton imported Mlle de Subligny and Balon. Other dancers in the company had also come from Paris, but the main attraction was the children, who were very young indeed. Marie Sallé, according to French official records, was born in 1707, so she was only nine when she made her debut in London, but she had a touching quality as well as talent, and the British public was very sentimental about child actors. After Marie and her brother had performed almost nightly for two months, their engagement came to an end, but three days later another announcement was posted: "In Consideration of the Diversion the French Children have given the Town, Mr Rich has engag'd their Stay in England for some time longer, and on Thursday next they will perform again." So they went on with the strenuous program until the middle of June, appearing once in a *French Scene* with their father and once as guest artists at the King's Theatre—more than a hundred performances in all.

As the child of a large theatrical family, Marie Sallé was already experienced when she began her first London season. Her uncle, François Moylin, known to the public as "Francisque," was a versatile comedian-harlequin-tumbler and the director of a company of itinerant actors who traveled around the small towns of France and turned up at yearly intervals to perform at the fairs in Paris. The troupe included Moylin's brother Simon, his sister and her husband the acrobat Sallé, and another sister married to the clown Cochois, whose son and daughters Babet and Marianne also went on the stage. A long history lay behind the wandering companies. Most popular and most persistent were the Italians, and there were laws governing their performances as early as the year 1200. Famous later on as Les Comédiens Italiens du Roi, they were banned by Louis XIV because of their bawdiness and their biting parodies which made fun of even the King's entourage, but they came back again and again, eventually evolving into the present day Opéra Comique. At the beginning of the eighteenth century, Italian, French, and other players all congregated in Paris each spring and summer for the Foire Saint-Germain, the Foire Saint-Laurent, and lesser fairs—showmen with trained animals, puppets and marionettes, rope dancers and jugglers, ballad singers, vaudeville artists, and actors in plays or operettas.

In this hurly-burly Marie Sallé grew up and got her early training. She is first billed at the fair in *La Princesse de Carisme* (1718), a three-act comic opera in which a number of children played minor roles, and her brother's name and hers have been discovered on the programs of two other operettas, *Deucalion* (1722) and *Claperman* (1724). From the very start she must have shown a special aptitude for dancing, because her family arranged to have her study with Françoise Prévost, Balon, and Blondy, and she even made a brief appearance at the Opéra one evening in July 1721, when the *première danseuse* was ill and offered her pupil "as a slight consolation to the public." It turned out that the audience was more than consoled, and the enthusiasm did not at all please Mlle Prévost, who was now past forty and resented the success of younger dancers.

But, at the moment, little Mlle Sallé was no threat to Françoise Prévost. She was to have four more years of touring the provinces; her uncle's troupe would also return for the annual run in Paris in spite of increasing hardships at the fairs. Each season the authorities passed new laws favoring the resident companies since the Comédiens-Français wanted no competition from other actors, and the Opéra objected to any rival production that included singing or dancing. Francisque tried out a dozen schemes to dodge the restrictions, was sent to jail, and for a while was obliged to take refuge in England.

In 1725 Marie Sallé and her brother went to London, too, remaining there from October of that year until June 1727. Once more they were welcomed at Lincoln's Inn Fields together with other performers from France, and again they went through their routine of solo dances and *pas de deux* between the acts, with additional roles in the featured pantomimes. Mlle Sallé was also seen several times in Françoise Prévost's old show piece *Les Caractères de la danse*.

When she returned to Paris it was for her debut at the Opéra, and she was no longer a wonder child but a young woman of twenty and a mature artist, though she would be confronting an audience for the first time without the support of her brother. She knew she would also have to face Mlle Prèvost's ill-humor, the challenge of the popular new ballerina Camargo, and perhaps a cool reception from the French critics, but her experience with provincials and good-natured Britishers had not prepared her for the corrupt atmosphere at the opera house in the Palais Royal. Parisians were still far from imagining the orgies of immorality that would mark the period of Marie-Madeleine Guimard, but already they seemed disappointed if a dancer did not openly flaunt a lover . . . or several; and backstage all the performers were competing for patrons and promotions. Modest Mlle Sallé preferred to avoid any sort of scandal, and people were quick to sense that only her art was important to her. If there were many partisans of Camargo's dizzying technical feats, there were soon nearly as many who understood and admired Marie Sallé's sincerity, gentle grace, and expressive miming.

During her first and second engagements at the Opéra (1727-30 and 1731-32) she had leading roles in nearly all the important presentations, and a special success with her own new version of *Les Caractères de la danse*, no longer a solo but rearranged as a *pas de deux*, with Antoine Laval, to give herself more scope for acting. She also had her share of roles in the ballets at court, where she was much admired. Her reputation was growing, and she made many friends, among them Fontenelle, Voltaire, and his young protégé Thieriot, who fell in love with her and remained her abject slave for a dozen years. She seemed, however, neither flattered by all the attention nor happy. She missed her brother, who had stayed behind in London to get married and so, she felt, was lost to her for good. Besides, the press and public and her friends all made too much of the rivalry between Camargo and herself. Lancret added to it by painting similar portraits of them, and even her devoted Voltaire was moved to dedicate a poem to both ballerinas:

> *Ah! Camargo, que vous êtes brilliante,*
> *Mais que Sallé, grands dieux, est ravissante! . . .*

Camargo might leap like the Nymphs, but the Graces themselves must have danced like Sallé, he concluded. Far too much was also said, publicly and privately, about her having no love affair that anyone could discover. Her aura of virtue, one of the "wonders of the Opéra," seemed a source of constant amazement. Was she amused or annoyed at being acclaimed as a vestal virgin or priestess of Diana? Was she perhaps leading a secret life and laughing covertly at everyone?

More than anything else, the Opéra itself was a cause of dissatisfaction. Only sixty years had passed since the first opening, but already it was suffering from a sort of spiritual paralysis. Many of the stilted and tedious aspects of the court ballets had survived during Lully's regime and, along with his operas, were still in vogue. "The

celestial music of Lully's times has degenerated, and is still degener-
ating," lamented the Marquis d'Argenson in 1739. As in Louis XIV's
day, the dancers still had their *entrées* to their preferred pieces of
music, whether or not these airs suited the action of the work being
performed or were even by the same composer. They refused to
consider any change and on the subject of costumes were just as
arbitrary. The taller the coiffures and feather headdresses, the more
voluminous the skirts and panniers, the more glittering with sequins
and jewels, the better pleased they were. Elaborate costumes had
become a matter of prestige, and no one cared if such regalia was
incompatible with the roles of ancient Greeks, for instance, or
Indians or peasants. Nor did anyone mind if freedom of movement
was hampered. The male dancers also wore traditional masks, which
deprived them of any emotional expression. To Marie Sallé all of
this was stifling, and she quarreled with the director.

Between her two Paris engagements she escaped to England for
several months to dance for the last time at Lincoln's Inn Fields and,
for the last time, too, with the beloved brother who had been her
comrade and partner since their childhood. Though her special claim
to immortality would not be apparent until 1734, her popularity in
London was now at its height. The royal family attended her benefit
performance, and there was a stampede for tickets in spite of the
fact that prices were almost doubled. The details, with all the customary embellishments of the Paris press, preceded her when she
returned to the Opéra, adding lustre to her reputation at home, but
she found conditions there as little to her liking as before. In June
came the blow of her brother's sudden death in London. He died
while she was far from him, and she was heartbroken. Nevertheless,
on July 8, she gave one of her best performances in *Le Ballet des
sens*. Voltaire saw her in that ballet and dispatched a letter about
it to his protégé. Astonishing and admirable, he reported. The public
was ecstatic, and even Mlle Prévost relented and expressed her

approval. "I have been to call on Mlle Sallé as often as possible," he told Thieriot. He found her not at all well and deeply affected by the loss of her brother.

Soon after, it was bruited around that the ballerina would depart for England again, but the rumors were premature. She left the Opéra at the end of 1732, and a full year passed before she crossed the Channel. In the meanwhile, her life was not lacking in excitement. Toward spring at the theatre of the Comédie-Italienne, preparations were under way for an entertainment with music by Mouret to be followed by *Le Bouquet*, a one-act play in verse by Riccoboni and Romagnesi. Mlle Sallé was invited to participate, and several reasons must have tempted her to accept. Apart from two private appearances for the Comte de Clermont and the Duc de Lorge, she had been idle for many months and certainly felt the urge to be dancing again. Besides, the authors of *Le Bouquet* were old friends. Jean-Antoine Romagnesi, son, grandson, and great-grandson of Italian actors, was playing at the fairs when Marie was a child performer there with her uncle's troupe; and Antoine-François Riccoboni was the son of the famous "Lelio," whom she saw often in 1727 while he was in London on leave from his theatre. She could be sure that the Comédie-Italienne would not only welcome her as a dancer but would be far more receptive to her ideas and her as yet unfulfilled choreographic ambitions than the reactionary Opéra had been. She had, however, overlooked the long-standing rivalry between the two institutions. The director of the Opéra was furious at what he considered her disloyalty. He sent a formal complaint to the King's minister, and the minister notified Mlle Sallé that she would be locked up in the prison of For-l'Evêque if she attempted to appear with the Italians.

At the same time, some foolish gossip was started about her marrying Riccoboni. Mlle Sallé had no such inclinations; and as for Riccoboni, he was soon to marry the beautiful and notorious Marie-Jeanne de Mézières whose career was later summed up by a malicious critic: "Mme Riccoboni, wit, author, courtesan, but a most incompetent actress, was cast as the romantic heroine some twenty-six years ago; because of age and overweight she had to give this up and play only the mothers, a role which she was never able to achieve in private life, although she worked at it tirelessly for forty-five years."

After all the commotion, *Le Bouquet* was presented by the Italians in August without the participation of Marie Sallé. A few weeks later she was off to London accompanied by the youngest of the three lively Malters [6] who was to be her dancing partner in place of the adored brother.

John Rich had moved to the new theatre at Covent Garden, and there Marie Sallé created the ballets which made her name one of the most important in ballet history. The season of 1733–34 began quietly enough with the usual offerings and few novelties, but when *Pigmalion* was presented on February 14, Mlle Sallé triumphed on three scores at once; she realized her dream of being a choreographer and had an unprecedented success, she was acclaimed as a dancer and mime capable of every nuance of feeling and expression, and she imposed her own notion of costume, which was the very antithesis of the tinsel and clutter so dear to the Opéra. She wore (she *dared* to wear, said a French journalist) a simple muslin dress, draped in the style of classic Greek sculpture, slippers without heels, and her hair, without any ornament, fell loosely around her shoulders. The ballet itself received the highest praise as a work of great originality, and was cited from then on as the forerunner of Noverre's invention, the *ballet d'action*—the type of ballet which really told a story, rather than being a series of unrelated *entrées*.

After a number of performances, *Pigmalion* was again on the program of Marie Sallé's benefit on March 21. Eyewitnesses never forgot the excitement of that gala evening. Crowds besieged the theatre and were unable to force their way inside. The ballerina appeared in a solo dance and a *pas de trois* as well as her own ballet, and at the end when she came out to bow and acknowledge the applause, she was pelted with flowers and gifts, and gold guineas rained down upon the stage. Within the week she was seen in another composition of her own, *Bacchus and Ariadne*, and both ballets remained the rage of London until the summer closing.

There were two rather mystifying occurrences before the season ended. On May 7 the widow of Marie's brother shared the proceeds of a benefit at the theatre with a Mrs. Cantrell. Nothing has been found out about the origins of this sister-in-law. Listed on the program of Covent Garden as: "Mrs Salle, the first time of her appearing on that stage," she may have been a small-town actress or was perhaps taking her chance at a completely new career. The benefit for a newcomer was obviously a friendly gesture toward Mlle Sallé and the memory of her popular brother, and must have been an almost too moving occasion for the ballerina. Then, on May 24, *The Necromancer*, in which she had a leading role, was abruptly canceled, and the theatre register noted: "by reason Madem Salle wou'd not come to the House." Could not because of illness or accident would be understandable, but "wou'd not" is very strange.

All in all, it had been Marie Sallé's most successful year. As was to be expected, the Paris newspapers again made capital of her triumphs. Wild tales were printed about her revolutionary ideas, about her salary, and about a huge sum supposedly offered by a would-be lover and refused because of the ballerina's unassailable virtue.

In view of such recognition it is a pity to inject a note of doubt concerning the originality of Marie Sallé's choreography and costumes. Yet it is necessary to point out that at Drury Lane Theatre, as early as 1717, the English dancing master and choreographer John Weaver staged the first of several works which must be considered action ballets. Mlle Sallé was dancing in London the year he pro-

duced his ballet-pantomime *The Loves of Mars and Venus*, and
whether or not she saw it has always been a moot question. And if
she did see it, could she really have been much influenced since she
was a mere child of ten at the time? It is more reasonable to assume
that she learned the details from Louis Dupré, who appeared in it as
Mars and fourteen years later became her dancing partner at the
Opéra. Nor is it likely that she was unfamiliar with Weaver's books,
in which he set forth many of the very principles which she and
Noverre later expressed—Marie Sallé in the ballets she composed,
and Noverre in his ballets, too, but mainly in his great treatise
Lettres sur la Danse. Furthermore, those flowing locks of Sallé's
which caused such a stir were not a novelty. England's lovely
actress-dancer Hester Santlow, who played Venus in Weaver's
ballet, was remembered long after in a published article: ". . . Santlow contrived to loosen her clustering auburn hair, and letting it fall
about such a neck and shoulders as Praxiteles could more readily
imagine than imitate, danced on, the locks flying in the air, and half
a dozen hearts at the end of every one of them." [7]

In direct contrast with 1734, Mlle Sallé's next season began well
and ended in catastrophe. Handel had been in London off and on
for many years; his opera *Rinaldo* was, in fact, the main feature of
the program at the King's Theatre when the two Sallé children
danced there in 1717. Now he was asked to join John Rich's company at Covent Garden, and betwen November and April the public
heard five of his operas, into which he inserted ballet numbers ex-
pressly arranged for Marie Sallé. First of these was a sort of pastiche
entitled *Terpsichore*, which he wrote for her as a prologue to his
Pastor Fido. Variously inspired by an earlier *Terpsichore*, danced by
Mlle Prévost at the Opéra, by some of Mlle Sallé's previous solo
pieces, and by the mime-dance version of *Horace* performed for
the Duchesse du Maine, it was nevertheless a moving and successful work, and is of special interest as the only complete ballet for

which Handel wrote the music. Mlle Sallé also revived many of the favorites of past seasons and even *Pigmalion*, but the temper of the audience had changed, and suddenly she was no longer an idol.

On April 16, in a ballet she devised for Handel's *Alcina*, she made the mistake of appearing dressed as a boy and experienced the humiliation of being hissed. Afterwards, several critics rebuked the spectators for their bad manners, and some suggested that the attack on the ballerina actually was directed against Handel by a rival opera group. The cabal, in fact, roused the press in defense of Handel, who lost his audience whenever Mlle Sallé was not posted. "Handel," said the *Old Whig*, March 20, "whose excellent Compositions have often pleased our Ears, and touched our Hearts, has this Winter sometimes performed to an almost empty Pitt. He has lately reviv'd his fine Oratorio of Esther. . . . But so strong is the Disgust taken against him, that even this has been far from bringing him crowded Audiences; tho' there were no other publick Entertainments on those Evenings."

Just the same, the angry reaction of the audience is more difficult to analyze than appears on the surface, since other women dancers in male attire, including Hester Santlow, were previously applauded. It is possible that Mlle Sallé, conscientious actress that she was, overplayed the role and that people were shocked by a too unfeminine performance. Possibly, too, there were already rumors afloat in London of what became a few weeks later a minor scandal. For, on the return journey to France, Mlle Sallé committed her first open indiscretion: she made the Channel crossing with a dancer from the Drury Lane Theatre, Mlle Manon Grognet, who later married the Marquis d'Argens, but at this time was the butt of Paris muckrakers because of her lesbian tendencies.

Immediately Marie Sallé was also lampooned in coarse and outspoken verse. The attacks were cruel, but at last, it seemed, there was a realistic explanation of her fame as a virtuous woman. Men who were in love with her felt foolish and cheated; they had publicized her faultless morals only to discover a different and humbling truth: she had no interest in them, and was simply a person with less conventional inclinations. Voltaire, past master of sarcasm, did not spare her; others turned against her, too, including Voltaire's protégé, though obviously he could not get along without her. Eight years later we still hear of him. He is described in her letter as "that boring Thieriot," sitting patiently with the woman friend who shared her life, waiting for Marie to return from a country weekend.

In the hostility of her homecoming from London, assailed by the press, which magnified every detail of the debacle at Covent Garden, and abandoned by her friends, she was more in need of encouragement and devotion than at any moment except after the death of her brother. Though she had never been happy at the Opéra, it may have assuaged her pride and hurt feelings to know that she was wanted there now. In August 1735 she began her last and longest Paris engagement, and there were three major compensations: Jean-Philippe Rameau, the first great composer since the time of Lully, had appeared, and she not only danced in his ballets but was also allowed to express some of her own choreographic ideas; she no longer had to contend with the rivalry of Camargo, who had left the Opéra and would remain in retirement for six years; and finally, in David Dumoulin, she had the best partner of her whole career, a performer who combined excellent technique with a rare gift of expression.

Sallé opened the season in Rameau's *Les Indes galantes*, as the Rose in the flower scene, a rather banal *divertissement* which she revised very successfully later in the year. The opera, almost a failure at the start, gained in popularity and was performed more than twenty times. The grace and finesse of Mlle Sallé's dancing also reconquered her fickle public. But "one swallow maketh not summer," says the proverb, nor did a work of Rameau, or even several, mean that the Opéra had abandoned its rigid policies. In the schedule of new ballets one mediocrity followed another, and soon all the old warmed-over fare was back on the program— *Thétis et Pelée* (1689) and even Madame de Maintenon's favorite, *Atys* (1676). And when Sallé was again permitted to choreograph a scene for herself in June 1736, it was not in the sort of ballet that she approved, a *ballet d'action* with unity of design, but in a revival of *L'Europe galante* (1697).

Louis de Cahusac, who shares with Noverre the distinction of being a great eighteenth-century dance commentator, described the scene in detail. "This tableau," he concluded, "fraught with art and passion, was all the more admirable in that it was entirely the invention of the *danseuse*. She had enhanced the poet's plan, and thus stepped out of the rank of mere performer and rose to the rare category of creative artist." [8]

In June 1739 Mlle Sallé informed the Opéra that she was giving the customary six months' notice of her intention to resign permanently. She was still very young, only thirty-two (compared with Mlle Prévost, who was fifty when she retired), but many considerations could have prompted her decision. No doubt she was weary of struggling against the limitations of her career. Possibly, too, she felt threatened, since there were always rumors that Camargo would come out of her self-imposed seclusion, and in a few weeks another dancer would make her debut, Barbara Campanini, whose feats, it was predicted, would put even Camargo to shame. Perhaps Marie Sallé merely longed for a peaceful private life. Shy and reticent by nature, she had been constantly on display from the age of nine and always subjected to more than her share of adverse as well as favorable publicity.

When December came round the Opéra would not let her go.

Her notice of resignation had been verbal and therefore not valid, they said. So she resigned again, in writing this time, and in June 1740 she was finally free. On retiring she was not eligible for the pension of opera performers with a record of fifteen years of consecutive service, but since she had always been a favorite at court the King awarded her a special pension as dancer of the Royal Ballets.

Until 1745 she lived quietly in Paris. She gave up her rooms in the Palais Royal and settled with her friend Rebecca Wick, her maid, her little dog, and her bird, in an apartment on the rue Saint-Honoré, opposite the present-day Hôtel St. James & Albany. She sat for two portrait painters; she received her friends at home; but for five years she neither danced nor was seen in public.

People were astonished, when, between 1745 and 1747, she reappeared at Versailles, performing with David Dumoulin in twenty ballets, after which her pension was doubled. Then once more she withdrew for a period of five years. In the autumn of 1752 she took part in four ballets when the court was at Fontainebleau. For these final appearances she danced once with Gaëtan Vestris, who had recently made his debut at the Opéra, and was only twenty-three, and once with old Louis Dupré. Two years earlier Casanova had already marveled at the long-drawn-out career of "*le Grand Dupré*," "*l'Apollon de la Danse*." Now, at Fontainebleau, he was fifty-five, and one of the courtiers described him as a tottering tower who inspired pity rather than admiration. Mlle Sallé herself was beginning to look like a dessicated spinster and was wise to stop dancing when she did.

It is curious that Sallé's best biographer, Emile Dacier, should have overlooked her much publicized first London appearances (1716–17),[9] especially as it was unusual for a dancer to begin as a featured performer at the age of nine. Apart from this omission, we must feel grateful to him for his patient research, which uncovered all the official French documents relating to the ballerina's life—contracts, pensions, her dress and food allowances as royal dancer, her death certificate and will, and the inventory of her belongings, details which give us added insight concerning her personality. It is disappointing, just the same, that none of her private correspondence was found. Lost, too, is one of her cherished possessions, a portrait in oils of the brother who played a crucial role in her life. Two years her senior, he was not only her dancing partner until she was twenty-four but, on account of the early disappearance of their parents, was probably also her mentor. It was a traumatic experience for her when he died, aged only twenty-seven, a fortnight after entertaining Lincoln's Inn Fields at his own very successful benefit performance. Her intense devotion to him could even explain her indifference to other men.

It was in the last will and testament that Dacier discovered the existence of Rebecca Wick. Manon Grognet appears to have been merely a brief attachment for Marie Sallé, although it may be assumed that they met as early as 1724, when both of them were acting at the fair. But the relationship with Rebecca Wick was one that endured. Five years before Mlle Sallé died she had already named this *"aimable amie"* as her sole heir, in spite of the fact that her surviving family included two uncles and an aunt, nieces, and a nephew, who had all been closely associated with her.

༈

We see Marie Sallé as her Paris public last saw her, because Jean Fenouil painted her portrait a few months before she retired, and the following year she sat for a pastel by La Tour. Petit made an engraving of the Fenouil portrait and later reissued the print as *l'Après-Dîner*, altered to fit in a series that included *le Matin*, *le Midy*, and *le Soir*. The painting vanished, according to Dacier, and although he says that no copy of *l'Après-Dîner* was ever located, readers of this book will find both prints among the illustrations. Even ardent admirers of Mlle Sallé agreed that she was never pretty, but her portraits reveal the intelligence and independence which animated the inventive choreographer and memorable ballerina. What is missing, what we can never retrieve from the past, is the artistry and delicate charm which captivated the audiences who saw her. Noverre, severest of critics, wrote that he was enchanted, and later writers have always been tempted to quote his comments. Her dancing, he said, "had neither the brilliance nor complexity of our times, but she replaced that ostentation with simple, touching grace; free of any affectation, her expression was noble, eloquent, and spirited. Her sensuous dancing displayed equal lightness and finesse; it was not by leaps and antics that she touched one's heart."

CHAPTER 3

Marie-Anne Cupis de Camargo
1710–1770

IN APRIL 1726, while Marie Sallé charmed London with her poetic dancing in *Les Caractères de la danse*, Marie-Anne Cupis de Camargo was preparing to make her debut at the Opéra in the same *ballet-divertissement*. Camargo's interpretation was very different indeed. The audience which first saw her on May 5 was electrified by her speed and fire, and by technical feats such as the *entrechat quatre*, which until then had been performed only by male dancers; and though the leading newspaper was cautious in reviewing such novelties, the public found her dazzling. Almost overnight the sixteen-year-old *danseuse* became the rage of Paris. She was the talk of all the cafés, was admired and petted by the ladies of the court; coiffures, bonnets, and new fashions in dress were named for her, and her shoemaker was said to be reaping a fortune.

Like Mlle Sallé, Camargo had her first triumphs as a very young child. Her father, Ferdinand Joseph de Cupis, though he came of a noble Roman family which boasted cardinals, bishops, and military men, had been launched on a useful career as dancing master and violinist by his mother, who was widowed and poor and hoped that he would soon be able to earn his living. Settled in Brussels, where Marie-Anne was born, he became a successful teacher and obtained such prodigious results with his daughter that, when she was only ten, ladies of the Belgian court offered the funds to continue her training in Paris with Mlle Prévost. After a few months of intensive study, father and daughter went home, and Marie-Anne joined the Brussels opera.

Reports of her amazing accomplishments soon spread abroad, and the year she was fifteen, Pélissier, opera director in Rouen, proposed engaging her as prima ballerina. The offer seemed a step in the direction of the Opéra de Paris, the terms were excellent, and there was also a position for her father, so they set off together for Normandy, little guessing how soon they would actually find themselves in Paris. In the mid-sixteenth century the ancient town of Rouen had been one of the main centers of art and culture in France, but war and Catholic-Protestant strife had been ruinous, and after the Edict of Nantes was revoked, many of the wealthy families emigrated. Pélissier now found it impossible to raise the money he had expected to collect for his opera house, and the venture collapsed. However, his leading performers were not stranded for long. Two of the singers taken on by the Opéra de Paris were the director's wife, Mlle Pélissier, later famous for her spectacular quarrels and total disregard of opera regulations, and the equally capricious Mlle Petipas, who came originally from the fair. A contract was also offered to Marie-Anne de Cupis, who formally adopted the name of her Spanish maternal grandmother, Camargo.

No one in Opéra circles was surprised that Mlle Prévost was roused to jealousy by the sensational debut of her former pupil. She revenged herself by relegating Camargo to the line of ballet girls. The final rift—an often-told story—came about during a performance when one of the Dumoulin brothers failed to appear at the moment of his *entrée*. On an impulse, Camargo sprang from her place in the *corps de ballet* to fill the breach, took the center of the stage, and improvised a variation which brought down the house. Not long after this Blondy found Camargo in tears because the Duchesse de Condé had asked to see her in a special *entrée*, and Mlle Prévost refused to rehearse it. "Forget that envious, hard-hearted creature who subjects you to so many humiliations," Blondy consoled her. "I'll teach you myself, and next week you will dance the *entrée* requested by Madame la Duchesse."

For a while Camargo's success was undisputed, but Marie Sallé returned from London and, in September 1727, began an engagement which was to touch off a rivalry that lasted until Camargo went into temporary retirement in 1735. The public, journalists, and friends all took sides. So many verses appeared in the newspapers to champion the graceful style of the one or the verve and technique of the other that it became a sort of battle of the poets, and long after both ballerinas had died critics were still furiously debating their respective merits. Certainly Marie Sallé suffered a great deal from the situation. It was one of the reasons for her several escapes to England. Camargo, less sensitive by nature and protected by powerful friends at court, no doubt enjoyed the challenge.

In any case, her private as well as her professional life kept her far too occupied to be bothered by thoughts of her rival. She had quickly adapted herself to the sophisticated ambiance of the Opéra, and already her liaisons were common gossip. She was involved, too, in the scandal of the Hôtel de l'Académie Royale. This building, erected in 1712 by order of Louis XIV, was the headquarters of the Opéra administration and housed a rehearsal theatre, the library, studios, and offices. Known as "the shop," it was also, after working hours, the scene of much revelry. In

June 1731 the director Gruer gave a supper there for a group of French aristocrats. To entertain them he also invited the composer Campra, the Duval du Tillet sisters and Marie-Anne Camargo of the ballet, and the singers Mlle Pélissier and Mlle Petipas. The party was very gay, the evening was unusually warm, and the champagne very intoxicating. Gruer dropped a hint, and with one accord the ladies dropped their clothes. After all, if he wanted them to appear in the garb of Venus, could they really refuse their director! In due course, reports of the party reached Louis XV, who was greatly amused, but around him there rose such cries of moral indignation that he felt obliged to make an example of the culprit. Gruer, who had looked forward to continuing in his thirty-year tenure of office, was summarily dismissed.

Marie-Anne de Camargo was twenty-three when she became the mistress of Louis de Bourbon, Comte de Clermont, Prince of the Blood and grandson of the great Condé, active military commander and an abbé as well. Half a dozen abbeys, including Saint-Germain-des-Prés, contributed to the vast income which he lavished on spectacular entertainment and especially on Camargo. A young man of many passing love affairs, he nevertheless remained devoted to her for nearly nine years. In the spring of 1735 he learned that his duties as Lieutenant-General of the King's Armies would compel him to leave Paris. He was, of course, aware that he was far from being Camargo's first lover. If he left her alone for months, perhaps even for years, he might find her in someone else's arms when he returned. Rather surprisingly, she acquiesced when he asked her to give up dancing while he was gone, and she retired to the Château de Berny, a safe distance from the Opéra and its temptations.

Six years went by, and Camargo was bored and longed for the footlights and public applause and Paris. Clermont's ardor had cooled, too, and when he returned to Paris his wandering eye settled on Mlle Le Duc of the *corps de ballet*. After that it was merely a matter of changing partners: Mlle Le Duc abandoned Bernard de Rieux for the Comte de Clermont; Camargo took up with Bernard de Rieux and went back to the Opéra.

Clermont's new mistress proved more enterprising than her predecessor, and much more demanding. When the armies called him again she prepared to disguise herself as a soldier and follow him to the battlefield, and was stopped only by an order from the King. Clermont then made the same request of her that he had once obtained of Camargo. But Mlle Le Duc objected. She preferred to give him up, she declared, rather than give up the Opéra. She would, however, accept his apologies. Her independent spirit did not displease her royal lover. In his capacity as Prince of the Blood, he bestowed upon her the title of Marquise de Courvay, and, *cela va sans dire*, she went on dancing. Nor did the pranks end there. Clermont fell ill and begged his relatives to send for his chosen confessor. When they discovered that the solemn figure who appeared at his bedside was none other than Mlle Le Duc disguised as a priest, a tremendous scandal ensued which was hushed up only later when it came out that the Count had married his little *danseuse*.

Camargo, in the meanwhile, had resumed her career in 1741 with undiminished success both at the Opéra and at court. Two other ballerinas might have become serious rivals—Marianne Cochois, Marie Sallé's cousin, who was Dupré's protégée, and Barbara Campanini, whose flamboyance and *entrechat huit* far outshone Camargo's achievements. But after one brief season Mlle Cochois departed for Berlin, and La Barbarina was a bird of passage, never a fixture at the Opéra. Camargo stayed on for ten years more and danced in seventy-eight different ballets before she finally withdrew from the stage.

The charming house where she lived during her retirement was in the most fashionable section of the rue Saint-Honoré. There, surrounded by her menagerie of dogs, parrots, doves, and canaries, she enjoyed all the ease provided by a pension from the King, a considerable fortune in money, jewels and silver, and a well-stocked wine cellar. For nineteen years she observed the passing world without playing any role in it. At the Opéra new ballerinas came and went—Vestris, Allard, Guimard, Heinel, and many more. When Marie Sallé died in 1756 Camargo was perhaps one of the few persons to hear of it—they were near neighbors on the same street. In 1754 her old friend the Comte de Clermont was elected to the Académie Française, an honor even for a Prince of the Blood, and that same year, his one-time secretary, Louis de Cahusac, produced his great treatise *La Danse ancienne et moderne*. Four years later Clermont suffered a crushing military defeat at Crefeld, and after that was always referred to scornfully as *"l'Abbé."* In 1763 the Opéra, which held so many memories for Camargo, burned almost to the ground; a temporary stage was hurriedly made ready in the Tuileries, pending the rebuilding of the Palais Royal, which might take five or six years. Madame de Pompadour died in 1764. The familiar faces and landmarks were disappearing.

With Camargo lived a faithful friend, last relic of her "thousand-and-one lovers." She bequeathed all of her dogs to him, reported Grimm, and it was he who used his considerable influence to arrange a magnificent funeral for her at the Eglise Saint-Roch, with the church decorated in the white hangings that symbolized virginity, a privilege reserved for those who have never married. The rites were all the more extraordinary because the Church took a dark view of the theatre in general and of dancers in particular. (When so illustrious a person as Molière lay dying his friends were unable to find a priest willing to administer the last sacraments to an actor and, in spite of the intercession of the King, his remains were not received for burial in consecrated ground. Many years later the same Eglise Saint-Roch, which honored Camargo with so much pomp, barred its doors to the ballerina Louise Chameroy. Her death at twenty-three had stirred public sympathy, and angry demonstrations continued long after the cortege was received by another church with a more lenient priest. In order to quiet the protests the Abbé Marduel, curé of Saint-Roch, was suspended for three months by the Archbishop of Paris, but Church prejudice, it will be seen, would continue to oppress dancers right up to the twentieth century.)

In any case, when Marie-Anne Camargo died, in April 1770, she was mourned by all her neighbors as "a model of modesty, charity and decent conduct."

∾

Voltaire, who had a wide experience in ballet, paid high tribute in verse and prose to the talents of La Camargo. "She was the first," he said, "to dance like a man"—that is, the first who displayed the strength and technical ability of the male dancers of her period. The admiration of contemporary critics was echoed by the *Anecdotes Dramatiques:* "Her figure unquestionably was the greatest possible asset to her talent; her feet and legs, her waist, her arms and hands, were most perfectly formed." On the subject of her dancing they stated that she had assimilated the principles of Mlle Prévost, Pécourt, Blondy, and Dupré, and then created a style of her own which embraced everything from *danse noble* to light comedy.

Her detractors included Noverre. "I saw Camargo dance," he reported. "The various authors were wrong who called her graceful. Nature had denied her everything which might have made her so: She was neither pretty, nor tall, nor well formed. . . ." He did grant that her dancing had gaiety and brilliance and went on to comment: "Mlle Camargo had intelligence and she made use of it in choosing a style which was lively and quick and never gave the spectators time to examine her and observe the shortcomings of her figure." Others who dismissed her as nothing more than a clever acrobat overlooked the fact that, like her brothers, Charles and François, she had inherited far more from her distinguished father than mere technique.

Though many later historians have made a point of attributing Camargo's verve to her Spanish ancestry, it should be observed that she was half Italian and that other Italian dancers had just as much temperament. Perhaps she also had gypsy blood. It would not be too far-fetched to imagine that one of her forebears may have acquired the name El Camargo from the Camargue, meeting place of the world's gypsies.

In trying to assess Camargo's contribution to ballet, it must be conceded that she was soon surpassed by other ballerinas and, judged by today's standards, her accomplishments would seem quite elementary. She was, however, the forerunner of today's stellar performers. She was also the first to shorten her skirts—to just above the ankles!—so that the spectators could study her technique. Even this slight abbreviation caused an uproar at the time. It brought about a police ruling that opera dancers must wear "precautionary panties," though it was not enacted soon enough to prevent a mishap when Mlle Mariette's costume caught in some scenery as she whirled across the stage, and she was left naked with a full house applauding the impromptu show.

Unlike Marie Sallé, who remained a rather obscure figure until recent times, Marie-Anne Camargo was never forgotten. Her name, more than any other, grew to represent the spirit of eighteenth-century dance. She was the subject of an opera and of a ballet choreographed by Petipa; an English ballet club was named for her, and *The Dance Encyclopedia* even lists a number of dishes created by Escoffier which bear Camargo's name.

CHAPTER 4

Barbara Campanini (La Barbarina)
1721–1799

EIGHTEENTH-CENTURY MEMOIRS disclose the fact that when Barbara Campanini arrived in the French capital some two hundred and thirty years ago she succumbed to a debilitating complaint which afflicts modern tourists, nowadays politely referred to as "Paris tummy." The malady had little effect on the unbounded energy of the sixteen-year-old ballerina; nor did the presence of her Italian traveling companion and partner curb her amorous adventures. She took the Paris ballet public by storm and immediately became the mistress of the Prince de Carignan, *Inspecteur Général* of the Opéra, and then went on to other conspicuous affairs.

The new *danseuse* and Rinaldi-Fossano made their debut together in July 1739. The time was propitious, since Camargo had not yet returned to the stage, Marie Sallé had already announced her intention to retire after six more performances, and operagoers were rather bored with Mlle Mariette, who was talented but unexciting, and had been around for ten years. La Barbarina was just the kind of sensational dancer that the audience craved. She was a perfect exponent of the almost acrobatic style associated with the Italian school. She had precision and elevation, she dashed off her *entrechat huit* with ease; she was very sure of herself. A novelty was the light comedy, or pantomime, a sort of dance dialogue which the partners enacted with real Italian brio. Apart from a few diehards who still yearned for the days of Lully and Mlle Prévost, and the discriminating ones who could never forget Marie Sallé, everyone adored La Barbarina. It went to her head, and she became absurdly spoiled and demanding.

Her liaison with the director of the Opéra was nothing more than a calculated affair to further her own interests. Carignan was generally despised as a lecher and squanderer and for his careless management and favoritism at the Opéra. Barbarina knew from the start that she would have to share him, not only with the dancer Mlle Rabon and all the women for whom he had a passing fancy, but mainly with Mlle Mariette, who had three children by him, and had been his mistress for so long that the public had nicknamed her *"Princesse."* When he had served her purpose Barbarina dismissed him casually and took up with Lord Arundel and others. Fossano, in the meanwhile, consoled himself with the more serious Mlle Constantini, granddaughter, daughter, and niece of celebrated actors who had been with the Comédie-Italienne since 1687. They were married and returned to Italy in November, leaving Barbarina to finish the season on her own.

Tales of her triumphs—the *entrées* which Rameau added specially for her to his operas, her success at court, her notorious amours —had not escaped the attention of John Rich. He went in person to Paris to fetch her for an engagement at Covent Garden, and she made her first appearance there on October 25, 1740. On opening night King George II was present with the Princesses Amelia, Caroline, and Louise, and during the following ten days there were two evenings "By Command of His Royal Highness the

Prince of Wales." Before the company dispersed for the summer Barbarina took part in seventy-five varied programs particularly suited to the London public. The English, at this time, doted on crude or comic dance turns with titles such as *Drunken Peasant*, *Wooden Shoe Dance, Laundress Visiting Day, Maggots*, and *Hornpipes*, often incongruously combined on the same bill with classical opera and Shakespeare. Barbarina obliged them with a "Comic Dance called *The Italian Peasants*," *Tyrolean Dance, Scots Dance, Les Savoyards, Tambourine, Satyrs and Nymphs*, as well as "A Grand Serious Ballet called *Mars and Venus*." Desnoyer, who had been a favorite at Drury Lane, was her partner, and on nine occasions the royal family went to see her.

No less a person than Servandoni was dispatched to London with offers to renew her Opéra contract and escort her back to France. Described by Diderot as a "great stagesetter, great architect, able painter, and sublime decorator," Jean-Nicolas Servandoni was idolized in Paris, and only Baron Grimm disposed of him as an unimaginative vulgarian, very inferior to the Italians. The scenery he produced during his thirteen years as chief designer at the opera house was considered marvelous by the French, and the whole city came to gape at the out-of-door *fêtes* he staged. To celebrate the birth of the Dauphin, artificial mountains towered in the middle of the Seine, spouting fireworks and surrounded by mermaids and sea monsters, and other works of his included chapels, theatres, and the decoration of princely houses. La Barbarina herself was not more arrogant and ambitious. She allowed him to persuade her, but on arrival was dismayed to find that she was no longer the center of attention at the Opéra.

Her former protector, the Prince de Carignan, had died in April, mourned only by Mlle Mariette, and the new director was sponsoring Marianne Cochois. Under Dupré's guidance, this cousin of Marie Sallé had blossomed into a finished dancer, and the reviewers announced that she combined the qualities of both Sallé and Camargo, and soon would surpass them. La Barbarina was only too pleased to leave in a hurry for England, where there was no competition and where she gave another fifty performances under continued royal patronage.

Her next major engagement was in Berlin and was the turning point in her life. Opera and ballet had been viewed with such disfavor by Frederick William I of Prussia that his son, the future Frederick the Great, was obliged to pursue such pleasures in secret. When the young King ascended the throne in 1740 one of his first projects was to establish an opera company which would outshine the Opéra de Paris. As advisor he enlisted the services of Voltaire and as director of court entertainment he chose another Frenchman, Jean-Baptiste Boyer, Marquis d'Argens,[10] a curious sort of ne'er-do-well and adventurer, whose qualification for the post was little more than his past experience as lover of several singers and dancers. After some false starts due to the stinginess of the King (he was unwilling to grant proper salaries or pay for a *corps de ballet*), it was agreed that Barbara Campanini would be engaged as *première danseuse*.

Barbarina was staying in Venice at the time. A representative of the King sought her out, and she signed a contract that called for her arrival in Berlin early in 1744. In the meanwhile, she had formed another romantic attachment with an English lord whom she was passing off as her husband and suddenly she refused to show up on the stipulated date. Frederick had no intention of giving in to such behavior. As the Venetian ambassador happened to be in Berlin just then, the King took countermeasures against him in order to force the Republic of Venice to deliver "the recalcitrant creature" to the Austrian frontier, and from there she was conducted under guard to Berlin.

La Barbarina was far too clever to show resentment over the

turn of events and within a few days she was exerting herself to captivate not only her new public but Frederick as well. So great was her success that after her debut, on May 13, the Prussian capital was at her feet, and the King was so enamored of her that he immediately hired a *corps de ballet* and gave Barbarina a three-year contract with the unheard-of salary of 7,000 talers a year and the revealing clause that she was not to marry during its term.

For a young person, twenty-three years of age, it could be said that she had already achieved an extraordinarily full life, but Barbarina was insatiable. Although she was honored and indulged in every possible way and remained Frederick's accredited mistress for four years, toward the end of that time she was involved with the son of the King's chancellor, Charles-Louis de Cocceji. The scandal assumed such proportions that young Cocceji's parents themselves requested his banishment, which did not prevent his marrying Barbarina secretly in 1749.

Since a great king is no better off in affairs of the heart than his humblest subject, Frederick, like others cast off by Barbarina, raged and grieved in vain and then had to seek solace elsewhere. Casanova asserted that *"Sa Majesté, après ses amours avec La Barbarina, devint entièrement négatif."* Nevertheless, Marianne Cochois, who followed her as *première danseuse*, did replace her to some extent in Frederick's affections. Casanova, on a tour of Potsdam Palace in 1764, saw portraits of both of them in the oddly miserable room where the King slept.

Marianne, after her single season at the Paris Opéra, reached Berlin two years before La Barbarina and settled there with her mother, brother, and sister, but as she lacked her rival's gift for self-promotion, her career developed more slowly and modestly. Eventually she married the ballet master Desplaces and flourished for a further ten years as Berlin's most esteemed ballerina. Frederick the Great even wrote a eulogy of her talents. Her remarkable sister Babet (sometimes called Barbe) was a poet, linguist, musician, painter, and a first-rate dramatic actress. She was not much more than thirty when she gave up the stage to marry the Marquis d'Argens, who was nearly twice her age, and whose intellectual attractions can hardly have compensated for his hypochondria, neuroses, and foolish superstitions. The King, by now, had become almost as dictatorial as his father, and he allowed his courtiers neither privacy nor independence. When he discovered that the Marquis had married in secret, without requesting his permission, he was exceedingly angry. He took revenge, year after year, by playing all sorts of cruel practical jokes on the poor old Marquis, who had no peace until he returned to France, where he fell ill and died.

As for La Barbarina, it could hardly have been expected that the course of her life would run smoothly with Count Cocceji. In 1759 they were formally separated, though it was not until 1788, when she was nearing seventy, that their divorce became official. At that time the King bestowed a last favor upon his mistress of happier days. He allowed her to keep her title, and she was thenceforth known as Countess de Campanini. Only then did she settle down to a quiet existence. She endowed a convent for impoverished ladies, much like the Closter memorably described in Isak Dinesen's "The Monkey." She assumed her final role as its prioress, and it is not difficult to imagine the tales with which she must have regaled her elderly charges.

❧

If the emphasis so far has been on the Paris Opéra, it must not be forgotten that ballet originated in Italy and continued to prosper there independently. We have seen that long before the Opéra was founded the first promoters of ballet in France were Italians (Beaujoyeulx was Belgiojoso, and Lully himself came from Florence as Lulli), but while the French went on to develop the *danse noble*,

the focus in Italy was on pyrotechnics. In this respect La Barbarina carried Camargo's achievements a step further and set new
standards in London and Berlin. As an Italian, she was also a
herald of later exportations, who would profoundly affect the
Opéra. First and foremost was the Vestris family, followed in
the nineteenth century by the great Romantic ballerinas Taglioni,
Grisi, Cerrito, and many others. Repercussions of this influence
were also to be felt in every capital of Europe: during Barbara
Campanini's lifetime Galeotti was setting the Royal Danish Ballet
on its path to glory, Angiolini was altering the destinies of ballet in
Vienna and St. Petersburg. Its continuity is apparent even today in
the teaching tradition of Maestro Cecchetti and in the magic of
Carla Fracci's dancing.

CHAPTER 5

Thérèse Vestris

1726–1808

FRANÇOIS-MARIE D'ESTE, Duc de Modène; le Marquis de Ricardy, Governor of Florence; Count Esterhazy; Mr. Horace Walpole; M. Civix des Forges, Comte de Mouzone; le Marquis de Monfenac; Pierre de Jélyotte, countertenor at the Opéra; Jean-Barthélemy Lany, ballet master at the Opéra; M. Bay de Curis, Administrator of the King's Armies; M. de Saint-Florentin, Minister of the King; M. Le Normant d'Etiolles (husband of Madame de Pompadour); Abel Poisson de Vandières, Marquis de Marigny (brother of Madame de Pompadour); Son Altesse Royale, le Duc d'Orléans; Charles-Anne de Montmorency, Duc de Luxembourg; Chrétien II, Duc des Deux-Ponts; Philippe-Henri, Marquis de Ségur; M. Coquelen; Mr. Robinson; M. de Laborde; Louis-Auguste, Vicomte de Rohan-Chabot; Lord Powerscourt; M. de Brissart, fermier-général; M. Hocquart de Coubron; M. de Sainte-Foix; le Comte de Ascligio . . . At first glance it reads like a section from the Almanach de Gotha or perhaps the guest list for a royal reception. It is, however, merely a roster

of the lovers of Marie-Françoise-Thérèse Vestris recorded by the
Paris secret police. As for the unrecorded lovers, it would be idle
even to hazard a guess. They were legion, no doubt, and the only
thing about them of which one can be certain is that they were all
men of means or influence. Thérèse was interested only in self-
advancement. Her portrait, as she herself would have expected, is
included in Boulanger's mural at the Opéra, but if ever she shone
as a ballerina, it was only in the reflected glory of her brother
Gaëtan. Her main claim to fame is as a courtesan.

The Vestris family arrived in Paris in 1747; that is, Mme Vestris
mère settled there at the time with five of her eight children; her
husband and the other three stayed behind in Italy and, as far as
ballet history is concerned, were not heard of again. Soon Gaëtan,
Thérèse, and Angiolo were all employed as dancers at the Opéra,
Violante sang in the concerts at court, and only Jean-Baptiste had no
professional stage career, modestly satisfied to be housekeeper for
the others. Four years after his debut Angiolo resigned, having quite
rightly decided that if he remained in Paris he would never be known
as anything but a less talented younger brother of Gaëtan. In 1761
he was engaged as *premier danseur* at the court of Württemberg, and
there he not only had the privilege of working with Noverre, but
also met and married Rose Dugazon, later one of the very successful
actresses of the Comédie-Française.

It was Gaëtan who rapidly made a name for himself at the Opéra.
Gifted, charming, as dedicated to his art as if it had been a religion,
he was also extremely vain and quarrelsome. His incessant demands
for money, recognition, and special favors were the bane of a long
series of opera directors, he was constantly having rows with the
ballet master Lany and even with the ballerinas, and several times
he was either dismissed or locked up in prison. But he was indispensable, and he knew it. "Le Grand Dupré" had retired in 1751
and, with the exception of Vestris' son, Auguste, all the male dancers

for the next fifty years were mediocrities compared with Gaëtan, whose own high opinion of himself was expressed very simply. "There are only three great men in Europe," he asserted. "Myself, Voltaire, and the King of Prussia."

Thérèse Vestris had all of Gaëtan's vanity, ambition, and bad temper, and practically none of his talent. Having made up her mind to reign supreme at the Opéra, she first consolidated her position there by having an affair with the ballet master Lany. As a result she hardly dared to attack his sister Louise-Madeleine. This particular rival was, in fact, quite unassailable. Apart from Lany's brotherly protection, she was famous for having perfected the *entrechat six*, and her reputation was confirmed when Noverre published his opinion that "Mlle Lany has effaced all those who shone by the beauty, the precision, and strength of their technique. She is the first dancer in the universe. . . ." [11] Thérèse therefore focused her jealousy and hatred on Mlle Puvigny, who had inherited one of Marie Sallé's pensions as well as Camargo's place as *première danseuse*. She, too, proved to be a redoubtable foe. She had been on the stage since the age of eight and knew every angle of backstage intrigue. If Thérèse won one round by persuading Lany to let her dance an *entrée* that belonged to Mlle Puvigny, then Mlle Puvigny lined up the powerful Prince de Soubise on her side and won the next bout. Eventually the directors grew tired of Thérèse's scheming and, along with Gaëtan, she was banished from the Opéra for a while.

Thérèse permanently gave up her far-from-admirable stage career in 1766, but as a courtesan she went on and on. At times she was juggling four or five lovers all at once, but "her heart had no part in these affairs. . . . She never had a lover whom she loved. Disdainful, indifferent to everything except profit, debauchery or show, she felt no tenderness for any of her adorers, and the only discoverable feeling, the only affection of which she seemed capable, was her constant devotion to her family." [12]

Loyalty, which was the one redeeming grace in Thérèse's character, was a trait shared by all five brothers and sisters. They all espoused each other's quarrels, all of them worked to promote their combined or separate interests, and they far preferred each other's company to any other. It is hard to say whether Baron Grimm's tone was ironical or reluctantly admiring when he reported to one monarch: "While the beautiful Theresina Vestris is in bed with a lover for money, her mother, devout as a saint, is saying her rosary in the adjoining room; her brother whom they call the Cook is preparing supper which their sister Violenta and the other brothers will come and share with Theresina and her lover, in the friendliest way in the world." [13] During the month when Gaëtan was in confinement at For-l'Evêque Thérèse went to the prison to see him every day and refused to appear on the stage. Jean-Baptiste's devotion went even further when Gaëtan's son was jailed at La Force. He managed to get permission to move right into the prison with Auguste in order to take care of him.

Thérèse lived to the age of eighty-two. Oddly enough, even in death it seemed that the family could not be separated. Thérèse, Gaëtan's wife (though she was twenty-six years younger), and Gaëtan himself all died within the space of a few months, and soon after Angiolo, too, followed them to the grave.

~

Thérèse Vestris as ballerina? No comment.

CHAPTER 6

Marie Allard

1742–1802

Let us not be too harsh in judging little Mlle Allard. If her private life was frivolous, *very* frivolous, it must not be forgotten that she was also a great ballerina and, by all accounts of her contemporaries, a delightful and warmhearted person. In her defense, let it be said that her conduct was merely typical of the times, and her love affairs, though numerous, should not be confused with the calculated commerce of a Thérèse Vestris.

The accepted view during the heyday of Marie Sallé—that every actress was expected to parade some eminent man as her paramour—by now had been carried to a preposterous extreme. Aristocrats and parvenus alike (especially the *fermiers généraux*)[14] all felt that their prestige would suffer fatally if they did not have a string of singers or ballerinas on the leash. The record holder, no doubt, was the Prince de Conti who "kept sixty recognized mistresses, without counting the 'minor,' the 'occasional,' and the 'imperceptible' ones," but there were others who did not lag far behind him. Houses, settled incomes, jewels, carriages (Lord d'Eggremont gave Mlle Duthé the magnificent coach with six horses that the Duc d'Aiguillon had ordered for Madame du Barry)—every sort of inducement was held out to the favorites, who often had only recently emerged from the poorest, most ignorant families. Small wonder that they succumbed.

The lure of riches also encouraged the rise of that detested watchdog, the "ballet mother," whose aim, far from trying to protect her daughter's virtue, was to see to it that she did not yield to someone she loved, but reserved herself for the highest bidder, after which the mother would claim her share. For a few more years the activities of these harpies were limited by the very regulations which also permitted vice to thrive. When Capon remarked that an engagement at the Opéra was "a passport to a life of evil and immorality" he had reference to an unwritten but strictly observed rule that remained in effect until 1775: Once she was 'on the list,' the Opéra girl was no longer subject to the authority of her parents nor even to the strictures of the police, and similarly a dissatisfied wife was rid of her husband's control if she managed to get inscribed as a singer or dancer. The rakes profited by the situation, "and if they wished to abduct a young girl, first took the precaution of getting her entered as a *danseuse* at the Opéra. When the elopement took place, and the parents appealed to the police to recover their erring daughter, they would be informed, in the course of a day or two, that she belonged to the Royal Opera, and therefore was under no authority except that of the King, or the gentlemen who formed the 'Committee' which regulated the royal theatres." [15]

Marie Allard's miserable childhood began in Marseille with parents who were not only poor but greedy and corrupt. She was barely ten when they farmed her out to the Comédie de Marseille and to Monsieur V——, a man with Lolita inclinations and a willingness to pay for them. Two years later, death having relieved her of her unscrupulous mother, Marie made her way to the opera at Lyon where, in spite of her youth and perhaps because she had caught the fancy of another protector, she was engaged among the *premières danseuses*. The theatre in Lyon had excellent standing among the great opera houses of Europe, and at various times had sheltered such talents as Rameau, Camargo, Mlle Lany, and Noverre. It seemed, nevertheless, not to offer sufficient scope for the prodigy Marie. By the summer of 1756 she had somehow arrived in Paris, was settled in a small apartment of her own, and had secured an engagement at the Comédie-Française. She was now all of fourteen.

In Paris her first lover gave her a monthly allowance, the second moved her into a larger apartment near the fashionable rue Saint-Honoré, the third was a duke and, according to the standards of the times, she was getting on in the world. But Mlle Allard had something more than social and financial aspirations. Having already proven herself a precocious dancer at two major theatres, her next object was to be received at the Opéra as a leading ballerina.

The best introduction obviously was Gaëtan Vestris, and the best introduction to Vestris was to study with him. As for the "*diou de la danse,*" [16] if he was pleased with the lively talent of his new pupil, he was even more delighted by her personality. "Her gay character and vivacious nature harmonized with his chatter and verve." Almost immediately they were living together in a state of semi-marital bliss which, however, did not prevent Vestris from having flirtations on the side nor Mlle Allard from succumbing to the blandishments of Dauberval. Jean Bercher, known as Dauberval, was also about to begin a career as dancer at the Opéra, along with an equally spectacular career as lover. All of his contemporaries would soon be speaking of him in superlatives. "Fashioned by the Graces and endowed with wit, taste, and intelligence," was Noverre's appraisal. "Added to the gaiety expressed in his dancing were gentleness and affability rare in a famous man," said another critic. Desarbres remarked that Dauberval "held a master's degree in philandering," and it is certain that many of the ladies at court, including Madame du Barry, vied with the ballerinas for his favors. He did not linger long with Marie Allard, and she, it must be admitted, was in no condition to detain him. On March 27, 1760, she gave birth to Marie-Jean-Augustin Vestris.

The appearance of Auguste (or Vestr'Allard as he was later known) was to prove a far greater event than his ambitious parents could have imagined; in the meanwhile, it caused his mother's debut to be postponed for more than a year. Even so, she was only eighteen when she finally stepped out on the stage of the Opéra (June 1761, in *Zaïs* by Cahusac and Rameau), a small sprightly creature, beguiling and pretty, with all the natural vivacity of the women of Marseille and a brilliant, buoyant technique. "She inspired joy the minute she came on stage," said one observer, "a feeling which did not detract from the admiration merited by her talent."

The audience fell in love with her at first sight, as did an extraordinary number of the town's connoisseurs of easy virtue. For one whom she rejected (he made such threats to shoot her and then blow out his own brains that she had to have a police guard) there were more than enough who were accepted and all too often with disconcerting results. Mlle Allard's contract was temporarily canceled by the management "on the ground that her deplorable habit of producing two children every eighteen months caused her to be constantly in a condition which was destructive of all stage effect. The almost chronic ungracefulness of her figure also estranged the affections of her lovers, and caused Sophie Arnould to say of her that 'she was like certain nations, always extending her borders but never retaining her conquests.'" [17] Sophie, whose fame has endured as a wit rather than as the Opéra's leading singer, made a number of apt jokes at the expense of Marie Allard, but she was mistaken about the fickleness of her admirers. Surely it was quite exceptional and a tribute to her character, too, that many of them did actually remain her lifelong friends. In particular, the Duc de Mazarin's attachment withstood many trials. It survived her infidelities, not to mention her pregnancies. The Duke also suffered a fractured skull when a jealous rival hurled him down the stairs at her house, but while he was still at home convalescing, he sent for a magistrate and notaries and settled a life annuity on her of 3,000 livres. His devotion persisted even when she abandoned him altogether for the one man who seemed able to inspire her with a serious passion.

Monsieur de Bontems was a person of consequence in his day, but his real nature remains somehow elusive. He was Gentleman in Waiting to the King and Governor of the Tuileries, and in the latter capacity was able to gratify one of the whims of his little *maîtresse*. She was now living on the rue Sainte-Anne, a few steps from the Tuileries gardens, which stretched along the Seine as far as the new Place Louis XV (today the Place de la Concorde), and beyond which lay the woods of the Champs-Elysées. It was a delightful place to walk, leaning upon the arm of a lover but, she complained, for rest and conversation there was no more inviting place to sit than some hard wooden benches or the grass. Bontems changed all that in a trice, and no less than four thousand chairs were set out under the trees. He also, like many another long-suffering individual, had done his stint as director of the Opéra (1755–57) in partnership with Levasseur, and so he was understanding of Mlle Allard's ambitions and problems as a dancer. Unfortunately their idyl was destined not to last. He died in 1766, and Marie Allard's grief was so intense that she applied for a leave of absence of six weeks "so that her tears might flow unhindered." The Duc de Mazarin had finally taken another mistress—Marie-Catherine Lachau, a *corps de ballet* girl known professionally as Mlle Adélaïde; nevertheless, as a sympathizing and loyal friend, he went daily to call on Mlle Allard for a long time after the death of Bontems.

Was Monsieur de Bontems really Marie Allard's last lover? Desarbres, who insists that he was, sometimes indulges in very unhistorical flights of fancy. No doubt it is touching to think of the ballerina as faithful to a romantic memory for more than forty years, but it seems very unlikely, considering her character, her past, and the fact that she was only twenty-four when Bontems died.

In the midst of her escapades and private joys and sorrows she never neglected the serious side of her life, which was the dance. A beautiful engraving was made to commemorate her *pas de deux* with Dauberval in *Sylvie* (1766 and 1767), a ballet in which the audience found both of them irresistible. Dauberval's deft, humorous, flirtatious manner of dancing was a perfect foil for Marie Allard, "that inimitable mime, and the only *danseuse* who composed her own *entrées*." [18] For indeed there were still those irrelevant *entrées*, as there were still incongruous costumes. Consider, for instance, Vestris dressed for the role of a peasant in "white taffeta with pink insets threaded in silver, a pink taffeta flounce puffed with striped tulle and trimmed with garlands of flowers and lace; a pink taffeta headdress decorated with motifs of brocaded tulle." [19] And male dancers still wore their static masks. All the reforms of Mlle Sallé had been forgotten, and would not be revived until after the advent of Noverre.

In her first ten years at the Opéra Marie Allard danced thirty-five different roles, always endearing herself more to the public. During that time she was also busy helping Vestris train their son Auguste, who was to become the marvel of the age. Baron Grimm devoted nearly two pages to the debut of Auguste: "A few days ago [September 1772] at the Opéra, an extraordinary phenomenon was to be seen: The great Vestris . . . was replaced by a child twelve and a half years old in the *entrées* of that dreary *Cinquantaine*. . . . The boy danced with the same precision, the same aplomb, and almost the same strength as the great Vestris, who was not humiliated at seeing himself eclipsed by a child. The fact is that the lad is not only his pupil but his son. He's of the pure breed of the Gods, conceived in the chaste loins of the plump Terpsichore Allard, greatest *sauteuse* of the century." [20]

Vestris introduced Auguste in a little speech on the stage; then he and Mlle Allard watched proudly from the wings while their son displayed his prodigious gifts. "What talent!" exclaimed Dauberval, who was standing nearby. "He's Vestris' son, not mine. Alas, he missed being mine by a mere fifteen minutes!"

As Auguste's career began, Marie Allard's was already starting to decline. She was, as Grimm indicated, putting on weight, and although the public continued to be indulgent, obesity was going to become her serious problem. She had seen many changes during a dozen years at the Opéra. Her debut was on the stage of the Palais Royal; after the fire she danced at the temporary Salle des Machines, and then she was back at the Palais Royal in the new opera house. In 1770 she was Médée when Noverre's novel *Médée et Jason* was given its first Paris performance by Vestris; and she was there in 1773 when Maximilien Gardel first discarded the mask (after which the tradition was abolished). Severer critics grumbled about her overgenerous curves, but the audience welcomed her with enthusiasm when she revived the favorite *Sylvie* in 1776.

That same year Noverre embarked on his stormy course at the Opéra. His triumphs in Stuttgart and Vienna were known and appreciated in Paris, but Queen Marie-Antoinette (to whom he had given dancing lessons in Vienna) appointed him as ballet master ahead of Gardel, who was next in line to succeed Vestris, so he was soon surrounded by enemies. When he choreographed *Les Petits Riens* in 1778 the ballet was well received (not least because of the scene in which a shepherdess in male attire bares her bosom to prove that she is not a boy), but Noverre felt that his work had been sabotaged. With Opéra productions usually so lavish, he was disgusted at having to use decors left over from three other ballets. Mozart was furious, too, when he discovered that half a dozen banal French airs had been tacked on to the original twelve that he composed for *Les Petits Riens*, and he swore he would never again write anything for the Opéra. Nor did it help matters that Marie Allard appeared in the ballet; by this time even her infatuated audience looked on with ill-concealed smiles whenever she danced.

At the end of three more years, she received the King's pension of 1500 livres, and that was the moment when she might have bade farewell and retired with dignity. She lacked the courage, however, to make the decision and so had the rather humbling experience of having the committee request her retirement the following year. If she was greatly disappointed at giving up her career when she was only thirty-nine, at least she had a compensation enjoyed by no other ballerina. Hers was the satisfaction of watching her son become the world's greatest dancer. No one could have been more conceited than Gaëtan Vestris, but even he acknowledged Auguste's superior gifts. "Gaëtan is his father, an advantage which nature denied me," was his explanation. And when someone remarked that Auguste soared as though he had wings, he replied: "If my son touches the earth at all, it is out of consideration for his comrades."

All of Marie Allard's apartments had been in the general neighborhood of the Palais Royal. There she was within easy walking distance of her work, the shops, the gay rue Saint-Honoré, and (alas for her) one of the great food markets. Most of the theatre people lived nearby, and as Mlle Allard was sociable and rather talkative she must have been pleased to run into many friends whenever she went out. After her retirement she moved to the outskirts of Paris, near what is known today as the Place d'Italie. At that time it was right at the city limits, with real country stretching beyond. Perhaps she felt that it would have revived too many nostalgic memories had she remained in the *quartier* where all the dancers were hurrying back and forth to rehearsals and performances. It is even possible that she chose to move away so that people would not be able to comment on how enormously fat she had become. In 1802 she died of a stroke brought on by overweight.

∾

It is hard to imagine why Marie Allard was not given a place of honor in Boulanger's mural of great ballerinas. No dancer was more highly praised by contemporary critics and observers, no one was more cherished by the public, and even her rivals conceded that she was outstanding and described her as an "enchantress." Apart from producing and helping to train the almost miraculous Auguste, her particular contribution seems to consist in having been the first typically French ballerina. Her dancing had the piquant, sparkling, and very feminine flavor which we tend to associate nowadays not only with the best French *danseuses* but with Parisian charmers in general.

CHAPTER 7

Anna Heinel

1753–1808

"MADEMOISELLE HEINEL," reported the much-quoted Baron Grimm in May 1768, "Mademoiselle Heinel, burdened with seventeen or eighteen years, two large, well-set eyes, and two shapely legs which support an extremely pretty figure, arrived from Vienna for her debut at the Opéra in *danse noble*. It was conceded that she displayed precision, sureness, aplomb and nobility comparable to the talents of the great Vestris. Connoisseurs of the dance declare that two or three years from now Mademoiselle Heinel will be the greatest dancer in Europe, and connoisseurs of charm are already competing for the glory of going bankrupt for her." Our informant, for once, is disappointing. He was three months late in getting around to Anna Heinel's debut, and by then the enthusiasm she aroused was such as to make his description seem meager. What most impressed the Parisians was her size. She was very tall, with a figure that was majestic rather than pretty, but perhaps Grimm did not notice this, being German himself and used to sturdy women. A greater omission was his failure to mention that she introduced the multiple pirouette, or *pirouette à la seconde*,[21] a novelty at the Opéra.

Anna Heinel was born in Bayreuth on October 4, 1753. At the age of fourteen she was already attached to one of the most splendid opera houses in Europe, at Stuttgart, where ballet as good as any that could be seen in France was being produced. Noverre was there as ballet master from 1760 to 1767 and left for Vienna only a few weeks before Mlle Heinel arrived; the designers included Boquet and Servandoni from the Opéra; and among the dancers who came and went were Dauberval, Le Picq, Angiolo Vestris, and star performers from London. Even Gaëtan Vestris appeared once a year for the Duke of Württemberg's birthday celebrations. In such surroundings Mlle Heinel was able to perfect her style and technique long before she went to Paris.

The French, noting a certain reserve in the new ballerina, immediately labeled her *"la Belle Statue,"* but she proved to be no marble maiden. Her first conquest was the Comte de Laraguais, for many years the lover of Sophie Arnould and father of her four children. Laraguais was a person who could have distinguished himself in any sort of career, but all his talents came to nothing because of his eccentricities. He wrote plays that no one could publish and controversial articles that landed him in prison; he loathed any sort of discipline, often offended Louis XV by his outspoken remarks, and ruined his chances in the ministries; he could not resist playing practical jokes and was continually in exile or in trouble. "He gave me a million kisses," sighed Sophie, "but made me shed four million tears." His infatuation with Anna Heinel was intense but brief. A dowry of 30,000 livres, 20,000 more for a brother she adored, a lavishly furnished apartment, and a carriage and pair, all lent weight to his courtship, but it was not long before he was bored with Anna's stolid Teutonic charms. He missed Sophie's humor and warmth and attempted one of his many reconciliations with her. He was, in fact, still trying to get her back thirty years later.

After Laraguais, Mlle Heinel simply followed the accepted *modus operandi* at the Opéra. She was one of the sixty who surrendered to the Prince de Conti, and simultaneously scattered her favors among other devotees. Sophie, writing to Laraguais (in exile once more?) was only too pleased to report the scandal: "There is such a chaotic mass of lovers that nobody can discover the truth," and Anna's biographers were even less able than Sophie to unravel the details.

One thing, however, was evident: by the end of her fourth year in Paris Mlle Heinel had developed into the spectacular ballerina foreseen by Grimm. Gaëtan Vestris resented her popularity. His vanity, inflated by twenty years of adulation, made him intolerant of any success except his own and his son's and he was foolish enough to think that as ballet master he was in a position to discredit her. When he tried to cast her in minor roles the audience, realizing his motives, were quick to take her side, and for several evenings he was hissed while Mlle Heinel got all the applause. Behind the scenes he raged and shouted vile names at the unoffending ballerina until the situation got so out of hand that the directors complained to the minister. Vestris was ordered to apologize, but after he humbled himself the quarrel merely grew worse. At last Mlle Heinel asked for a leave of absence.

Like other frustrated dancers at the Opéra, she took refuge in England. She braved the stormy winter Channel crossing in the rickety little sailboat ferry, kept her engagement at the King's Opera House, December 17, 1771, in the "New Grand Ballet by Mlle Heinel . . . By Command of Their Majesties," and then succumbed to the London fog. When she got over the grippe, her weekly schedule was composed of all the favored exotic mishmash: *Venetian Dance, Turkish Dance, A Spanish Character, Dutch Dance, Chacone,* and the *Grand Jacone.* English enthusiasm may have consoled her for the lack of classic repertoire but even as stalwart a girl as Anna Heinel must have felt shaken at times by the rowdy ways of the audience. If a billed performer did not appear, either because of bona fide illness or out of pique, the spectators were likely to be in an uproar for hours. A local news item described what was not an unusual occurrence: "A fellow . . . threw a Keg (which he had brought full of liquor into the House) over the Gallery front. It fell upon a lady's head, who sat in that part of the Pit which was railed into the Boxes, but the Lady's hair being dress'd in high *ton,* the artificial mountain luckily prevented the mischief that otherwise might have been occasioned. . . . As the custom of throwing mugs, bottles, apples, etc. from the galleries of the theatres is equally as wanton and wicked and is frequently the cause of great mischief, it is thought the present culprit will be made an example of." Another newspaper complained that latecomers, finding the doors shut, "begin a violent noise with their sticks. . . . Thus a riot is commenced, which frequently stops the play. . . . The orange girls shamefully encourage it."

In June, having come to the end of her contract, Mlle Heinel was persuaded to give one more performance, and on the occasion thanked the public prettily "for the flattering reception she has met with in England." The King's Opera House did not announce her for the 1773–74 season, but in March she was back in a *Polish Dance* and some of her hits of the previous two years; and finally she was billed in May 1776 in the *Grand Chaconne* (by which time the program-maker had learned to spell, though he still did not mind his genders).

During the time when Anna Heinel was abroad, the Paris newspaper hacks found plenty to say about her private life. They hinted at a love affair with her London partner, Fierville; they reported that she married and had a child by him; and they accused her of callously leaving the child behind when she returned to France. The Opéra audience either ignored or disbelieved the tales and welcomed her back with joy. She was especially admired as Roxane in *Apelles et Campaspe,* which Noverre staged in October 1776, as his first offering in Paris. She displayed all her best qualities in this ballet to make up for the misconduct of Maximilien Gardel, who purposely botched his role in order to emphasize his resentment of Noverre.

Meanwhile, Anna's old feud with Vestris was finished and forgotten, and the former enemies discovered that their hatred had turned to love. The astonished public learned that the two dancers were living together and then heard that both of them had applied for permission to retire. Vestris was fifty-three, and had given more than his share to the Opéra in thirty years of service, but Mlle Heinel was only twenty-nine. She had already gone far in her career, and there was general dismay at the thought that no one would see her dance again.[22]

A few years later people were even more amazed to learn that the ballerina had gone into retreat in a convent "for a brief period of 'deconcubination,'" after which she and Vestris were married. One reason for the marriage was to legitimize their year-old son, born in May 1791, and christened, in honor of various relatives, Adolphe-Apoline-Marie-Angiolo; but there is no doubt that the *"diou de la danse"* and his wife were happy. Anna Heinel was cherished as part of the semi-sacred if wicked community of interests which was the Vestris family. Auguste, who was Marie Allard's son, must also have felt a special affection for his stepmother; long after all the older generation died he married a Mlle Tuillière and inscribed himself on the marriage certificate as the son of Gaëtan Vestris and Anna Heinel.

ᔥ

Mlle Heinel, who had forty roles at the Opéra besides her performances elsewhere, is chiefly remembered as the exponent of the *pirouette à la seconde* but, apart from this bit of bravura, she was a strong dancer with a very personal style. Grimm, a good judge of ballet, grew more ecstatic in his descriptions as he observed her progress. "After all," he claimed, "Mademoiselle Heinel is the glory of Germany, which gave birth to her, the solace of France, which benefits by her talents, and the foremost dancer in Europe. If I were less busy, I'd go to the Opéra each time she appears there, if only to watch her enter and leave; the grace and distinction of her bearing are ravishing and enchanting: *incessu patuit dea*." [23] Her ability to revolve very slowly in perfect balance also aroused great admiration. Horace Walpole remarked: "She can turn as slowly as the Zodiac," and couldn't resist adding: ". . . but she is not the Virgin."

Though Mlle Heinel retired at an earlier age than other ballerinas, she may have been right to disappear when she did, leaving a flawless image of her youth, grace, and beauty.

CHAPTER 8

Marie-Madeleine Crespé (Mlle Théodore)
1760–1796

IN CONTRAST TO OTHER *danseuses* of the eighteenth century, Mlle Théodore was a highly moral person, impervious to flattery, indifferent to gifts and favors. Campardon, usually a wellspring of precise information, declares that she was obstinate and difficult in her relations with people, but all the evidence indicates that she was gentle and sensitive and that the public and her fellow performers loved and esteemed her. The cause of her semi-comical quarrel with Mlle Beaumesnil has never come to light, but in her trouble with the Opéra directors it is obvious that she was not to blame.

In 1776, when she was sixteen, Théodore was briefly a member of the *corps de ballet*. She left the theatre to continue her studies with Lany and also to think matters over and make sure she was choosing the right career. Reading actually took up more of her time than dancing, and she was especially interested in the new ideas of Jean-Jacques Rousseau. As no one had ever heard of an intellectual dancer, still less a *danseuse*, Théodore was spoken of respectfully as "the philosopher in satin ballet slippers" or the "free thinker in skirts."

She was very much shocked by her first glimpse of the goings-on at the Opéra, so when Lany convinced her that she had a promising future as a ballerina she immediately wrote a letter to Rousseau. How, she asked him, was she to cope with the problems and temptations of her new surroundings? The old philosopher, who had spent a lifetime giving advice where it was often unwanted, was surprised and pleased to be consulted and sent her a long, humorless reply full of solemn warnings.

Mlle Théodore did not stay with the Opéra long enough to reach the rank of *première danseuse*, but her debut in *Myrtil et Lycoris* (December 1777) confirmed Lany's faith in her, and she acquired a devoted following who were as much impressed by her sensible conduct as they were by her talent for dancing. Once only, forgetting the recommendations of her mentor Rousseau, did she allow herself to be drawn into a backstage scandal. Whatever was said or done to provoke the quarrel was so offensive to Théodore that she challenged Mlle Beaumesnil to a duel. Possibly the cause of the trouble was Dauberval, with whom Théodore was already in love. In any case, it was nothing new for women to settle their differences with pistols. Opéra patrons had not forgotten that one woman was seriously wounded and her opponent exiled after their duel over the singer Chassé. When every effort to dissuade Mlles Théodore and Beaumesnil failed, they and their seconds repaired to the usual meeting place for such affairs, a field near the Porte Maillot, on the outskirts of the city. Jean-Baptiste Rey, the assistant conductor of the orchestra,[24] went along in a last attempt to prevent the spilling of blood and took the added precaution of placing the weapons in a spot where the grass was very wet. As a result of his foresight, both pistols misfired. There was a moment of stunned disbelief, and then the two antagonists burst out laughing, kissed, and made up.

In 1781 Noverre finished his exasperating term as ballet master at the Opéra. His revenge was to take some of the best dancers with him when he left, in the spring of 1782, for the King's Theatre in London, and there Théodore found herself in the familiar company of Pierre Gardel, Nivelon, Antoine Bournonville, and other friends. Noverre's ballets, new works as well as revivals, had an immediate success, a gratifying change after the aggravations of Paris, although Mozart's music was so little appreciated that another composer had to be hired to write a new score for *Les Petits Riens*. For Théodore the stay in England was a happy, relaxing interlude which she hoped to prolong. She shared in Noverre's triumphs, particularly when she danced the title role in *Rinaldo and Armida*, and not the least of her rewards was the praise he accorded her in his book. She was, he said, ". . . the very image of Terpsichore, such was her ease, facility and brilliance. She had the resilience of a ball. She performed with such lightness that without even leaping, by the mere elasticity of her instep, one had the impression that she never touched the ground." [25]

It was a relief too, she discovered, to be far from the Opéra, where Dauberval's presence was a daily reminder of her unhappy passion. She was seriously in love with him, but his philandering habits horrified her, and when he hinted that he would be only too pleased to add her to his list of conquests, she made it very clear that nothing but marriage would be acceptable.

The fact that her salary at the King's Theatre was almost double what she earned in France was a further reason for her wanting to get permission to remain abroad, and her correspondence with the Opéra management soon grew to enormous proportions. First she requested a yearly leave of eight months in order to be available for the entire London season. When this was refused, she asked to be allowed to withdraw from the Opéra for a period of three years, and finally she sent in her permanent resignation. When all of these efforts came to nothing she dispatched a petition to Queen Marie-Antoinette, who handed it over to the minister, who passed it on to the Opéra director, who signified his disapproval to Mlle Théodore, and then the whole process began again. At last, and largely through the Queen's intervention, her contract was canceled "with no conditions or restrictions."

As soon as the London theatres closed for the summer Théodore left for Poinchy, in Champagne, to stay at a château which belonged to Dauberval, and it was then that the Opéra authorities began to regret the annulment of her contract. They had counted on her remaining in England, and now that she was in France again and no longer under their jurisdiction, they were afraid of her becoming a bad influence. Soon all the dancers might feel free to resign or demand long leaves or exorbitant pay. After a hurried consultation, they decided to make an example of her. An order was issued for her arrest, a police officer was sent to Poinchy to escort her to La Force prison, and a letter went off to Dauberval to reprimand him for sheltering her.

The minister had made a foolish miscalculation. There was an immediate outcry from the public, who wanted to know how it was that the authorities could first take issue with Théodore for remaining in England and then put her in jail for coming back to France. They wanted to see her dance again and demanded her reinstatement. The minister also underestimated Mlle Théodore. The letter she addressed to him from prison was a splendid piece of sarcasm. Perhaps it escaped his memory, she said, that she was in possession of a signed release from the Opéra "with no conditions or restrictions," and was she not therefore entitled to come and go without hindrance? She had a further surprise in reserve for him, too: Dauberval himself had gone to London to fetch her and had married her at Poinchy a week before her arrest.

In his hurry to lock up Mlle Théodore the minister actually forgot the clause which allowed her complete freedom of action, and it now took eighteen days and as many letters to undo his mistake and arrange her discharge from jail. As a last precaution, he stipulated that she was to go direct from La Force prison to Poinchy and was not to set foot in the capital for a period of eight weeks. If she did not obey, he threatened to withhold her passport the next time she wanted to leave for England.

Like Noverre, Mlle Théodore had her little revenge. She took the adored, the irreplaceable Dauberval away with her when she turned her back on the Opéra. She also had the pleasure of saying no when the minister gave in to the public's insistence and begged her to come back.

Dauberval's next post was as dancer, ballet master, and choreographer in Bordeaux, with Théodore as his *première danseuse*. It was a huge, luxurious theatre, with a following that was even more spoiled and unruly than the audiences in London and directors who were just as inflexible as those in Paris. Occasionally there were the inevitable moments of friction, and at times, when Théodore and her husband felt homesick for friends and the opera house in Paris, they made halfhearted efforts to return there. Apart from these minor griefs, they enjoyed almost too much adulation. "The people of Bordeaux give us more applause than we deserve," said Dauberval with a modesty that was new to him. He also gave up philandering and took pride in his wife's wit and erudition and in her sparkling performances. But if they lived happily it was not, as the fairy tales have it, ever after nor even for very long. Théodore died when she was only thirty-six. The disconsolate Dauberval, who was eighteen years older, survived until 1806.

❧

Although Mlle Théodore was highly regarded for her *ballon* and a style which combined the speed and precision of Mlle Lany with the humor and coquetry of Mlle Allard, present-day balletomanes think of her principally as Lise in the original production of *La Fille mal gardée.* This two-act ballet-pantomime by Dauberval has had such a long and interesting history that a few details may not be out of place here. Except for Galeotti's *The Whims of Cupid and the Ballet Master,* preserved by the Royal Danish Ballet, *La Fille mal gardée* is the only eighteenth-century work that survives in the modern repertory. First produced in Bordeaux, in 1789, it was revived two years later by Dauberval and Théodore in London, and in Italy by Viganò in 1792. The Paris Opéra did not stage it until 1828, by which time a version of it had also reached New York. It was rechoreographed by Petipa and Ivanov in St. Petersburg in 1882, and a new adaptation of the theme was made by Frederick Ashton for the Royal Ballet, Covent Garden, in 1960,[26] and the list could go on and on. The leading role has been danced by Fanny Elssler, Pavlova, Alicia Alonso, Irina Baronova, and Nadia Nerina, to name but a few, and there is little doubt that, for many years to come, ballerinas will be carrying on the tradition of Mlle Théodore's Lise.

CHAPTER 9

Marie-Madeleine Guimard
1743–1816

Today the rue de la Chaussée d'Antin starts off near the opera house, but takes its character from the opposite end, which is down by the squalid railroad station. It is a street of tawdry shops and noise, of grinding traffic snarls and surly moods—a mean survival of the street it used to be. Two hundred years ago the Chaussée d'Antin was only a country road, with isolated farms and churches scattered across the surrounding fields, but sometime around the year 1770 it underwent the first of several transformations. Among hurriedly planted parks and gardens, a row of palaces soared, and for a few decades the pleasure-seekers of Paris rode out there in their gilded carriages. Then, almost as suddenly, the great houses began to vanish. The nobles, the financiers, and courtesans who lived in them were swept away by the Revolution, the palaces were torn down or crumbled from neglect. And the street, after its brief golden hour, sank into bourgeois anonymity.

In 1772 the newest marvel of the Chaussée d'Antin was the

Temple of Terpsichore. The King's architect Le Doux designed it, and the most famous artists sculpted and painted the decorations; it had a winter garden and private theatre that could accommodate five hundred persons, and every luxury that an extravagant imagination could devise. "The house of Mademoiselle Guimard is nearly finished," noted the diligent Baron Grimm in his March 1773 letter to Berlin. "The entire salon is painted with murals, and Mademoiselle Guimard appears in them as Terpsichore with all the qualities that can show her off in the most seductive way in the world." The pictures were still unfinished, continued Grimm, when she quarreled with the painter Fragonard, dismissed him, and hired another artist. Sometime later Fragonard slipped into the house unobserved to see how the work was getting on, and the sight of his successor's palette and paints suddenly inspired him to revenge. With a couple of deft brush strokes he transformed Terpsichore's smile into an angry scowl, and had just made his escape when Marie Guimard herself arrived to show the painting to some of her friends. Her indignation at seeing her portrait so disfigured was comical. The more she raged the more she resembled the ugly Terpsichore.

Except for some hearsay picked up by Edmond de Goncourt, no precise descriptions remain of Mlle Guimard's other house at her country estate in Pantin. Nevertheless it is possible to reconstruct some aspects of it from accounts of the festivities there. The ballerina, decked out in diamonds and the dresses which set the Paris fashion, presided over three magnificent weekly suppers, one of them for her friends and admirers at court, another for intellectuals, artists, and writers, and a third for her own intimate circle of courtesans and their protectors. As at the Chaussée d'Antin, there was a private theatre where only the most obscene plays were staged. There were screened loges for those who wished to see without being seen—court ladies and churchmen who feared for their reputations—and Sophie Arnould, Marie Allard, Dauberval, the *maîtresse de maison,* and their friends provided the ribald entertainment. Usually the Paris public took a good-natured view of Mlle Guimard's extravagance and excesses, but it became a real grievance that the best actors of the Opéra and the Comédie-Française were constantly out at Pantin. At first the police threatened to close the theatre on moral grounds, and finally the minister issued an order forbidding the actors to appear anywhere except in their own theatres without special permission from the King. The minister might have guessed that it would be useless to try to restrain Marie Guimard. She had more than enough allies at court, and only a few days went by before the order was rescinded with the King's sanction.

Before acquiring her astonishing wealth and influence, the ballerina had known long years of want and misery. She was the illegitimate child of a woman who called herself the Widow Guimard (though M. Guimard was still in evidence some twenty years later), and whose main object seems to have been to exploit her daughter. Marie was fifteen when her mother consigned her to a pair of dissolute men who made a practice of helping young girls in order to have them available as mistresses later on; and it was they who placed her in the *corps de ballet* of the Comédie-Française in 1758.

No doubt the Widow Guimard enjoyed going to collect her daughter's earnings at the theatre, where she can hardly have failed to notice the flowers and jewels and carriages of actresses who were kept by wealthy patrons. But all her visions of a glittering future dissolved when Marie eloped with a penniless dancer. Campardon's careful records of the Comédie-Française and Opéra fail to list Marie's abductor, Léger, though he danced at both of these theatres and made quite a stir at the time. Perhaps, as later scandals suggest, his prowess was amorous rather than balletic. Marie Guimard, at any rate, must have loved him sincerely, since she was willing to share a bleak, almost hungry existence with him for several years. Léger was also the father of her first child, born in the middle of winter in a bare, unheated garret on the rue du Jour. The street, contrary to its name, was a mere alley where day never seemed more than a sort of perpetual twilight, but almost next door Marie had a gay, warm-hearted neighbor in Marie Allard. The two girls were already friendly rivals at the Comédie-Française, as they were soon to be at the Opéra, too, and many years later, when Mlle Guimard had moved on to the splendors of Pantin and the Temple of Terpsichore, they were still very devoted.

It was the Opéra which brought about an abrupt change in Marie Guimard's public and private life. She appeared there for the first time in May 1762 as Terpsichore in *Les Fêtes grecques et romaines*, replacing Mlle Allard, who had injured her foot, and within a few years of her debut became the dancer whom opera-goers preferred to any other. Her rapid rise as a ballerina kept pace with her spectacular career as an *amoureuse*, and it would be hard to say whether she bewitched her lovers with the eloquence acquired in the theatre or whether she captivated the audience with the wiles she practiced as a professional charmer of men.

That she was a consummate actress is evident from all the comments of the period, but even the critics were astonished by her performance in the elder Gardel's *La Chercheuse d'esprit* in 1778. Though she had by then become a symbol of worldliness and sophistication, and was in her sixteenth year at the Opéra, her portrayal of the simple farm girl, Nicette, was a masterpiece of coy innocence, naive and touching, but never silly. "La Guimard's talent made one forget the shortcomings of the ballet," said Grimm.

An exceptional group of dancers made up the original cast of *La Chercheuse d'esprit*, and in view of what we know of them today, it may be amusing to pause for a moment to consider them.

Marie Allard, already stout and marked by middle age, was the

Farm Wife, mother of Nicette (she must have been very displeased with her role); Despréaux played old Subtil the Notary, who tries to marry Nicette (and Despréaux did in fact marry Marie Guimard eleven years later, when she was nearly fifty); Dauberval played Eveille, the flirtatious young man who hands the bouquet to Nicette (and in real life Dauberval was Marie Guimard's more than flirtatious lover). The cast also included the two celebrated Gardel brothers, of whom one died young and the other was ballet master for forty years and lived to see the great moments of the Romantic ballet. And finally there was Mlle Dorival in the role of Nicette's sister.

Two years before, this same Mlle Dorival was sent to prison at For-l'Evêque after an argument with Gaëtan Vestris, who obviously had treated her unfairly. The next night the *"diou de la danse"* discovered that he was not as sacrosanct as he imagined. When he came out on the stage without the *danseuse*, he was assailed by an uproar of hissing and catcalls. "To jail with Vestris!" the audience shouted. "Let's have La Dorival! La Dorival!" Fearing a real riot, Vestris and a police officer rushed to For-l'Evêque but the prisoner, it seemed, was very reluctant to leave her prison. A crowd of friends had arrived to console her, and a champagne supper was in progress, with most of the guests already far from sober. Only if Vestris shared a bottle with them would the ballerina consent to go back to the theatre. When the audience had waited for more than an hour, Vestris and Mlle Dorival finally appeared, hand in hand and visibly tipsy, and cheers and applause welcomed them both.

The eighteenth-century craze for writing memoirs left an almost inexhaustible miscellany relating to the ballet. Statesmen, nobles, artists, and travelers of every kind wrote down their impressions of opera-ballets and performers; but it is mainly in the less accessible records of M. de Sartine, preserved in the French National Archives, that the private or secret lives of the dancers are revealed.

Antoine-Raymond-Jean-Guilbert-Gabriel de Sartine, Lieutenant-General of Police, Counselor of State, and later Minister of the Navy, was described by Marmontel as a man whose minor talents added up to nothing more than mediocrity. However, there has probably never been, in any large city, at any time, a man who had greater power and abused it less. M. de Sartine knew everything about everyone. His vast network of police inspectors was spread all over the city, following people and watching every house. They noted how many guests arrived, who they were, and whether anyone stayed for the night. They had spies in the kitchens and spies who eavesdropped in public baths. They found out about every intrigue and love affair and exactly what bribes or presents were exchanged. No detail was too insignificant for inclusion in the reports which they brought each day to the office where their chief presided, a seriocomic personality in his solemn robes and long curled Louis XIV wig. M. de Sartine's wigs were a standing joke; he kept an entire closetful from which he chose according to his mood or the importance of the occasion. In the morning M. de Sartine himself presented the previous day's gleanings to the King, and it was generally known that Louis XV so enjoyed reading the bulletins about his subjects that he often neglected to attend to matters of state. The King was especially amused by reports that dealt with the Opéra, since most of his courtiers were involved with the singers or ballerinas.

Through the zeal of M. de Sartine's inspectors, the details of Marie Guimard's affairs were filed away in the National Archives; and since she was also an obvious target for gossip writers, all sorts of stories about her passed into the public domain. The tales, true or false, were seldom malicious. She escaped much of the slander that attached to Opéra performers because of the affectionate esteem she inspired as a dancer, and because her kindness and charity to the poor were well known.

Her sudden quarrel with Mlle Dervieux did, however, provoke a venomous battle of the poets. Mlle Dervieux at this time had already made her mark as a dancer and singer, but she resigned from the Opéra when she was only twenty-three to devote herself to a courtesan's career. She was very pretty, she had the unforgivable advantage of being nine years younger than Mlle Guimard, and she set her cap for the very men whom the older ballerina was hoping to add to her own list of gallants. For months the vilest of insults were exchanged by the partisans of both dancers. Then, just as suddenly, the two were friends again. Mlle Dervieux was back at Pantin helping to entertain the guests and, except for another bulging file in the Secret Archives, all was as it had been before.

Of Marie Guimard's many lovers four were more or less serious, and only one played a significant role in her life. She was twenty years old, and the Opéra had just appointed her as *danseuse seule*, when she became the mistress of Benjamin de Laborde, First Gentleman in Waiting to the King, Governor of the Louvre, and Farmer General. For ten years she had the unswerving devotion of this man, who was handsome, gentle and charming, generous, talented, and rich as well. According to his contemporaries, there was no end to M. de Laborde's virtues and accomplishments, and his only fault, if indeed it could be called a fault, was that he was a very second-rate composer who insisted on hearing his music performed in public. It was he who lovingly supervised the building of the Temple of Terpsichore, and its owner's every caprice was the law by which he lived. He spent his entire fortune on her, endured and forgave all of her infidelities, and finally, when she had no further use for him, his whole existence dissolved in emptiness. He stopped composing, abandoned his friends and his career, and set off on lonely, aimless travels far from France.

When M. de Laborde's money first proved insufficient, Mlle

Guimard accepted a large income from the Prince de Soubise and during the next five years contrived to keep both lovers enslaved and avoid any outbursts of jealousy. Eventually her demands strained even the Midas treasury of the Prince and then she availed herself of a more sensational source of funds. The Bishop of Orléans, it seemed, was no more immune to her wiles than other men, and the prodigious revenues of his diocese became hers to squander.

The insatiable ballerina's desire for money and more money was not merely a matter of indulging her own selfish extravagance. She was, remarked Campardon, "in spite of her disorderly life, far from being without good qualities. She had a kind heart, and her charity knew no limits." It was generally known in Paris that the entire sum which the Prince de Soubise sent to Mlle Guimard as a New Year's gift in 1768 was given by her to the poor, and that she climbed the stairs to all the miserable garrets in her neighborhood, carrying food and clothing to the sick and needy. Her acts of kindness were commemorated in many ways—notably in a poem by Marmontel and in an engraving entitled *Terpsichore Charitable, ou Mademoiselle Guimard Visitant les Pauvres.*

By a curious twist of fate, many years later, it was Marie Guimard who offered assistance to the desperate Prince de Soubise when his son-in-law was declared bankrupt in one of the worst scandals of the century. With the approval of other dancers, she drew up a long letter recalling the past favors of the Prince and the pensions he had secured for all of them. It was now their wish, she informed him, to contribute these pensions to help pay off the three thousand creditors involved in the disaster.

Several writers have suggested that Marie Guimard's concern for the poor was inspired by memories of the wretched years she spent with her first lover. The humiliation of her illegitimate birth may also account for her impatience to establish the legal status of the daughter she had by Benjamin de Laborde. Her own position had to be clarified first, and this would serve to explain why her father turned up at this time after neglecting her for twenty years. It is even probable that she sought him out and offered him money. Certainly it was not, as he pretended, "his desire to continue the marks of friendship and personal tenderness which he had always felt for her" that made him agree to sign the papers she needed. She was twenty-two when it was finally set down in the records that Louis, by the Grace of God, King of France and of Navarre, has acceded to the request of Demoiselle Marie-Madeleine Guimard "to efface the stigma of her birth and permit her to enjoy the privileges and advantages enjoyed by our other legitimate subjects. . . ."

A similar document was filed later for the ballerina's daughter, with the reservation that she was not to inherit her father's estates and was to retain her mother's name given to her at baptism. Nothing further was heard of the second Marie-Madeleine Guimard until 1778, when a certificate was issued for her marriage to a jeweler called Robert Drais. Surprisingly, she was only fifteen, and it may be assumed that her mother, remembering her own precarious girlhood, was anxious to see her settled. A year after she married, young Mme Drais died as obscurely as she had lived. Her death was nevertheless the one really tragic event in the life of Mlle Guimard, who felt no attachment to her own parents, never regretted her cast-off lovers, and was even able to maintain a sort of heedless gaiety during the dark days of the Revolution.

Compared with the loss of a much-loved child, to part with a house was a minor matter. Marie Guimard arranged the sale of the Temple of Terpsichore so that it seemed an amusing public event rather than a calamity. In 1786, finding herself on the verge of bankruptcy (and not for the first time), it occurred to her that a far larger sum might be realized through a lottery than by surrendering the house to a single purchaser. Having gone through the tedious process of obtaining permission from the authorities, having fatigued herself by personally signing two thousand five hundred tickets (two of which are conserved in the Bibliothèque Nationale), and having sat through the final drawing, which lasted from ten in the morning until ten o'clock at night, she may well have deplored the undertaking. A total of 300,000 livres resulted from the lottery, but Comtesse Lau, who held the winning number, sold the house almost immediately to the banker Perregaux for almost double the sum. Just the same, Mlle Guimard was much more fortunate than she realized. In less than three years, under the Revolution, the Temple of Terpsichore would have been confiscated, and she might have received no compensation at all.

The problems faced by the Opéra management during the second half of Marie Guimard's career made all of their past aggravations seem insignificant. They had coped with the pretensions of the Vestris family, the pregnancies of Marie Allard, the independence of Mlle Théodore, elopements and feuds, but they knew no way of dealing with Marie Guimard. Unruly dancers could be fined, sent to For-l'Evêque, or even exiled, but La Guimard was beyond their reach. Shielded by court favor, she enjoyed stirring up trouble.

In 1776, when Noverre took up his post as ballet master, she sided with him against his enemies; to appear in the ballets of Europe's most famous choreographer would obviously enhance her own reputation. But as his prestige in France declined, she saw she had nothing to gain and joined the group that wanted to oust him from his job. Knowing that the authorities would never dare to ignore her complaints, she accused Noverre of incompetence, of trying to sabotage the ballets of Gardel, and of neglecting her own interests in favor of younger dancers. After four years of persecution, Noverre summed up his griefs in a seventeen-page letter to the minister and then, having received neither his promised pay nor any other satisfaction, resigned in despair.

Equally the victim of Marie Guimard's displeasure was Jacques de

Vismes, a brother-in-law of her former devoted friend Benjamin de Laborde. Instated in April 1778 as Opéra director for a period of twelve years, M. de Vismes survived in office for a mere twenty-three months, and of all the troubled regimes his was the most chaotic. The leading performers met secretly in Mlle Guimard's house to air their grudges against the new director and decided not only to get rid of him but not to replace him at all. Self-government was their aim. Failing that, they would refuse to dance or would even resign. The King, who usually arbitrated when matters got out of hand, finally lost patience. "That rabble!" he said, dismissing the subject.

It remained for M. de Vismes to mete out the penalties, which made him more hated than ever. Marie Guimard, of course, could not be called to account, but Vestris *fils* was conducted to For-l'Evêque, and the singer Mlle Duplant was dismissed without her pension. Dauberval, a leader of the revolt, was forbidden to enter the opera house even if he bought a ticket. On March 6, 1779, the musicians supported the dancers by refusing to play, and Gluck's *Iphigénie en Tauride* could not go on. To add to de Vismes' troubles, an open war broke out between the partisans of rival composers. Supporters of the Italian Piccini, who had been hired by the director, were pitted against admirers of Gluck, whom the Queen favored because he was Viennese. Demonstrations in the theatre and violent attacks in the press only subsided when Gluck left the city. He swore he would never go back to Paris, and never did.

De Vismes resigned—escaped, one might say—just in time to avoid a final calamity, which provoked , another rebellion. Once again, on June 8, 1781, the home of the Académie Royale de Musique et de Danse was burned to the ground, and this time a number of persons were killed or badly injured. When the fire broke out Mlle Guimard was in her dressing room, and had removed her costume, but she was saved by a quick-witted scene-shifter who flung some

curtains around her and carried her out. The most extraordinary out-
come of the fire was the feat of the architect Lenoir. He offered—
in fact, guaranteed—to build a new opera house in ninety days, and
kept his promise. Work commenced at the Porte Saint-Martin on
August 2, and exactly eighty-six days later, on October 27, the theatre
opened its doors to a crush of six thousand people.

   In the meanwhile, the greatest worry was how to keep the singers
and dancers out of mischief while the Opéra was closed. They
might be tempted to go abroad and never return at all. London and
Stuttgart were always luring them with offers of better pay and
greater personal freedom. The obvious solution was to forbid them
to leave the city, but to the performers, who were already in a state
of revolt, this was the worst kind of provocation. When they also
found out that M. de Sartine's police inspectors had orders to
shadow them day and night, they all made plans to escape. The
baritone Lays was arrested at the frontier, but another singer, Rousseau, and the dancer Nivelon both managed to cross into Belgium.
Nivelon was twenty-one, a young Adonis with an enormous following, and the opera officials fell into a sort of panic when
he eluded them. They knew the whole town was laughing at them
and felt that they had to get him back and make an example of
him, if only to save their prestige. But, by the time letters had been
exchanged by the director, the minister, and the King's envoy in
Brussels, by the time permission had been obtained for French police
to operate on Belgian soil, Nivelon had given them the slip, and was
safe in England. A year later, he returned voluntarily, and was forgiven because he was needed, but his troubles did not end there. The
success of his escapade, his popularity, and the fact that too many
women were in love with him all tended to make him overconfident.
He refused to perform one day on the grounds that he was free to
dance or not, just as he chose, and he was carted off immediately to
La Force prison.

Mlle Guimard became absurdly arrogant, too, and when the Opéra reopened she was a continual source of annoyance. Like Nivelon, she insisted that it was her privilege not to dance. She added that certain roles belonged to her and if she herself did not appear in them, neither could anyone else. The ballet in question would then have to be canceled, and another program substituted at the last minute. She was just as intractable on the subject of her costumes, which were a severe strain on the director's budget. In a single year, 1779, her stage wardrobe cost 30,000 livres, although she was then in mourning for her daughter and stopped performing for several months. Eventually every request took on the tone of an ultimatum. Although male dancers traditionally had higher pay than ballerinas, she asked for the same salary as Auguste Vestris and, at the first hint of a refusal, sent in her resignation.

The director's dilemma was that he couldn't afford to meet her demands but neither could he afford to let her go and, in any case, there was no one to take her place. Allard and Heinel had retired, Mlle Peslin was getting decrepit, La Dorival drank and was unreliable, and the others were all too inexperienced. Marie Guimard was unique. In 1783, after twenty-one years at the Opéra, she still gave an illusion of youth and charm. "Everyone acknowledges her talent," said Papillon de la Ferté, the harassed Surintendant des Menus Plaisirs du Roi, whose name was as whimsical as his title. "She still looks very young on the stage; if her technique is not outstanding, her gracefulness makes up for it; she is very good in action ballets and pantomime, is enthusiastic and works hard, but she is an enormous expense to the Opéra, where her wishes are obeyed with as much respect as if she were the director." [27] Twice, however, her career just missed ending on a tragic note. She contracted smallpox toward the end of 1783 and later fell down a flight of stairs and injured her knee. But she came back to the stage as delightful and even more presumptuous than ever.

When she took final leave of the public it was in a way that no-body could have expected. For several years, during the Opéra's summer holiday, she had been going to England, where her arrival always created a flurry. The Duchess of Devonshire, a ballet enthu-siast, set the trend, and then the ladies of London vied with each other to entertain the amusing French *danseuse*, who counted the French King and his court among her friends, and could always report on the latest Paris fashion. Noverre was again at the King's Theatre as ballet master and, in view of Mlle Guimard's past mistreatment of him, it was odd to find her dancing happily under his direction. She could afford to be generous with him, since his popularity in London was at least as great as hers, and she was, besides, in unusually high spirits. At forty-six, she was carrying on successful flirtations with Nivelon, who was twenty-nine and a handsome spoiled boy, and with Despréaux, who was thirty-one, witty and wise for his age, and a poet. It was very flattering and, almost in spite of herself, her attachment to Despréaux was becoming serious.

Unforeseeably soon, the season was over. She danced *Annette et Lubin* with Nivelon as her partner on April 28, 1789, *Les Caprices de Galathée* in May, and in June the King's Theatre suffered the Opéra's frequent fate and burned to the ground. Most of the dis-banded company returned to Paris, arriving there on the eve of the Revolution. In the meanwhile, Mlle Guimard had made up her mind to marry, and the career which had survived age, illness, ac-cidents, and intrigue was brought to an abrupt end by the Church and Despréaux.

Perhaps the eternally young Mlle Guimard might have continued dancing for many more years. The real responsibility for her retire-ment lay with the Church, which persisted in its stringent policy toward the acting profession. Not satisfied with depriving actors of the burial service, churches also refused to marry them unless they "recognized through divine mercy that the art of representation in the theatre is contrary to the profession of Christianity" and vowed to give up their careers. One of the rare efforts to change the situation was made by Mlle Clairon of the Comédie-Française, in 1765, when she went to consult her doctor in Geneva, a city where all theatrical performances were forbidden. At Voltaire's house in nearby Ferney, she drew up a plan by which she hoped to circumvent the Church. The King was to be persuaded to give the title of Royal Academy of Dramatic Art to the Comédie-Française, whose actors would thus have the status of members of the royal household and be legally exempt from excommunication. One of the ministers promised to hand the proposal to Louis XV, and the Archbishop agreed to let the matter take its course, but it was fumbled through a series of meetings and finally dropped. Although Mlle Clairon was still in her prime as the leading actress of France, she had made several earlier attempts to resign from the Comédie-Française. This time, when she saw her project collapse, she was adamant.

All this was strangely incompatible with the fact that the Bishop of Orléans had been Marie Guimard's lover, and many other churchmen had liaisons with actresses, that cardinals hired professional singers and dancers to entertain their guests, and some of the most erudite books on theatre and ballet were written by priests. Nevertheless, since the ban remained officially in effect, La Guimard and Jean-Etienne Despréaux were obliged to renounce the stage before they were married, in August 1789, in the Church of Sainte-Marie du Temple.

During the long and terrible years of the Revolution, Despréaux and his wife were hidden away in a tiny apartment at the top of Montmartre. One of his poems described their placid existence, high above the city roofs, where paved streets merged with country lanes, and fields, hamlets, and forests reached to the far horizon. "Peaceful from morning till night," he wrote. "Under the vault of greenery, with hoe and watering pot in hand." At times they were very poor, because dancers' pensions, under the new regime, at first were paid irregularly and then not at all; but La Guimard gave no sign of regretting the luxuries of her past. Busy with gardening and keeping house and simple amusements, she was perhaps discovering happiness for the first time.

In their contented life together, the two dancers seemed oddly detached from the horrors of the Revolution, but Marie Guimard's heart had always been stirred by the misfortunes of others, and she must have suffered deeply over the accumulating deaths and tragic events. Surely she mourned the King, who had shielded her from a dozen angry ministers and indulged all her caprices; and surely she wept for the patient, generous lover who was the father of her child. Benjamin de Laborde made the mistake of returning to Paris, and the scaffold claimed him, as it had claimed Papillon de la Ferté and too many others.

When Despréaux and Magdelaine (it was his name for La Guimard) moved down to the city after eight years, they settled near the opera house, but it was no longer the Opéra they had known. In 1794 the Committee of Citizens of the Republic abandoned Lenoir's miracle theatre, though he had guaranteed it for a period of at least thirty years. Instead, they chose one on the rue de la Loi (rue de Richelieu) which belonged to a Mlle Montansier. The lady was notified of their decision, and a price was discussed, but when she failed to evacuate the premises quickly enough, she and her partners were taken to jail, and the building was confiscated—a faster and cheaper method. Renamed Le Théâtre des Arts, the new Opéra was inaugurated in August of that year.

The citizens soon discovered that running an opera house was not as simple as they thought it would be. They lacked M. Papillon de la Ferté's gifts for intrigue and compromise, they had little understanding of the finances, and even less knowledge of what the public wanted. Their first offerings at the Porte Saint-Martin had flaunted such titles as *L'Offrande à la Liberté* and *Le Triomphe de la République*; at the Montansier they presented a couple of patriotic cantatas and then not a single major addition to the repertoire for the next two years. The more resounding name of Théâtre de la République et des Arts, adopted in February 1797, obviously did not help matters, and many of the performers resigned and went abroad. The remaining singers engaged in a vicious struggle with the dancers for a leading place on the programs; several managements failed; and the enterprise was verging on chaos when a veteran director was appointed.

Marie Guimard must have been very surprised indeed to learn that, after nineteen years, her old enemy de Vismes was back at the helm, though he no longer was Anne-Pierre-Jacques de Vismes de Valgay and proud of his relationship with Benjamin de Laborde, but plain Citizen Devismes, for whom it was safer to forget any of his past connections. As with the opera house, a bourgeois name produced no visible improvement in the citizen director. He took charge in September 1799 and, in spite of a conscientious effort, went out unmourned in December of the following year—the first year of the incoming century. The date was a memorable one for ballet history, because the debut of Emilie Bigottini portended a new phase.

At a time when the Opéra and almost every aspect of city life seemed painfully changed, Despréaux's love for Marie Guimard remained constant and reassuring. She proved by her charm that time could be made to stand still, said one of the poems he published in 1806, when they had been married for seventeen years. "*Oui, c'est la pure vérité/J'adore mon amie,*" he declared. His *amie* was sixty-three, but we have his word that she was still sweet-tempered, graceful, and gay, though their money troubles had worsened, and they verged on absolute need.

There was a brief hope that their fortunes might improve when the Republic and Empire were swept away, and the Bourbons came

back in the person of Louis XVIII. The King had known and admired Mlle Guimard in pre-revolutionary days, when he was the
Comte de Provence, and she reigned as first ballerina of the Académie Royale de Musique et de Danse, but she did not live long
enough to receive any mark of his remembrance.

Long before Marie Guimard died she came to personify not only
the corruption, the extravagance, and artificiality of the eighteenth
century, but also the qualities for which it was called "the divine
century"—the exquisite taste, wit, and elegance of an age which
also belonged to Mozart and Marie-Antoinette. At the time of her
death, on May 4, 1816, the public had forgotten her. She was buried
without fanfare, and a brief, banal obituary made no mention of her
achievements.

There could be no better epitaph for Marie-Madeleine Guimard
than the words her sorrowing husband wrote to a friend seven
months after her death. The letter is also a sort of epitaph for the
ballet of the eighteenth century. He pleaded that his head was aching
from grief, and then went on: "I am firmly persuaded that theatrical
dance was at its height during the last twenty years before the
Revolution. . . . Among women dancers Mme Guimard-Despréaux
was superior to all the others because nature had endowed her with
intrinsic and, one might say, spiritual grace. She lacked the stature of
the beautiful Heynel, but her charming figure suggested the Medici
Venus which was at the Museum in Paris for some time. As a *demi-
caractère* dancer, Mlle Allard, the mother of Auguste Vestris, was
the liveliest, nimblest, and most delightful one could see. There were
several others besides. But to return to your question about the
dance, I shall say that present-day dancing in no way resembles what
I saw from 1770 to 1790 or '92. . . . Talent in dancing is not in
knowing how to perform all sorts of steps in time to some rhythm

or other; the merest ballet girl can do that, and speed is only a minor asset. . . . Simple, correct execution is what is needed: to be able to leap very high is a poor gift. . . . It was with *terre-à-terre* dancing that Mlle Guimard beguiled a discerning audience for more than twenty-five years, in the gavottes of *Armide* and two hundred other ballets. She was always new, and I don't mean just in the way she used her feet, which amounted to little in comparison with the charm of her head and figure. . . . Her expressive face conveyed all the emotions she felt or was supposed to feel." Despréaux's letter was long and rambling; he was, after all, lonely and confused and unable to sleep; he ended by saying that Mlle Guimard never approved of the modern mode of raising the foot to hip level: "These exaggerated movements distort the body, and the only effect of such attitudes is to astonish the spectators." [28]

As Despréaux penned these lines, Pierre Gardel was concluding his forty-fifth year at the Opéra, and Auguste Vestris had been before the public for forty-four. Though they and other survivors from the heyday of Mlle Guimard were making a last attempt to preserve the old forms and style, the gentle seduction of the Romantic era was already in the air. Young dancers were exploring a new technique which would alter the whole course of the ballet. They were making the first tentative efforts to dance on point.

Part III
EMPIRE AND RESTORATION

CHAPTER 10

Emilie Bigottini
1784–1858

THE OPERA HOUSE on the rue de Richelieu remained in use for twenty-six years (1794–1820), a period which spanned all the regimes from the Revolution to the Restoration, and along with succeeding governments, the Opéra changed its name from Théâtre de la République et des Arts to Académie Impériale de Musique et de Danse and then back to the title it originally had under Louis XIV. After the patriotic bombast of the Republic, Napoleon's neoclassicism set the trend. The Greek-Roman-Egyptian influence on painting, furniture, dress and jewelry design affected the Opéra, too, and once again the program featured mythological titles such as *Le Retour d'Ulysse*, *Vénus et Adonis*, and *La Fête de Mars*.

All this was very much to the taste of two relics of the eighteenth century: Auguste Vestris, who did not retire until 1816, and Pierre Gardel, who kept his post until 1829. For nearly forty years Gardel's ballets dominated the repertoire, an advantage he was only willing to share with his assistant ballet master Milon. His egotism deprived France of the creative gifts of Louis Henry and Didelot, and his determination to preserve all the old traditions was the reason the Opéra remained a stronghold of anti-Romanticism.

Elsewhere in Europe fresh life was being infused into the ballet. The dance-dramas staged in Milan by Viganò, from 1812 to 1821, were so impressive that Stendhal compared him to Shakespeare, and Louis Henry, who emigrated to Italy, was also experimenting with new forms and styles. Didelot fled to St. Petersburg and, under his guidance (from 1801 to 1811 and 1816 to 1829), the Imperial Ballet and its school were making the strides which eventually would lead to Russia's world supremacy.[29]

In Paris, in spite of the reactionary attitude of Gardel and his sup-porters, the Opéra was not without its splendid moments. The in-spired dancing of Louis Duport, Albert, and Paul often made up for the mediocrity of the ballets they were obliged to interpret. Most of the *danseuses*, until Milon produced *Nina* for Mlle Bigottini, had to content themselves with showing off their technique (which was no longer a novelty) or by attracting attention to their notorious private lives which, in fact, were anything but private.

Like her husband, Mme Gardel, the former Mlle Miller, was a survivor from pre-revolutionary days. She was mentioned in 1788 in a report on the Opéra personnel drawn up by the director for the information of a newly appointed minister: "Mlle Miller—Excel-lent dancer though rather cold. She works tirelessly to become a *premier sujet*. She demurs at nothing to make herself useful." [30] Mlle Miller achieved her ambition to inherit the place of Marie Guimard and to become the wife of Pierre Gardel and for thirty years was a fixed star in the Opéra's constellation. "Her feet flash diamonds, so to speak; her performance has exquisite finish," said Noverre. He might have added that she was still a cold, ambitious woman who would stop at nothing to make trouble for younger dancers.

In 1810, six years before she retired, Mme Gardel was obliged to share her position as *première danseuse* with Mlle Clotilde [31] whose sentimental adventures and tussles with the director almost equalled those of La Guimard. There was never a shortage of picturesque gossip to print about Mlle Clotilde. It was said that Prince Pignatelli set her up in a house with a monthly income of 100,000 francs, that she received a gift of 400,000 francs from Admiral Mazaredo, and that a French banker gave her 100,000 francs yearly for the privilege of "being present as a mere spectator while she had her meals." She astonished everyone when she married the young composer Boieldieu, who had no fortune to offer her, but as she refused to give up her dissolute life and was just as loath to relinquish her husband, he escaped to Russia and stayed away for seven years.

At the Opéra, where she might have relied on her astonishing beauty to dazzle the audience, she was nevertheless a serious artist, though limited by the formal style she acquired from her studies with Vestris. Noverre, at the end of a long, fruitful life, had retired to a house in Saint-Germain-en-Laye. The twenty-mile journey by carriage was arduous for a man of nearly eighty, but he attended the Opéra faithfully and followed Mlle Clotilde's career with interest. Though she reminded him of the goddess Diana and had a perfect technique, he felt she could learn to be more expressive. With a sly allusion to her love affairs, he suggested that she should try to display on the stage the feelings and passions which she was able to inspire in individuals.

Mme Gardel and Mlle Clotilde both won places on Boulanger's wall of fame, but there were three who did not achieve this honor, although they were celebrities in their day. Fanny Bias, so thin and limber that she was called *"la Désossée,"* so spoiled and temperamental that no one could ever be sure whether she would dance or not, was at the Opéra from 1807 to 1825 and attained the rank of *première danseuse*. Geneviève Gosselin's exceptional talent made her the chosen victim of Mme Gardel, but she had the devotion of the critics and public and was on the verge of surpassing all the others when she died suddenly, in childbirth, at the age of twenty-seven.

Her younger sister, Constance, known as Mme Anatole, remained an accomplished exponent of the traditional *danse noble* until the start of the Romantic ballet.

In this hierarchy of brilliant Opéra dancers Emilie Bigottini was a curious anomaly. She was not outstandingly beautiful, and her technique left much to be desired. In an atmosphere of jealousy and intrigue, she was gentle and generous. Furthermore, her particular talent, which was for mime rather than pure dance, was not at all suited to the demands of the classical repertoire.

Her surprising advance from a seventeen-year-old debutante in 1801 to solo roles in 1804 was only in small part due to her eagerness to improve and the fact that the audience found her very appealing. The driving force was her brother-in-law, the ballet master Milon, who taught her himself and was determined to save her from the dreary nullity of her family's professional life.

Emilie's father was one of the hundreds of Italian actors who kept drifting to France in search of better living conditions. Luckier than most, he was hired in 1757 at the Comédie-Italienne to play harlequin roles, but proved so inept that he was dismissed almost immediately and had to resign himself to touring the provinces. When he was re-engaged, in 1777, he was hardly more successful. During the intervening twenty years he had acquired the speed and dexterity of a prestidigitator but, after the first astonishment wore off, the public found it boring, and the leading critic protested that such stunts slighted the dignity of the theatre and were fit to be seen only at fairs. Baron Grimm, who despised the Comédie-Italienne, but felt that he ought to forward the news to Berlin, complained that: "There is no comparison between Bigottini's acting and that of Carlin, whom he's supposed to replace. He has neither the same grace, nor the same finesse, nor even the same natural quality." To add to his troubles, Bigottini was reprimanded for appearing without a mask [32] and then was demoted to minor roles and the job of assistant machinist. Finally, in 1780, when the Italians merged with the Opéra Comique, the poor old actor was discharged once more and had to go back on the road.

His daughter Louise was even less fortunate. In 1784 (the year her half sister Emilie was born) she was on the Opéra program as Mlle Bigotiny in the *corps de ballet*. Six years later she was still in the *corps*, and by the time Emilie was launched on her career, Louise was Mme Milon and merely an odious presence backstage with all of Mme Gardel's propensity for trouble making.

With Milon, on the contrary, one success followed another. He had been a favorite dancer for nine years when the Opéra produced his *Héro et Léandre* and also appointed him ballet master to assist Gardel. The next year he staged *Pygmalion*, a one-act version of which he tried out earlier in a small theatre, with Emilie, aged fifteen, making her first public appearance; and during the first weeks of 1801, he created *Les Noces de Gamaches*.[33] As ballet master, he was now in a position to further the interests of his pupil and protégeé, and she made her debut in Gardel's *Psyché*. More than half a century later, a singular letter signed by Mlle Bigottini was discovered in the Opéra archives by Alphonse Royer, who was director from 1856 to 1862 and later wrote the *Histoire de l'Opéra*. The letter was dated Nivose 2, Year X (December 23, 1801), and although it was only a short time after her debut, she informed the Minister of the Interior that she was dissatisfied with secondary roles and requested a promotion.

It was soon apparent that Mlle Bigottini would always get everything she wanted. By 1812 she had the coveted title of *première danseuse*, and had starred in many of the new ballets, eleven of them by Gardel and three by Milon, though there was still something lacking in her performance which made her fall short of being a truly great ballerina. Even Noverre failed to understand her particular problem. He died in 1810 and so missed seeing her moment of triumph, but a few years earlier he remarked: ". . . The public encourages her by its applause, but lovers of the ballet would like to see her pay more attention to her head, arms, and shoulders, which she could use to the best advantage, and would also prefer her to be more turned out, which would add brilliance to her *entrechats*." [34] What she needed, however, was not this improved technique, but a vehicle that would give her a chance to display her extraordinary gifts as an actress. In this respect, she was like Marie Taglioni who, in spite of her unique qualities, needed only *La Sylphide* in order to become the revered symbol of the Romantic movement. On November 23, 1813, Milon staged *Nina, ou la folle par amour* [35] for Emilie and, from one day to the next, she fulfilled all of his hopes for her.

Nina was a sentimental story-ballet, a precursor of the type that was to wring the hearts of the Romantic ballet audiences. The heroine goes mad when the Count, her father, banishes her beloved, preferring that she should marry the son of the Governor. The hero throws himself into the sea, is rescued, and finally there is a happy ending, with Nina and her friend Georgette united to the men of their choice. As recently as 1938 Cyril Beaumont suggested that it would be worthwhile to revive *Nina*. "The first act is of particular interest," he said, "for certain of the dramatic scenes have much in common with those in *Giselle*. Nina's suddenly coming upon the duel between Blinval and Germeuil causes her to swoon from terror. On regaining consciousness she has lost her reason. She recovers a little and believes herself still to be dancing at the recent festival. This succession of incidents is so similar to those in the first act of *Giselle* as to suggest that Vernoy de Saint-Georges received inspiration from *Nina* for some of his situations." [36]

Apart from the fact that Milon's ballet has none of the poetry of the second act with the Wilis, *Giselle* has the added advantage of surviving in a superb version by Petipa, who was familiar with the original production. A revival of *Nina*, on the other hand, could never be anything but a patchwork of inadequate source materials or an entirely new interpretation of a very silly libretto.

In the year 1813, however, *Nina* was not only just what was wanted for Mlle Bigottini, but also exactly right for a public surfeited with the artificial conventions of ballets based on mythology. Far more plebeian in their taste than operagoers of pre-Revolutionary days, they enjoyed a good cry over the human tribulations of Nina. Berlioz, in his *Memoirs*, tells how the mood was rudely shattered one evening: "The playbills had announced that the solo violin part in the ballet *Nina* would be played by Baillot. Either because of illness or for some other reason, the virtuoso couldn't perform, but the management thought it all right to notify the audience by nothing more than a tiny strip of paper pasted on the poster at the door to the Opéra, which nobody ever reads; so most of the people were expecting to hear the great violinist. . . . Not even Mlle Bigottini's touching pantomime could make us forget Baillot. The scene was almost over when: 'Wait a minute, what about the violin solo?' I said loudly enough to be heard. 'He's right,' said someone. 'It looks as if they've left it out. Baillot! Baillot! The violin solo!' . . . And then the whole audience stood up and shouted to have the program carried out as announced. While this uproar was going on, the curtain came down, and at that the noise grew worse. The musicians, terrified by the fury of the crowd, abandoned the field in a rush, whereupon the enraged public invaded the orchestra pit, hurling chairs in all directions, knocking over the stands and smashing the drums. . . . The rioters didn't stop until they'd destroyed the whole orchestra, leaving the instruments and chairs in ruins." [37]

Such demonstrations in the theatre were rare at this time; audiences were much better behaved than during the eighteenth century and they were all the more quiet and spellbound as they watched Mlle Bigottini, because they had heard it said that the emotions she portrayed so vividly on the stage reflected her own personal grief over the recent death of her lover, Général Duroc.

Emilie's private life was no mystery to the public. Noverre himself had chided her for the frequent absences from the theatre, which were detrimental to her progress as a dancer, absences which in the main were due to her being with child. The father of two of the children was Géraud-Christophe-Michel Duroc, Duc de Frioul, Grand Marshal of the Tuileries, and Napoleon's friend as well as one of his most trusted generals. Wounded at the Battle of Bautzen in May 1813, he died the following day at a nearby farm. Napoleon bought the farm and erected a monument to him there, but Mlle Bigottini, in spite of the tales about her sorrow, did not mourn him for very long. Prior to her liaison with Duroc, she had a child by the Comte de Fuentes. (He was none other than Mlle Clotilde's Prince Pignatelli, of the proud Spanish family that produced several distinguished ambassadors and also the Marquis de Mora, lover of the perversely strange Mademoiselle de Lespinasse.) When a similar *force majeure* again obliged her to ask for a leave of absence, the dancer Albert was blamed, though less for the indiscretion than for depriving the public of Mlle Bigottini's performances. *"Quel enfantillage!"* remarked Jacques Arago. Other affairs were known, or guessed at, and there was endless speculation about the fortune which the ballerina was amassing. All in all, it was a far cry from the arrogant assertion in the letter she wrote to the minister in 1801: "My talent will be my dowry. I have no wish to live at the cost of my honor."

While Emilie Bigottini's acting in *Nina* was "searing the spirit of the spectators so that they left the theatre heavy of heart, red-eyed and wan," this same audience might better have saved its tears for the graver tragedies being enacted on the battlefronts of Europe. In October 1813, only a month before the première of *Nina*, Napoleon had met disaster at the Battle of Leipzig, his great empire was falling apart, and before long Paris would surrender to the enemy. During the happier days of his reign, Napoleon had been one of Mlle Bigottini's patrons and admirers, and a much circulated story which made everyone laugh concerned his gift to her of a collection of French classics in sumptuous bindings. Afterwards, when he asked if she had been pleased, she replied: "Upon my word, Sire, not very much. I was paid in '*livres*' and I should have preferred francs." By the spring of 1814 the Emperor was an exile on Elba, and his stepson, Eugène de Beauharnais, one of Emilie's most devoted lovers, had retired to Munich, where he remained until his death. Historic events, however, seemed not to disrupt the careers of favorite dancers. Summer was barely ended when Talleyrand set out for Vienna to defend the interests of France, and while, in the words of the Prince de Ligne, "the Congress danced," Emilie was dancing there, too.

That autumn, when the statesmen of Europe assembled for the Congress of Vienna, the Austrian capital took on the air of a carnival. Emperor Franz I was said to be spending 16,000,000 gold gulden on military displays, fireworks, theatre and dance festivals, staged to celebrate the peace and amuse visiting royalty and the four hundred and fifty diplomats, while embassies and Austrian nobles vied with each other in arranging hunts, banquets, and balls. Lured by the most glittering audience Europe had ever seen (it included four emperors and empresses, four kings, and an extraordinary number of princes and dukes and all their courtiers), Jean Aumer arrived from France to assume the post of ballet master. He was forty-one, with a long experience behind him as dancer and choreographer in Bordeaux, Paris, Cassel, and Lyon, and now at the Kaernthner Thor opera house, he staged a series of splendid ballets, augmenting the resident company with foreign guest performers—Mlles Chevigny and Bigottini from Paris, André Deshayes from the King's Theatre in London, as well as three dancing Aumers of his own immediate family.

Standards for ballet were high in Vienna. Hilferding, Angiolini, and Noverre all had left their mark, and people had never forgotten the furor over the visits of Viganò and his beautiful wife, the dancer Maria Medina. With her impassioned pagan nature, her flashing eyes, her swirling, clinging, revealing costumes, she had the whole city in love with her. Never again, they said, would there be anything like the "Viganò-Terpsichore" but now, a dozen years later, the gentler Mlle Bigottini was dancing and breaking hearts and getting her share of adulation. Emperor Franz I himself announced that he wished to see her dance, Talleyrand invited her to dine at his house, her name was linked with one of the great Austrian princes, and in the theatre world she was as much a reigning queen as any who had arrived in state to officiate at the Congress.

As the season in Vienna wore to an end, with the affairs of Europe being settled somehow in spite of the mad frivolity, as Napoleon escaped from exile and proceeded north in triumph toward his inevitable final disaster, the mean little microcosm of the Opéra de Paris went on pursuing its own intrigues, unconscious of major events. It was a never-ending sequence of Gardel, Milon, Gardel and Milon, and more Gardel. A few weeks after Napoleon left Elba, Milon staged *L'Epreuve villageoise*, and in July, only a few days after Napoleon departed for St. Helena, the two of them staged a ballet together—the twenty-sixth for Gardel, with many more still to come.

Nevertheless, in the persistent monopoly of the two choreographers, there was a curious interlude during the following December. Didelot returned from Russia and, in spite of every effort to sabotage his work, succeeded in staging his *Flore et Zéphire*. First produced in London in 1796, and revived in St. Petersburg in 1808, it was Didelot's favorite ballet and one which he had always longed to show in Paris, where he had been snubbed and thwarted by Gardel. As on all previous occasions, the ballet created a sensation because of the flying dancers. Aerial effects, of course, were not new; they had been used since the days of Louis XIV's expert machinists, but Didelot was the first to invent a system of wires which were next to invisible. "At so novel a spectacle, the secret of which the observers are still far from solving, the public was unable to control its emotions," reported a leading critic. "The applause lasted way beyond the intermission and burst forth again with renewed energy when Zéphire, returning in the same way as he ascended, soared upward a second time carrying Flore in his arms. This marvel, even more striking than the first, raised the enthusiasm to its highest pitch." [38] Such a success with both the public and press must have infuriated Gardel; and Didelot, having scored his point, returned to the pleasanter atmosphere of St. Petersburg. *Flore et Zéphire* was memorable, too, because of the dancing of the ill-fated Geneviève Gosselin; during the three years of life that remained to her, she was one of the very first to be making efforts to rise on point.

Although Milon continued producing ballets, it was only with *Clari, ou la Promesse de Mariage,* in 1820, that he achieved a work as suited to Emilie's personal style as *Nina.* He was to stay in his post at the Opéra until 1827, but this was the swan song of his choreographic career. However, before *Clari* was staged, the Opéra had to move again, this time because of an assassination. The Duc de Berry, nephew of Louis XVIII, younger son of the future Charles X and husband of Caroline, daughter of the King of Naples, had long been a ballet enthusiast, whose interest was not limited to performances. His many flirtations with dancers culminated in a serious liaison with Mlle Virginie who had a son by him.[39] On February 13, 1820, he left the opera house early to accompany the Duchess, who was *enceinte,* and as he handed her into their carriage he was stabbed by a man later identified as Louis Louvel, a saddler. The audience, unaware of the tragedy, sat on through the end of an opera and two ballets, while the mortally wounded Duke was transported to one of the Opéra's business offices, and the Archbishop of Paris was sent for. The old feud between Church and Theatre was still unresolved; when the Archbishop arrived he would only administer the last rites on the condition that the building never be used again for theatrical purposes. The opera house on the rue de Richelieu therefore was closed, and its demolition begun immediately.

In temporary and rather confining quarters on the rue Favart, the Opéra resumed its schedule in April with *Oedipe à Colone*, a three-act opera by Sacchini which dated back to 1787, and the ever-popular *Nina*. Six novelties—four operas and two ballets—were presented during the thirteen months' stay at the Théâtre Favart. *Clari*, the first of these, was a double triumph for Milon and his sister-in-law. Like *Nina*, it was a sentimental story-ballet. The peasant-girl heroine, deceived by the Duke of Mevilla's promise of marriage, goes to live in luxury with him at his castle, but as he fails to keep his word, she feels disgraced by her compromised situation. After a series of highly emotional incidents, she escapes and returns to her parents, but Clari's father spurns a daughter who has lived in sin. The Duke, discovering in her absence that he sincerely loves her, pursues Clari and gives his pledge to her father that he will marry her.

As the young innocent Clari, Mlle Bigottini surpassed even her earlier acting as Nina, though she was now a mature woman of thirty-six and the mother of four children. No one seemed to notice the curious irony of her portrayal of Clari's grief and shame at being the Duke's mistress, a role which Emilie had filled happily in her private life for many years. Her performance also recalled the sophisticated Mlle Guimard, who was thirty-six, too, when she triumphed in the part of naive Nicette in *La Chercheuse d'esprit*.

After the Congress of Vienna, Aumer was persuaded to extend his engagement at the Kaernthner Thor for five years, but Paris was still the mecca of the ballet world, and he wanted not only to show his ballets there, but also launch his daughter Julie. He first revived *Les Pages du Duc de Vendôme*, and though the Théâtre Favart was miserable and inadequate compared with the stately opera houses he was used to, he was compensated by the lively cooperation of Fanny Bias as the heroine Elise, and Emilie Bigottini, in boy's attire, as the page Victor. The rather slight one-act ballet, padded out with too many special *pas* and *entrées* was not the success it had been in Vienna. The first impression was that Aumer was far less gifted than Milon, but the public, which associated Mlle Bigottini with the pathetic roles of Nina and Clari, was amazed and delighted to watch her going through the pranks of the Duke's page.

The Opéra then presented four evenings in the Salle Louvois, in May and June 1821, pending the completion of its new building, which was rising rapidly on the rue Le Peletier. During its fifty-two years of existence, August 1821 to October 1873 (when it, too, went up in flames), this opera house was to be the scene of the great innovations of the Romantic period as well as the decline of ballet in Western Europe. Heine, who inspired *Giselle*, the finest ballet ever staged there, had nothing good to say of the theatre. "The Académie Royale de Musique, the so-called grand Opéra," he wrote, "is located, as everyone knows, on the rue Lepeletier [sic], near the middle, and just across from the restaurant of Paolo Broggi. . . . The building is not distinguished by any brilliant luxury, it has rather the exterior of a very substantial stable, and the roof is flat. On this roof are perched eight big statues which represent the muses. The ninth is missing,[40] and alas! it is precisely the muse of music. Concerning the absence of this honorable muse, the most extraordinary explanations are circulated. Prosaic folk say that a storm blew it off the roof. More poetic natures declare that it was Polymnia who flung herself down in an access of despair brought on by the wretched singing of M. Duprez." [41]

An opposite, more flattering, view of the theatre was taken by the opera historian Alphonse Royer, with whom the majority of the French proudly concurred. "The auditorium on the rue Le Peletier was the first in Paris to be lit by gas," he noted, ". . . this beautiful theatre, so elegant in its proportions and with such marvelous accoustics."

The new opera house, in fact, stood midway down a narrow street, with a minimum of space surrounding it, without any sort of dignified approach, and with its banal façade marred further by an enormous awning against inclement weather. On gala nights the street was completely blocked by carriages and seething crowds of frustrated ticket holders, ticket speculators, loiterers, and pickpockets. But if the outside of the theatre was unimposing, the interior at least was very attractive, with its four tiers of boxes and seating for nearly two thousand persons, a huge crystal chandelier, and a more than adequate stage. It had cost the then vast sum of almost 2,300,000 francs, in spite of the economy of salvaging structural material, loges, columns, and ornaments from the demolished Salle Richelieu.

After the limitations of oil lamps and candles, the gas lighting was a marvel in itself. Because of this innovation, it would soon be possible to effect the magical moonlit scenes of *Robert le Diable*, *La Sylphide*, and *Giselle*, though gas would also cause the deaths of many celebrated dancers—Clara Webster and Emma Livry among others, whose inflammable tarlatan skirts burst into flames when they hovered like moths too close to the dangerous footlights.

It was on the rue Le Peletier that the Foyer de la Danse acquired its international reputation. During daytime hours some of the ballet classes were held in this large room next to the stage, but at night the foyer vibrated with excitement when all the *danseuses* were warming up before displaying themselves to the public. Foreign princes and diplomats, local celebrities and young men about town all enjoyed the privilege of congregating there before the curtain call. As lovers, would-be lovers, or mere admirers, they came to pay court to their favorites under the watchful scrutiny of the "inevitable ballet mothers."

In these surroundings Mlle Bigottini created her final roles. Of the ten new works presented before she retired, four were ballets, and most of the operas had dance *divertissements*. She appeared in two of the operas, and when Aumer revived his *Alfred le Grand*, Emilie, who had enjoyed playing the page Victor, took the part of King Alfred's page. She was surely as delightful as ever, but the ballet, in spite of its grandiose presentation, was disappointing. *Cendrillon*, with Mlle Bigottini as Cinderella and Paul doubly in evidence as the choreographer and Prince, was far from a masterwork, though the public enjoyed it; and *Aline, Reine de Golconde* was barely redeemed by Mlle Bigottini's efforts to dignify the absurd Queen and even more foolish plot. It was becoming apparent that neither Aumer nor Paul could ever supplant Milon, as indeed it was very evident that there was no dancer-actress to replace the enchanting Emilie.

For over a hundred years it had been a tradition to stage benefit evenings, originally designed to augment the often inadequate salaries of the performers. If, as was sometimes the case, the recipient was not at all in need, the benefit was nevertheless a way of paying tribute to an admired artist. It was the custom for well-known theatre personalities to lend their services for such occasions, and among the celebrities who volunteered for Mlle Bigottini were Mlle Mars, the adored leading actress of the Comédie-Française, and La Pasta, one of the greatest nineteenth-century singers. As was fitting, however, Emilie herself was the star of the event. She regaled the gala audience with a vivacious rendering of Suzanne in a new ballet, *Le Page inconstant* (actually a restaging by Aumer of Dauberval's ballet based on *The Marriage of Figaro*), and, as the surprise of the evening, she acted (again as a page) in a speaking part alongside Mlle Mars.

Twentieth-century balletomanes have often seen dancers embark on acting careers—Tamara Geva in plays, musicals, and movies, Zorina as a narrator, and Maria Karnilova in *Fiddler on the Roof*—but, except for some dancers who became singers, it was a rarity in the days of Mlle Bigottini. She made this single attempt and delighted everyone with a new and unsuspected talent. At the conclusion of the program she stepped out on the stage again to thank the audience as well as her fellow performers, who placed a wreath on her head while a farewell poem was read aloud. The public, which so often had wept unashamedly for Nina and Clari, shed tears at the end for Mlle Bigottini. She had let it be understood that she was retiring.

The celebration in her honor was held on December 18, 1823. Emilie would soon be forty, and there was little she could add to the triumphs of her long career. Ten days after the benefit she made her final appearance, leaving the saddened spectators with a moving last impression of her as Nina.[42]

Nearly half of her life still lay ahead, and although it was known at least that she owned a city and a country house, and had laid aside enough of her fortune to be able to have whatever she needed, history is silent as to how she passed the remaining thirty-five years. All of the eminent men with whom she had liaisons had died or were scattered far from Paris, but perhaps she attracted new loves, for she was still an alluring woman when she retired from the Opéra. And, no doubt, she frequently saw Milon, who survived to the age of eighty-four, and kept in touch with her former dancing partner and lover, Albert, who, after his turns as ballet master in Naples, Marseille and London, came back to the Opéra in 1842 and staged a ballet for Carlotta Grisi.

When Emilie Bigottini died, in April 1858, she had long outlived the *danseuses* who were her contemporaries, and during the span of her seventy-five years had witnessed the most astounding changes in her country and in her profession. Born under Louis XVI, she could recall the evil days of the Revolution and the Republic, the parvenu ostentation of Napoleon's Empire, the reigns of Louis XVIII, Charles X, and Louis-Philippe, and lastly the start of the Second Empire. With the deaths of Vestris and Gardel she had seen the end of the stranglehold of the classical ballet; and by the time of her own death, the golden age of the Romantic ballet had come and gone.

☙

Of the five younger dancers who might have inherited her place, the two leading contenders were Lise Noblet and Amélie Legallois, whose liaisons gained them as much celebrity as their dancing. Général Claparède, the lover of Lise, and Général Lauriston, the lover of Amélie, both made such efforts to promote the careers of their favorites that the public spoke of the rivalry as "the War of the Generals." A true child of the Opéra, Mlle Legallois was already on stage at the age of five as one of Antony's children in Aumer's *Les Amours d'Antoine et de Cléopâtre* in 1808. At nineteen, she made her debut as Clari, and a few months later was seen as Nina, but her talent never fulfilled the hopes of her Général. Though trained by Milon himself, she made a rather poor showing in Mlle Bigottini's roles.

Lise Noblet had a brilliance and verve in the theatre which contrasted oddly with her serious private life. Her twenty-three years at the Opéra included many successes, especially the mime role of Fenella in *La Muette de Portici*. Besieged by a host of despairing admirers, she was nevertheless still faithful to Général Claparède when she retired in 1841.

Three years before Mlle Bigottini left the Opéra, Pauline Paul made a first quite dazzling appearance there and, though momentarily eclipsed by Mlle Mercandotti, she soon came into her own again. The wonderfully gay, sprightly quality of her dancing and the combined influence of her brother Paul, "*l'Aérien*," and her lover, the opera director Lubbert, ensured her lasting popularity. Known as Mme Montessu after she married a dancer of that name, her greatest claim to fame was her interpretation of the sleepwalking Thérèse in Aumer's *La Somnambule*.

Maria Mercandotti's career was as brief as it was sensational. Adopted and brought to England by Lord Fife, who discovered her dancing in Spain as a child prodigy, she was given her ballet training by the ablest French teachers and launched at the Opéra (1821–22) with her own private claque of British balletomanes and dandies. Her engagement at the King's Theatre, London, the following season, ended abruptly when she eloped with one of Lord Fife's rich, rakish young friends, Edward Hughes Ball-Hughes, the marriage ending as sadly and rapidly as her stage career.

Last to appear, in 1823, was the voluptuously beautiful Julia de Varennes, known as "the virtuous Mlle Julia." Along with her sound technique and great physical charm, she had a strange fatality for finding herself in awkward situations and provoking the not always good-natured comments of the press. "Mlle Julia narrowly escaped injuring herself the other day when she foolishly wanted to ape the new steps of Mlle Taglioni, which Paris is mad about just now," said a critic who would have condoned a similar lapse in almost any other dancer. "In trying to stay on point Mlle Julia just missed falling and making a clumsy spectacle of her useless imitation. Let's not push our talent too far. Let this dancer begin by merely having some talent, and then we'll see what happens." [43] In spite of such minor mishaps, Mlle Julia was much in demand for nearly sixteen years, and appeared in Italy, too.

For four years after Mlle Bigottini retired, choreography at the Opéra was at its lowest ebb, only four works being staged in all that time and none of them outstanding. A dreary one-act ballet, *Le Sicilien*, was memorable only because it provided the setting for Marie Taglioni's debut. Nor did the five interim ballerinas contribute anything new to the art of dancing, though portraits of three of them would one day adorn the Foyer de la Danse—Mlles Noblet and Julia, and Mme Montessu, who was still living in 1875 when the final opera house was inaugurated. Emilie Bigottini, who deserved it most, was enshrined there, too.

If only Noverre had lived long enough to see Mlle Bigottini interpreting her two great roles, he undoubtedly would have conceded that she was one of the rare dancers to realize his most cherished precepts. As Marie Sallé had done a hundred years before, Mlle Bigottini discarded the stilted conventions of the past and aspired to convey human emotions. But, whereas Marie Sallé's ideas were lost to many ensuing generations of dancers, the achievement of Mlle Bigottini was a very immediate link with the future.

1. *Marie-Thérèse Perdou de Subligny*

2. *Isaac de Benserade*   3. *Jean-Baptiste Lully*
4. *Decor:* Vénus Jalouse, *Act III*

5. *Françoise Prévost*

6. *Barbara Campanini (La Barbarina)*   7. *Choreography by Magny, 1765*

8. *Marie Sallé*

9. *Marie Sallé, Terpsichore*　10. *Marie Sallé*

11. *Marie Sallé, revised print*   12. *Theatre at the Saint-Laurent Fair*

13. *Auguste Vestris, 1781*   14. *Anna Heinel, 1772*   15. *Gaëtan Vestris*

16. *Marie-Anne Cupis de Camargo*

VUE DE LA MAISON DE MADEM.LE GUIMARD

17. *The House of Mlle Guimard*   18. *Residence "in exile" of Mlle Camargo*

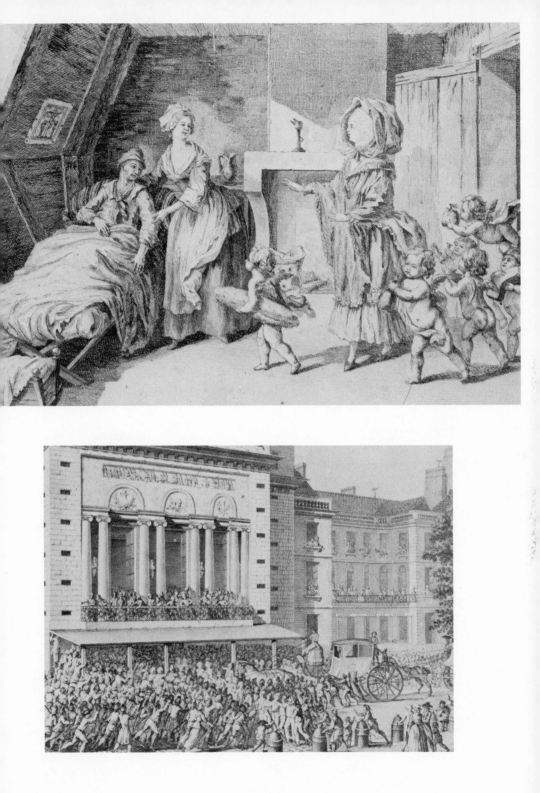

19. *Mlle Guimard, visiting the poor*   20. *The Opéra during the Revolution*

21. *Dauberval and Mlle Allard in* Sylvie   22. *"Pirated" portrait of Gardel*

23. *Emilie Bigottini*

24. *Emilie Bigottini in* Les Pages du Duc de Vendôme

25. *Fanny Bias in* Les Pages du Duc de Vendôme

26. *Maria Medina, Viganò-Terpsichore*   27. *Amalia Brugnoli*

Part IV

THE ROMANTIC BALLET

CHAPTER 11

Marie Taglioni
1804–1884

ROMANTICISM, THE IMPETUS for the new ballet, was wafted to France on the wings of the German literary fairy tales. Unlike traditional folk fairy tales, which tended to be earthy and moralistic, the stories of Novalis, Tieck, Brentano, and Hoffmann were an attempt to escape from the prosaic aspects of life. Reality was unpleasant, so the prose poets dispensed with it and substituted a world of their own make-believe. They conjured up mysterious landscapes peopled with exotic or magical creatures, and their everyday heroes met with extraordinary adventures which suddenly revealed the dormant or unsuspected poetry of their natures. The purveyors of these fairy tales found an immediate response among the artists and intellectuals of their country; during the first two decades of the nineteenth century the influence spread, became German Romanticism, and then crossed the frontiers of other countries.

In France, where the Revolution had failed to produce the hoped-for ideal state, and Napoleon's dream of Empire had ended with

Waterloo, bourgeois materialism was on the rise, combined with a sudden, surprising wave of prudery and hypocrisy. "To what degree of depravity have taste and morals come for someone to sign such an article and for a magazine to dare to publish it?" asked one of the leading reviewers, when *La France Littéraire* brought out Gautier's piece in praise of François Villon. "When you open *Lélia*," said a critic of George Sand's novel, "see to it that your library door is locked (lest others become contaminated)." [44] Demands followed for censorship of literature and the theatre, and the police were authorized to raid the bookshops for works by various contemporary writers and even the books of Voltaire and Diderot. Obviously a change of direction was needed, and the young intelligentsia felt that Romanticism was the answer, and since they were far less passive than their German neighbors, they espoused the new cult not as a form of escapism but rather as a call to open revolt.

One of their early battlegrounds was the theatre of the Comédie-Française in 1830, during the run of Victor Hugo's *Hernani*, when they turned out to support the author, their chosen spiritual leader. Gautier, who was then an art student, later described the affray in his *History of Romanticism*. "Whoever was young, brave, in love, or poetical was filled with the spirit of *Hernani*," he said. "What shouts! What hoots! What hissing! What bursts of bravos! What thunders of applause! The leaders of the contending parties insulted each other like the heros of Homer before they came to blows . . . ." [45] Wearing a scarlet vest (his conservative tailor at first refused to make it for him), with his hair streaming down over his shoulders, and followed by a horde of long-haired, bearded, wildly clad "ferocious Romanticists," the nineteen-year-old Gautier was on hand for thirty performances in order to demonstrate against the "academical and classical baldheads." Battles were still being fought in 1834 between the partisans of Marie Taglioni, the established high priestess of the Romantic movement, and the supporters of her rival, the newcomer Fanny Elssler, but by that time Romanticism was firmly entrenched in France, and had profoundly affected not only the arts but also morals and manners and human nature.

Apart from Romanticism, the most important influence on the ballet was the introduction of dancing "on point." Today the question is: who invented it? and the answers are many and confusing. For a long time it was generally believed that the originator was Marie Taglioni—a normal assumption, since her world-wide reputation attracted attention to her use of point dancing when it was still a novelty. Basing their opinions mainly on old prints, modern historians have proposed a number of other likely candidates. Both Lillian Moore and Walter Terry have indicated pictures of an unidentified dancer in Sweden (1790), Mlle Parisot (1796), Maria del Caro (1804), Fanny Bias (1821), all of whom seem to be dancing on point—or nearly so. But pictures are not conclusive evidence, since too much depends on the whims of the artists who have always wanted the dancers to appear as ethereal as possible. Typical are prints in which idealized dancers float among clouds, emerge dripping from mountain streams, or tread on flowers which do not bend beneath their weight. Naturally they also seem barely to skim the earth with the tips of their toes.

A better proof is offered by eyewitness accounts of persons competent to judge what they were seeing. Amalia Brugnoli learned from Armand Vestris, said the magazine *I Teatri* in 1829, ". . . the sort of dancing which was lost with the celebrated Mlle Gosselin, and which places upon the extreme point of the toe the weight that others sustain by the entire foot." And nine years after the premature death of the same Geneviève Gosselin, the *Journal des Débats*, reviewed Taglioni's dancing (August 3, 1827), and observed: "It reminds one of the elder Mlle Gosselin, the astonishing flexibility of her limbs, the muscular strength which enabled her to remain poised during one minute on the very tip of her feet. . . ." One minute!

Obviously Mlle Gosselin made only the merest beginnings in a technique which Amalia Brugnoli had mastered a few years later. Taglioni herself saw Brugnoli in Vienna in 1822 and grudgingly admitted in her memoirs: "Mlle Brugnoli was a dancer who presented a *new* kind of dancing; she did very extraordinary things on the point of her foot, which was long and narrow, very advantageous for this sort of dancing. . . . I did not find her graceful because, in order to rise on point, she had to make great efforts with her arms. . . ."

We need not pay attention to Marie Taglioni's reservations—her remarks about other dancers were always tinged with malice. A less biased report came out in the 1827 *Almanacco* of La Scala, when Brugnoli appeared in Louis Henry's *Dircea*. After describing her triumphs abroad, the article went on: "This phenomenon . . . is La Brugnoli, whom our directors hastened to present together with her husband, the dancer Samengo, and the *danseuse* Vaque-Moulin. All the most perfect that can be seen in dancing in the way of strength and nimble footwork resides in La Brugnoli. Actually working on the point of her foot, her steps, her attitudes, her turns acquire an airy something which strikes and astounds the imagination. In this dancer, trained in a strict school for graceful lines of arms as well as body, not even the severest critic can find the slightest artistic erring, not even those lapses which occasionally we may prefer to perfection."

Leaving aside the hide-and-seek game of finding the inventor, it remains evident that toe dancing had the almost magical effect of transforming the earth-bound ballerinas into the airy sylphs who, as much as any poet or musician, were the luminaries of the Romantic era in Paris.

Dr. Louis Véron, an oddly materialistic, unromantic, and controversial figure, presided over the Opéra during these days of exciting change. His appointment as sole administrator was hailed with particular joy, because he replaced a director who had been under orders to the despised Intendant of the Royal Theatres, the Vicomte Sosthène de la Rochefoucauld. Not only had the prudish Vicomte obliged all the *danseuses* to let down their skirts to ankle-length in the hope of subduing the carnal thoughts of the spectators, not only did he have two stairways built backstage to separate male from female performers, but he also obtained a royal edict forbidding access behind the scenes or in the foyers to anyone who was not in the employ of the Opéra. "I won't remind you," remarked Marcel Bouteron, "of the terrible danger to the peace of Europe caused by this ban. The diplomatic corps rose to a man; the Russians threatened France with invasion; the British murmured the word blockade; the Austrians prepared a note for the Holy Alliance; and the Italians swore they'd resort to the Jesuits." [46] Dr. Véron immediately restored the privileges and, during the four and a half years of his directorship, succeeded in turning the Foyer de la Danse into the most fashionable gathering place in the city.

It was under Véron's administration that the Opéra became a private enterprise rather than a government-run institution. On accepting the post he put up a large borrowed sum as guaranty and, on the promise of an additional annual government subsidy, he undertook the whole financial responsibility. The hatred which he inspired in many quarters was in great part due to jealousy, his most unbearable sin being the ease with which he made money. Almost all of his speculations turned out well and, although Opéra directors traditionally retired leaving enormous debts, Véron resigned in 1835 with a personal profit of nearly 1,000,000 francs.

"Dr. Véron, under whose management the Paris Opéra rose to a degree of perfection it has never attained since; Dr. Véron who, as someone said, was as much part and parcel of the history of Paris during the first half of the nineteenth century as was Napoleon I of the history of France . . ." [47] was already a doctor of medicine at thirty, had founded the very successful *Revue de Paris*, and had acquired a more than casual knowledge of art, theatre, music, and politics. An astute businessman, a *littérateur*, a celebrated gastronome, he had a rare gift for making the generous or flamboyant gesture that was oddly at variance with his stolid, almost gross appearance. His flair for publicity, something quite new in his day, aroused a lot of sarcastic comment and was almost superfluous at the Opéra in view of the assets he inherited from the previous director.

Dr. Véron's legacy from Lubbert was the greatest assemblage of talent that had ever been seen in Paris, and was to be equaled only once again when Diaghilev, in the twentieth century, presented Chaliapin in *Boris Godunov*, a company of the world's most gifted dancers and choreographers, and artists such as Bakst and Benois. At the Opéra in 1831, the singers included the "angel-voiced tenor" Nourrit and Levasseur, Mme Damoreau and Mlle Dorus; in the ballet were Mazilier and Jules Perrot, the most brilliant male dancer of the Romantic period, Marie Taglioni, Pauline Leroux, and Pauline Duvernay, who made her debut a few weeks after Dr. Véron took over; and never since the time of Louis XIV had there been such sumptuous, magical scenery as that produced by the inventive architect-designer Duponchel (later he served two terms as Opéra director) and the stage artist Pierre Ciceri.

To top all this Dr. Véron fell heir to *Robert le Diable*, which Lubbert had commissioned from Meyerbeer. "It would have required more brains to fail than to succeed with this opera," said Charles de Boigne and went on to describe it as "an immense, prodigious, dizzying successs." [48] It was the third act which made the deepest impression. The setting was a macabre ruined cloister bathed in moonlight; dead nuns, who in life were unfaithful to their vows, rose from their graves and performed a ghostly dance of seduction until the hero, Robert, lured on by their abbess, stole a talisman from the tomb of the convent's patron, Sainte Rosalie.

To understand the effect of this scene and the virtue triumphant of the finale when the cathedral doors swung open, and Robert, absolved of his crime, saw his beloved waiting for him in her bridal robes, to realize the impact of all this on Dr. Véron's public, one must bear in mind the semi-hysteria of Paris of the 1830s—the emotional climate of Gautier, George Sand (she made Prosper Mérimée take her to see *Robert le Diable*, carrying her sleeping small daughter in his arms), Hugo, Alfred de Musset, and all the sentimental Romantics for whom "Passion was king, as Reason once had been, and the Irrational was worshipped as a God." [49] *Robert le Diable* introduced the first of the eerie moonlit fantasies and it set the mood for the art, the ballets, and the legend of Marie Taglioni.

"Legend has completely triumphed over fact," said André Levinson, celebrated ballet historian. ". . . A literary fiction has colored the truth regarding this great person; the lyrical outbursts of poets exalted the 'Sylphide' to the seventh heaven; the engravings which adorned *Keepsakes* masked her real features beneath a likeness of pure convention. The complex and private life of a human being is submerged under a monotonous and verbose phraseology, because mediocrity in literature had never sunk so low as during the aftermath of 1830." [50]

Levinson was right about the myths that have surrounded Marie Taglioni. Where he was wrong, where chauvinism defeated his better judgment, was in asserting that La Taglioni was a product of France. ". . . People loved to think of her as a foreigner; it was a mistake," he declared. "Marie Taglioni is much the greatest glory of the French school, and occupied the same position as that formerly held by a Camargo or a Gaetano Vestris, despite their foreign origin. Her father, Philippe, had long been attached to the staff of the Opéra." [51]

Such comparisons are absurd: Camargo began in Paris, aged sixteen, and except for the time when she moved to the country to please her lover, her whole career of twenty-five years was at the Opéra; Vestris, too, danced regularly at the Opéra for thirty-three years, apart from the year and a half when he was sent away as punishment for his obstreperous behavior; Mlle Taglioni, on the other hand, had developed her own original style during five successful years in Vienna and Stuttgart before she was ever seen at the Opéra (for six debut performances during three weeks), after which she returned to Stuttgart for nearly another year, and, as we shall find, the greater part of her dancing career was in countries other than France. As for Philippe, he was a man of fifty who had made a name for himself as dancer, choreographer, and ballet master in most of the great cities of Europe before he went to Paris in 1827 to present his daughter. Until then he had been at the Opéra only briefly and in minor roles; after dancing in Italy for five years, he arrived in Paris as a youth of twenty-two and, realizing that an outsider had little chance to compete with Vestris, Gardel, and Aumer, was only too pleased to leave, in 1803, to become ballet master in Sweden.

It was in Stockholm that Philippe Taglioni met and married Sophia, daughter of the leading opera singer Christoffer Karsten, and it was there, too, that their daughter Marie was born in April 1804. Eight years in Vienna followed, where Gustave and Paul were born, and in Cassel, where Philippe remained as ballet master until the dangers of war made him decide to settle his family in Paris while he continued his nomadic career in Italy, Stockholm and Copenhagen, Munich and Vienna.

Marie's life from this point on has been described in almost too picturesque detail by Léandre Vaillat, who thought he had come to the end of available information about the ballerina when he made an unhoped-for lucky find: chance suddenly brought him Mlle Taglioni's birth and marriage certificates, passport and will, her contracts, her collection of newspaper clippings, the diary she kept during her girlhood, and many other items, including the book in which her father recorded all of his own and Marie's performances, with his personal comments and the list of all their earnings and expenses. The biography resulting from this store of information could have been a quite perfect source for later historians, except for the fact that its author was so much in love with his subject that he either glossed over her imperfections or carefully avoided mentioning them at all.

Marie, according to Vaillat's discoveries in her diary, was nearly twelve when she started her first ballet lessons with Coulon. She was a thin, stoop-shouldered, unprepossessing child, and it did not help matters that she often played hooky from class and failed to make a sufficient effort whenever she was present. Mme Taglioni, lonely without her husband and suffering from the recent sorrow of losing her son Gustave, was bound to spoil Marie. With a mother's partiality, she had no doubt that the girl was making brilliant progress, and her reports to the absent Philippe were rhapsodic.

It was therefore a shock when Marie was seventeen, a normal age for a debut, to discover that she was not at all ready to be seen in public, not even in a *corps de ballet*. Mme Taglioni had inquired of the Opéra's newly appointed ballet master, Jean Aumer, whether her daughter might be among the student dancers chosen to go to London as ballet girls. "*Chère Madame*," said Aumer, after a few minutes of watching Marie in class, "do you want me to speak to you as a friend and give you good advice? Well, then, make a dressmaker of your daughter, for she will never be a good dancer. I know your husband too well not to be sure that he would never want his child to be merely someone hanging about backstage." [52]

In the meanwhile, Philippe had taken Aumer's place in Vienna. With the security of a three-year contract, he felt able to send for his family and, encouraged by his wife's accounts of Marie's dancing, he also arranged for the young girl's debut at the Kaernthner Thor. However, not even a last-minute concentrated course of extra lessons with Coulon had prepared Marie for her father's critical eye. Many years later, when she had retired from the stage, she wrote a description of the rigorous training which Philippe at once imposed on her. A heartless taskmaster, he kept her at work six hours a day for six months before he allowed her to appear in the theatre. She was sometimes almost unconscious from exhaustion. Her explanations of this teaching, too long and detailed and perhaps too technical for inclusion here, indicate a general similarity with the Cecchetti method in use today. At the time it was unique and generated an entirely new approach to dancing.

"Like the artists of the great periods of painting," said Dr. Véron in his *Mémoires*, "Taglioni *père* founded a new school of the dance, entirely different in its style and philosophic thought from the school of a Gardel or a Vestris. The two schools actually presented a striking contrast: Vestris taught elegance, seduction; he was a sensualist; he insisted on provocative smiles, poses and attitudes that were almost immodest and shameless. I have often heard him say quite cynically to his pupils: 'My dears, be charming, coquettish; display the most alluring freedom in every move you make; you must inspire love both during and after your *pas* and make the audience and orchestra desirous of sleeping with you.' The school, style, and language of Taglioni *père* were exactly the opposite. He demanded graceful ease of movement, lightness, elevation, and especially *ballon;* but he did not allow his daughter a single gesture or pose which might be lacking in decency or modesty. He told her: 'Women and young girls must be able to watch you dance without blushing; your performance should be marked by restraint, delicacy and good taste.'" [53]

Entry in the journal of Philippe Taglioni: ". . . For the first time that my daughter Marie appeared on the stage, she obtained the very greatest success." [54] Marie, aged eighteen, cured at last of her stooping posture and properly trained in her father's new method, sewn into her costume by her anxious mother, and a wreath of pink roses on her head, had begun her career on June 10, 1822, in *La Réception d'une nymphe au temple de Terpsichore*, a ballet ideally suited to a debutante. And who, at the time, would have guessed it to be one of the most important dates in ballet history? For the next year and a half young Mlle Taglioni continued to merit her father's approval and the plaudits of the Viennese public. She gained assurance and poise, dancing with various partners in ballets by Gioja, Henry, and Armand Vestris, as well as in *pas* composed by her father, and she profited by observing such experienced dancers as Mlles Millière and Heberle, and especially Amalia Brugnoli, her model for point dancing. In March 1823, Fanny Elssler, who was not yet fourteen, and so far had been seen mainly in children's ballets, made a second debut. And again, who could have imagined the fierce rivalry that would develop when Taglioni and Elssler met again in Paris?

After leaving Vienna, Marie danced for three months in Munich and then, in October 1824, with only a month to spare before an engagement at Stuttgart, the Taglionis hurried to Paris. Their journey had the double purpose of fetching Paul, who had spent a year there in school, and of trying to arrange a debut for Marie at the Opéra, where Philippe was received with such disdain and discourtesy that he abandoned the project altogether.

Stuttgart, however, more than made up for the disappointment of Paris. The tiny capital of Württemberg, a lavish center of ballet since the days of Noverre (and destined, as a mid-twentieth-century German industrial city of over a million, to become a ballet center again under the aegis of John Cranko) provided an audience for Marie as discriminating as and even more receptive than the Viennese. As partners she had her brother Paul and the handsome Stuhlmüller, later celebrated as the lover of Fanny Elssler; and as material evidence of her own success she had gifts from Württemberg's royal family: two sets of diamond earrings, a gold chain and cross, gold comb with amethysts, brooch, and three gold bracelets. All of it duly noted in Philippe's account book, it was the modest beginning of the imposing collection of jewels she owned when she retired.

She would remember these years in Stuttgart (November 1824 to March 1828) as the happiest of her whole career for, in spite of the fanatical adoration she later inspired as a dancer, she was to be the victim of jealousies and a tragic marriage and more than her share of troubles. But for the present, her ambitious father kept her working, working to perfect the point technique and gossamer style which would literally cast a spell over the public and critics of Paris.

Paris indeed! A friend of Philippe's had insisted on negotiating the traditional six trial appearances without which no dancer could hope to obtain an Opéra contract; the Opéra was under new direction, he had assured Philippe, who was still smarting from his reception there, and it had even been agreed that Marie would dance only in *pas* composed by her father. During the summer holiday months of their last year at Stuttgart the family therefore set out for Paris again. For her daily practice class Marie went back to her first teacher, Coulon, who had also taught her father in 1799, and one can imagine his surprise and admiration on discovering her progress and the new direction her dancing had taken. When she showed him the *pas* to be inserted for her in *Le Sicilien* for her first appearance, on July 23, he warned her not to let anyone watch her rehearse it. Its novelty would arouse such jealousy, he said, that he feared an attempt might be made to prevent her debut.

"Total success," Philippe noted laconically in his diary the morning after *Le Sicilien;* "a more than total success," after the fifth evening; and after the sixth and last performance he recorded the fact that someone had tossed a wreath of flowers onto the stage for Marie.[55] By then the public had worked up a wild enthusiasm for the new *danseuse*, and the critics had outdone themselves in raving about her graceful, floating, modest manner of dancing and the astonishing feat of rising on point which, they said, no one but Mlle Gosselin had attempted before. But Coulon had been right in predicting the jealousy of the Opéra's personnel. After Marie's first success,

Lubbert explained to Philippe that it would be impossible to allow her to continue her debut performances unless she was willing to prove herself in one of the Opéra's classic *pas*. The *prix de la danse* in Spontini's opera *La Vestale* was chosen, and it was fortunate then that Marie had years of practice dancing with all sorts of partners, old and young and trained in a variety of schools. In a deliberate effort to make her appear inept she was assigned an inexperienced beginner as partner and, worse yet, she was about to step out before the footlights when one of the dancers whispered to her: "Be careful! I don't know what there is on the stage but it's very slippery." It was all too true: the next day someone informed Philippe that bits of soap had been scattered on the stage and, in fact, three dancers had fallen just before Marie's *entreé*.

Nevertheless Mlle Taglioni was engaged at the Opéra as *remplaçante*, to begin as soon as she finished her term in Stuttgart. The effect of her performances in Paris and on tour in the major French cities during the two ensuing years was best conveyed by the reviewer who said that "a breeze wafted her onto the stage"; and in London, where she was to become as much or more of a cult than in Paris, the impression was much the same. First seen there in *Flore et Zéphire*, on June 3, 1830, she danced "with such extraordinary ease, and with the airiness of thistledown, that it would scarcely have increased our wonder and delight had she ascended as a spirit," [56] and she was reengaged at the King's Theatre for four months the following April.

The first time Mlle Taglioni and her parents returned to Paris from London there was a new king on the throne of France: Louis-Philippe had replaced the exiled Charles X. When they came back the second time Lubbert was no longer at the Opéra, Dr. Véron had been in charge for several months, and preparations were under way for staging the opera *Robert le Diable.* Philippe Taglioni heard the score of the strange third act on August 20; six weeks later he had the ballet ready for rehearsal; and six weeks after that (perhaps it was too soon, in spite of all the director's precautions) the première took place. From Dr. Véron's day to the present, the story of that fateful evening has been told a hundred times over. "The opening night of *Robert le Diable*," said Dr. Véron, "was a series of dreadful happenings which might have had the direst results." He recalled that in the third act a brace carrying a dozen lighted lamps with glass shades crashed to the floor as Mlle Dorus was coming on stage and just missed falling on her head; a little later a flat dropped from the flies, Mlle Taglioni was barely able to leap aside and escape serious injury, and the curtain had to be lowered; finally Nourrit, who should have remained on stage to marry the princess, was so carried away by his role that he plunged through a trap door where only Levasseur was supposed to vanish. A shout went up from the stage: "Nourrit is dead!" No one was hurt, however, and there was one humorous moment when Levasseur saw Nourrit come hurtling down and inquired: "What the devil are you doing down here? Have they changed the plot?" [57]

During the year prior to *Robert le Diable* only one role of any real interest was created for Mlle Taglioni, that of Zoloé in Auber's opera *Le Dieu et la Bayadère* and, although received with enthusiasm by the public and press, even this was not totally satisfactory, since much of it depended on miming rather than dancing. Nor did she care for her role in the ballet of the nuns, despite the fact that her father had composed it especially for her. The supreme moment of her career was not far distant, however, and in the meanwhile, two matters of crucial importance were settled. Philippe signed a contract for Marie by which she was bound to appear at the Opéra for its main seasons, from August 1831, for a period of six years, and the astute Philippe not only obtained a tremendous salary for her and exclusivity of her roles, but also had himself hired as ballet master so that he could be sure of choreographing her ballets. Settled, too, was the question of her marriage. Marie had fallen in love, and as far as can be ascertained, it was a new experience. Naive in such matters, misled by the young man's aristocratic name, his ardent courtship, and high-handed manner, she became engaged to Comte Gilbert de Voisins. He was to prove a thoroughly worthless person, sarcastic, unkind, and even unscrupulous.

La Sylphide, by which Marie Taglioni was transfigured as the most immortal of all dancers, was not merely a sort of fairy tale about a youth in Scotland, able to see and converse with a magical sylph-like creature who remained invisible to other people; it was the expression in ballet form of the whole spirit of German Romanticism, and perhaps, too, of the dreams and yearnings which have always haunted mankind, and always will. *La Sylphide* is the story of James Reuben, who is about to marry his cousin Effie with whom he is not really in love. As he is sleeping in a chair by the fireside, on the night before his wedding, he has a dream-vision of a beautiful winged sylphide who hovers around him lovingly, and when she kisses him he awakens and sees her vanish up the chimney. As the wedding preparations go forward, the vision reappears, and James feels himself torn between his loyalty to Effie (the earthly and prosaic) and the lure of the sylphide (poetry and the longing of mortals for the unattainable). At last, he follows the sylphide into the forest, but he carries with him a fatal and symbolic gift. The wicked witch has handed him a rose-colored scarf, explaining that if he places it around the shoulders of the sylphide, her wings will fall off, and she will be his forever. Of course, the airy being dies when she loses her wings, and as her sister sylphs descend from the skies and bear her away, James is left standing alone in the forest, listening to the distant strains of the wedding procession of Effie, who has married his rival. The symbolism is clear: an airy vision without its wings is no longer valid, and he who turns his back on the world to chase after dreams is apt to find that the world is no longer waiting for him. It was, nevertheless, this very pursuit of the unreal, the ideal, which satisfied the cravings of the Romanticists and ensured the success of the new ballet.

The singer Nourrit, who was a poet in fact, as well as in the interpretation of his roles, wrote the libretto for *La Sylphide*. It has always been said that he was inspired by *Trilby*, a tale by Charles Nodier, but the resemblance between the two is rather strained. In any case, Nourrit, a modest and self-effacing man, soon dropped his claim to the authorship, and only Philippe Taglioni's name remained on the program. Neither expense nor effort was spared to produce the ballet, which was to be the first true vehicle for Mlle Taglioni and a fabulous one, in the most literal sense of the word. Philippe had already planned his choreography before he entered into discussions with the composer Schneitzhoeffer. This musician had produced a number of works for the Opéra, was a familiar figure on the Paris scene, and the butt of endless jokes, because the French found his name unpronounceable. It was said that he grew so tired of it that he had visiting cards printed which read: "Schneitzhoeffer (pronounced Bertrand)." His score for *La Sylphide* is no longer used for present-day revivals, having been replaced by an adaptation of the one commissioned by Bournonville from Løvenskiold in 1836 for the Royal Danish Ballet, but at the time of the original Paris production it elicited more praise than censure. The floating white costume of the sylphide, now known the world over as the Romantic *tutu*, was an essential element of this first production, and has been generally attributed to Eugène Lami; and for the settings, Ciceri, who designed so many masterworks for the Opéra, outdid himself in the moonlit forest scene, where the effect was enhanced by Dr. Véron's new gas reflectors and the flight of dozens of sylphs drifting about the treetops on invisible wires.[58] Dr. Véron himself admitted that he was hardly able to sleep during the night preceding the première. Although he had personally verified every detail of the flying apparatus, he was still obsessed by the series of mishaps that had upset the opening night of *Robert le Diable*.

The one participant who seems to have been neglected in all the excitement was Mazilier. Why he was given the leading male role is not quite clear. He and Perrot both joined the Opéra in 1830. Perrot had proven an extraordinarily brilliant dancer, Mazilier had not; but Mazilier was very handsome (*"beau comme M. Mazilier,"* was the saying), whereas Perrot was almost ugly. Whatever the reasons for choosing Mazilier, it is more than likely that Perrot was not chosen because Mlle Taglioni was neurotically jealous of his success. It was his misfortune that, the year before, in *Flore et Zéphire*, he had received more applause than she did and that the press had commented on it. When he was given an ovation for his dancing in *La Révolte au sérail*, 1833, she made a terrible scene with Dr. Véron, and a number of writers of the period stated quite frankly that she was largely to blame for Perrot's departure in 1835, thereby depriving the Opéra of one of the greatest dancers and choreographers. "La Sylphide was afraid; she didn't want anyone else to be able to take the least little part of the public's devotion away from her." [59]

As for the Sylphide herself, if Paris had been wildly enthusiastic about her before, the furor rose at this time to the pitch of near insanity. Earlier, a new verb was coined: *taglioniser,* i.e. to dance or move with the lightness of La Taglioni; now another word was added to the current vocabulary: *sylphide;* there were sylphide coiffures, dresses, flowers . . . moods; and the public persuaded itself that Mlle Taglioni was not only the theatre incarnation of the airy, pure, unsensual creature, but that she embodied all the qualities of the sylphide in her private life. Never before or since has there been such a gush of febrile, overwrought prose as that which flooded the Paris press from then on for years to come. "The flight of birds or the airy passage of butterflies cannot be described in words; they

must be seen. It is the same with Mlle Taglioni: language is power-
less. . . . She speaks to the soul; she makes one dream." . . . "To
describe Marie Taglioni one would have to dip a hummingbird quill
into the colors of the rainbow and inscribe it on the gauze wings of
a butterfly." . . . "She was so pale, so chaste, so sad," sighed the
author Jules Janin, one of her staunchest admirers, adding that when
she expired in the final scene of the ballet, it made him think of "the
death throes of a beautiful lily." Typical, too, was a letter the ballerina treasured from a youth who claimed he was dying of his hope-
less love for the "celestial" creature—"Farewell, farewell, beloved
Marie. Your image, the image of Taglioni, will be close to me in
the tomb."

La Sylphide had its première on March 12, 1832; less than a month
later the Sylphide was in flight—not soaring as usual above Ciceri's
stage trees but in actual flight away from Paris. The dreaded cholera
broke out early in April, and Dr. Véron sent off his leading singers
and dancers for an extended holiday, while he himself stayed on to
encourage the remaining artists and to provide some sort of entertainment for the few people who were brave enough to attend the
theatre. With justifiable pride, he noted in his *Mémoires* that he took
care of all of his staff without asking for help from anyone, although
often during the seven months of the epidemic the box office took
in as little as 500 francs in an evening.

Mlle Taglioni went first to Berlin, where her brother Paul was
settled, married to the dancer Amalia Galster and father of Marie's
namesake, who was two, and would in turn also become a celebrated
ballerina. A few weeks of furious activity included dancing in *Robert
le Diable* and *La Sylphide*, dinners and balls with the royal family
and diplomatic corps, with avalanches of flowers and gifts, and then
the entire family proceeded to London, where *La Sylphide* was
staged again, with Paul as his sister's partner and Amalia as the home-
spun Effie. But more significant than all the triumphs and festivities
of this London season was Mlle Taglioni's marriage, on July 14, to

Alfred, Comte Gilbert de Voisins, in a Protestant church ceremony. Because of objections on the part of Gilbert de Voisins' father, the civil ceremony, without which no marriage is valid in France, was deferred until August 28, 1834, in Paris. By that time Alfred was already bored with his captive sylph and eight weeks later he left her to make a six months' journey to Constantinople with his brother.

For La Taglioni there now began the winter of her discontent. Shocked and grieved by the departure of her husband, she was also forced into a mortifying competition with Fanny Elssler, who made her debut on September 15. An unusually clever publicity campaign by Dr. Véron and the partisanship of the critics and public whipped up the rivalry until everyone was divided into two opposing camps—Taglionists and Elsslerists—reminiscent of the earlier clash between Sallé and Camargo, but much more violent. Charles Maurice of the *Courrier des Théâtres*, who had been almost viciously anti-Taglioni from the beginning, now took particular pleasure in extolling the newcomer; and erstwhile faithful supporters went over to the "enemy." Marie, far from pretty, past thirty, and still suffering the aftereffects of a mild case of cholera contracted during the summer in England, Marie, who had fumed at sharing any part of her laurels with Perrot, saw half of the public madly in love with Mlle Elssler, who was only twenty-five, incredibly pretty, with feminine allure and a flashing staccato style of dancing that could also be very voluptuous and appealing.

In the spring of 1835 Dr. Véron decided to resign, and was replaced in September by Duponchel, who had much less patience with Mlle Taglioni's pretentious vagaries; and in May the wandering husband reappeared. "There was a scene," confided Philippe to his diary, followed by a brief reconciliation which resulted in Marie's famous "*mal au genou*," a trumped-up knee ailment which baffled all the doctors while Mlle Taglioni kept to her chaise longue for nearly six months. Little Marie, known in the family as Nini, was born the following March, and from then on in ballet circles "*mal au genou*" became the jocular expression for the pregnancy of a *danseuse*.

Although she always kept his name, and eventually her remains were placed in the Gilbert de Voisins tomb, although her son Georges (by whom?), born in October 1843, inherited the title, Marie Taglioni's husband never came back again after their one reunion in the spring of 1835. Nine years later he obtained a legal separation and, for the rest of his dull, insignificant life, he never missed an opportunity to make derogatory remarks about La Taglioni.

In June, while Marie was still convalescing after the birth of her daughter, her rival, Fanny Elssler, created her most spectacular role, dancing the *cachucha* in *Le Diable boiteux*; but less than four months later Mlle Taglioni was ready with her retort: *La Fille du Danube*, in which she became as much of a water nymph as she had ever been a sylph of the air. Her father had been preparing this ballet for some time with the help of the writer Eugène Demares. The diary first mentions this young man at a dinner on May 1, and not long after, it was common knowledge in Paris that he was the ballerina's lover. Gilbert de Voisins, when the gossip was repeated to him, is reported to have commented nothing more than that Demares certainly had not chosen a pretty mistress.

A mixed reception greeted the new ballet, and Mlle Taglioni did not take kindly to any sort of adverse criticism. Neither did she enjoy the constantly mounting tide of comparisons drawn between herself and Fanny Elssler, all too often favoring the latter. Her engagement at the Opéra was becoming a strain, and Duponchel, whose patience had run out over the *"mal au genou"* and her frequent refusals to dance for one selfish reason or another, was in no hurry to renew her contract. Counting the early Vienna-Stuttgart years as the first phase of her dancing career, the second, or Paris, phase was evidently coming to an end, and she welcomed an offer to appear in St. Petersburg.

It is obviously impossible in a mere sketch of La Taglioni's life to give details of all her performances in hundreds of ballets, but we cannot let her fly off to Russia without a brief mention of two special galas connected with this period. On July 3, 1833, at a benefit for the singer Mme Devrient-Schroeder, the sumptuous fare offered to the London audience included Beethoven's *Fidelio* and one act each from *Otello* and Weber's *Euryanthe*, sung by Mlle Malibran and La Pasta (who appeared ten years earlier in Mlle Bigottini's benefit), and two *divertissements* danced by Mlles Taglioni and Elssler together. The other extraordinary occasion was Mlle Taglioni's own benefit at the Opéra, when the program announced the beloved tenor Nourrit, a new ballet, *Brazila, ou la Tribu des femmes*, a *pas de deux* by Fanny Elssler and her sister and, as the great event of the evening, the seventy-five-year-old Auguste Vestris dancing a minuet and gavotte with Marie Taglioni.

Of course, Eugène Demares accompanied Marie Taglioni to Russia, as did Taglioni *père*, Mme Taglioni, Nini, the little dog, and an astounding baggage caravan of personal effects, costume trunks, furnishings and rugs, and the jewel coffer, carefully guarded by Philippe. Travel was not simple in 1837. From the day of departure Eugène was not only the official lover, but also the self-appointed indispensable impresario, publicity agent, manager, librettist, and major-domo; and his reports to his newspaper friends in Paris were the best, if somewhat euphoric, accounts of La Taglioni's reception when they reached their destination.

As Philippe had once noted down an earlier debut of Marie, now it was Eugène's turn. "Immense, immense success! Incredible success! Such as has never been seen before . . . ," he wrote, and this time he did not exaggerate. So great was the fervor aroused by the new *danseuse* that etiquette was swept aside. The decorous audience forgot itself and shouted; the Czar left the royal box to sit in the front row of the orchestra in order to watch at close range and also went up onto the stage to congratulate Mlle Taglioni. Three thousand portrait prints were distributed (what happened to all of them over the years?), and a cascade of jewels began to fill the ballerina's coffer to overflowing—tributes from generals, princes, ladies of the court, with the Czar himself presenting diamond and emerald brooches and earrings, and notably a garland of diamond and turquoise forget-me-nots for La Taglioni to wear in her hair.

Marie had her lover and family to watch over her and not even a rival *danseuse* to trouble the atmosphere. Duponchel, when news reached him concerning Philippe's *La Gitana*, had countered with Mazilier's *La Gipsy* with Fanny Elssler at the Opéra,[60] but in Russia Mlle Elssler was a remote specter, hovering on a snowbound horizon, a thousand miles away. After such an auspicious first season, Mlle Taglioni's St. Petersburg contract was renewed for four more years, with plenty of time during the spring-summer holiday for triumphant tours to Poland, Vienna, and London. The most wishful ballerina could not have imagined a more perfect existence, but for Marie the dream was suddenly shattered. Eugène Demares fell ill with what would seem to have been cerebral meningitis, and after two terrifying weeks he died, leaving Marie almost mad with grief.

Eugène's death was a sad blow for Philippe, too. He was vigorous and youthful for his sixty years but, in addition to the problems of reviving his early ballets and constantly staging new ones for Marie, he would now be saddled with all the responsibilities that Eugène had been pleased to assume. Besides, he had grown fond of the young man, who was more of a son-in-law to him than the worthless Alfred had ever been. However, like traditional good troupers, father and daughter had to go on with their work. Philippe was finishing *L'Ombre*, and only a few weeks later Mlle Taglioni made her first appearance in that strangely apropos role—a young girl's ghost, drifting hither and yon, seeking her lost lover.

The Sylphide—she always remained that in people's minds, no matter what roles she danced—had three more winters to spend in

St. Petersburg and many visits to make to Vienna (where forty young aristocrats unhitched the horses and proudly pulled her carriage through the streets), to London (where the glitter of all the jewels she wore onstage almost outshone her performance), to Milan [61] (where she held her own against the twenty-four-year-old Cerrito), and to Stockholm (where she was hailed as a returning native daughter). It seemed she was endlessly crisscrossing the vast snowy plains of Russia, and on one of these journeys she had an adventure so picturesque that we give it here in her own words, as she told it to Albert Vandam. She was leaving St. Petersburg with her father, two violinists, and her maid and, in spite of the warnings about Trischka, a former steward of Prince Paskiwiecz turned leader of a fearsome band of highwaymen, Philippe had insisted on bringing along all of Marie's jewels and a great deal of money. In the middle of the second night "all of a sudden, in the thick of a dense forest, our road was barred by a couple of horsemen, while a third opened the door of our carriage. It was Trischka himself. 'Mademoiselle Taglioni?' he said in very good German, lifting his hat. 'I was told you were coming this way. I am sorry, mademoiselle, that I could not come to St. Petersburg to see you dance, but as chance has befriended me, I hope you will do me the honour to dance before me here.' 'How can I dance here in this road, monsieur?' I said beseechingly. 'Alas, mademoiselle, I have no drawing room to offer you,' he replied, still as polite as ever. 'Nevertheless,' he continued, 'if you think it cannot be done, I shall be under the painful necessity of confiscating your carriages and luggage, and of sending you back on foot to the nearest post town.' 'But, monsieur,' I protested, 'the road is ankle-deep in mud.' 'Truly,' he laughed, showing a beautiful set of teeth, 'but your weight won't make any difference; besides, I dare say you have some rugs and cloths with you in the other carriage, and my men will be only too pleased to spread them on the ground.'

"Seeing that all my remonstrance would be in vain, I jumped out of the carriage. While the rugs were being laid down, my two companions, the violinists, tuned their instruments, and even papa was prevailed upon to come out, though he was sulky and never spoke a word.

"I danced for about a quarter of an hour, and I honestly believe that I never had such an appreciative audience either before or afterwards. Then Trischka led me back to the carriage and, simply lifting his hat, bade me adieu. 'I keep the rugs, mademoiselle. I will never part with them,' he said." [62]

Mlle Taglioni left Russia for the last time in 1842, swathed in sables which she had received from the Czar, with a jewel collection fit for a queen, and with enough money saved to pay Gilbert de Voisins' debts, which she had assumed, and also, so she believed, to take care of the future needs of a lifetime. She invested part of her funds in a house on the shore of Lake Como, where she rested between engagements, and in two *palazzi* in Venice, where she hoped to spend winters after she retired.

Two years later she took her last leave of Paris, too. In the interim, Théophile Gautier had become the leading ballet critic. For Taglioni's return in *La Sylphide* he produced one of his typical effusions: "The few years which have elapsed since her departure, and which have left us with a furrow on our brow and a wrinkle at the corner of our eye, have taken no toll from her. Fortunate woman! Always the same elegant and slender form, the same calm, intelligent, and modest features; not a single feather has fallen from her wing; not a hair has silvered beneath her chaplet of flowers! . . . What airiness! What rhythmic movements! What noble gestures! What poetic attitudes and, above all, what a sweet melancholy! What lack of restraint, yet how chaste!" Of the final scene, where the sylphide loses her wings, he said: "The theme of this very poetic *pas* is almost certainly borrowed from the natural history of insects. Virgin ants shed their wings after the love-flight. So nature has foreseen everything, even to the endings of ballet." [63] Philippe must have snickered when he read it.

Other critics were neither as gushing nor as kind. ". . . Her performances gave rise to many a spiteful epigram," said Vandam, "for she herself invited comparison between her former glory and her decline, by dancing in one of her most successful creations, *L'Ombre*." [64] "Don't speak to me anymore about your old Taglioni, that forty-six-year-old sylphide, who is always being thrown at other dancers, the way Molière is thrown at playwrights," [65] wrote Albéric Second, maliciously adding six years to the age of the poor ballerina. Perhaps her dislike of France arose from these cutting reviews, combined with the troubles she had recently had over the legal separation from her husband. Nevertheless, though even her ardent admirers would have conceded that her powers were waning, two spectacular achievements still lay ahead of her.

Jules Perrot, who had roused her jealousy during her early days in Paris, was now settled in London, where he and the composer Cesare Pugni had a virtual monopoly of the ballet, Perrot choreographing twenty-one works during a period of six years, while Pugni produced the music for twenty-four. Together they had already turned out ballets for three of the foremost living dancers—Carlotta Grisi, who created the role of *Giselle* in Paris, Fanny Cerrito, who was the idol of London, and the Danish Lucile Grahn, newly arrived in England after her conquests of Copenhagen, Paris, and St. Petersburg.

Now Perrot and Pugni were directed by Benjamin Lumley, manager of Her Majesty's Theatre, to produce a ballet in which all three of the spoiled, temperamental stars would appear together, and Mlle Taglioni as well. Lumley had resorted to every diplomatic maneuver, for, as he said, "these were subjects who considered themselves far above mortal control, or, more properly speaking, each was a queen in her own right—alone, absolute, supreme!" And Perrot, too, was coming to the end of his rehearsals with unhoped-for calm, when a quarrel suddenly erupted between Cerrito and Grisi over the matter of precedence. There had never been any doubt that Taglioni would have the prestige of dancing the last variation. The question was who was to dance the next to last. Lumley was able to settle the matter by deciding that each of the four would take her turn according to age—a suggestion which made all of them equally reluctant to claim the honor, and was a finely drawn point, since Grisi was actually only two days older than Grahn. From the moment the four ballerinas came onstage, all in a line and holding hands, the densely packed audience never stopped clapping, cheering, and stamping, at times the stage was so heaped with bouquets, wreaths, and garlands thrown by the public that there was hardly room to dance; and for a month the main topic in London was the *Pas de Quatre*,[66] "the greatest Terpsichorean exhibition that was ever known in Europe."

Following upon the success of the *Pas de Quatre*, Lumley had Perrot and Pugni stage *Le Jugement de Pâris*, a ballet first conceived five years before by the manager's predecessor, Pierre Laporte, with the idea of having Mlle Elssler as one of the three goddesses. In July 1846, it was Taglioni, Cerrito, and Grahn who danced in the now-famous *Pas des Déesses*, with Arthur Saint-Léon (recently married to Cerrito) as Pâris. Perrot, who, along with Mazilier, Lucien Petipa, Paul Taglioni, and Russian partners, once danced opposite Marie Taglioni in *La Sylphide*, appeared with her for the last time in this ballet in the role of Mercury, but the ovation he received on this occasion was for his choreography.

Exactly a year later, after a very disheartening tour on the continent, La Taglioni was back at Her Majesty's Theatre for two revivals of the *Pas de Quatre;* and on August 21, having been persuaded by Prince Troubetzkoy (later to become her son-in-law) to set a term of twenty-five years on her dancing career, she took her final leave of the public, appropriately in her role of goddess.[67]

The year-by-year details of a career do not constitute a portrait of the person. What counts, to be sure, is the artist's contribution to his art and the inspiration imparted to those who have witnessed the performance. People are eager, nevertheless, to learn something about an artist's private life and personality, and it is not always idle curiosity, since character traits often elucidate the motivating forces that render an artist creative. What sort of person was the most celebrated of ballerinas? It must be admitted, first of all, that she was abnormally jealous. She was not embarrassed to fly into tantrums over Perrot's successes, and her memoirs and innumerable, long gossipy letters are full of withering and unjustifiable criticism not only of Brugnoli, but especially of Mlle Duvernay and Fanny Elssler.

Perhaps her lack of attractiveness off-stage was one of the reasons for her being an exceptionally dedicated dancer, to the exclusion of anything else. It was not Marie Taglioni's fault that she was not good-looking, allowed Albert Vandam after dining with her at Dr. Véron's house in 1844, "but she might have tried to make amends for her lack of personal charms by her amiability. She rarely attempted to do so, and never with Frenchmen. Her reception of them was freezing to a degree, and on the occasions—few and far between—when she thawed, it was with Russians, Englishmen, or Viennese." It was less surprising, felt Vandam, that Gilbert de Voisins abandoned her than that he should have married her in the first place. "The fact was," said one of his friends, "that De Voisins considered himself in honor bound to make that reparation, but I cannot conceive what possessed him to commit the error that made the reparation necessary." [68] Twenty years after the unfortunate marriage, the two happened to meet at a dinner party. "Who," asked Gilbert de Voisins of his neighbor, pointing at Mlle Taglioni across the table and not recognizing her, or pretending not to do so, "who is that old-maidish sort of governess?"

Marie Taglioni retired to the villa at Lake Como in 1847, but her professional life was not at an end. Far from it. In 1858 she was settled in Paris again, receiving at weekly parties and being entertained as a revered guest of honor. In lieu of the Opéra director Royer, who was detained at home by illness, her old friend Dr. Véron presided at a dinner for her attended by fifty celebrities of the ballet world, which was followed by dancing, the eight participants of the *quadrille* including La Taglioni herself and her first *Sylphide* partner, Mazilier. During this season she was also busy making plans for a new career as *Inspectrice de la danse* at the Opéra, a position which was officially confirmed in 1859, and which she retained until the Franco-Prussian War of 1870, becoming also a teacher of the most advanced classes.

What had lured her back to Paris was the account of a sixteen-year-old *danseuse*, Emma Livry, described as a reincarnation of the original sylphide. Mlle Livry did indeed become Marie Taglioni's disciple and spiritual daughter; the one ballet choreographed by the great ballerina was for this young girl; and it was a major tragedy for La Taglioni when Emma Livry died as a result of burns incurred when her costume caught fire.

One of Pavlova's treasures was an autograph page of Taglioni's replies to a parlor game questionnaire dated 1872. What she filled in was mainly very banal, even quite priggish, but her answer to the question: your chief characteristic? is striking in view of what she did during the closing years of her life. *"La résignation dans l'adversité,"* she wrote but, rather than resignation, it was the most extraordinary courage that she displayed. It would appear that while she was busy as *Inspectrice de la danse* in Paris, her father, who was past eighty and had become very eccentric, was tempted into some foolish speculations, and all of the ballerina's fortune and possessions were lost, the only thing saved in the debacle being the house at Como, which fortunately had been deeded to her daughter Nini, Princesse Troubetzkoy. Undaunted, Marie Taglioni moved to London, 6 Connaught Square, where she established a school for dancing and deportment, giving private lessons and attending to all the correspondence and bookkeeping herself, and at the same time continuing a hectic round of social activities until she was seventy-six years old.

Philippe, having survived to the age of ninety-four, died in 1871, but Nini and her daughter, young Georges Gilbert de Voisins and his wife and little son took turns visiting her in London. At last, in 1880, she went to live with Georges and his family in Marseille and died there four years later.

Even in the semi-exile of that faraway city she was not forgotten by the friends of her glamorous past. She answered a letter she received there from Perrot, addressing him as "dear old friend," and he replied:

My dear Countess,

Just because we have known each other for more than half a century is no reason to treat a long-time friend as an *old* comrade. Watch out, if one were to take that seriously, one might believe it to be a reality. For you as much as for myself, you must permit me to spurn the word *old*, which my youthful imagination repudiates. Here I am then, with a heart which feels almost adolescent, and with happy memories of our past, joining my family in reminding you of my sincere affection. . . .

With this, a kiss on each cheek! Believe me, my dear friend, as in the past, so still in my thoughts at least,

Your young and passionate Zéphir of 1830.

Jules Perrot.

Nowhere is the spirit of the Romantic ballet better expressed than in the words of Ivor Guest when he speaks of the four greatest dancers of the period, of whom Marie Taglioni was the innovator and leader: "Technique with them, though never neglected, was concealed and took second place; they were creative artists in the full sense of the term, making a greater contribution to their art than did any choreographer of their day except Perrot, by setting up new standards and serving as models to their lesser companions. They brought new values to rejuvenate an art in which technical 'correctness' had assumed undue preponderance; they breathed the life of Romanticism into the cold marble of Classicism. 'Formerly,' explained the *Morning Post* in 1843, 'dancers' evolutions were as precise as those of soldiers—in their feats they bounded and leapt in the perpendicular line. . . . Now dancers have discovered that the line of beauty in dancing is like that of Hogarth in painting—and that the more it is waving, undulatory, and inclined, the more it is graceful and captivating. They have gone one step further and laid down this axiom: that dancing excels exactly in proportion as it resembles flying. That is the source of all the present triumphs.' " [69]

CHAPTER 12

Fanny Elssler
1810–1884

Bon *jour cher Gentz, tu es bien etonner, que je t'ecriez en francais, n'est-ce pas? tu voir comme je suive tes conseilles . . . adieu lieber Gentz ich küsse Dich deutsch und bleibe Deine deutsche Fanny."* ("Good morning, dear Gentz, you are very astonished that I write to you in French, aren't you? You see how I follow your advice . . . adieu, dear Gentz, I kiss you in German and remain your German Fanny.") The misspelled, awkward little letter was sent in 1830 by Fanny Elssler to Friedrich von Gentz, one of the most brilliant political and financial minds on the European scene. Gentz, who was to have an important influence on Fanny's life, was born and educated in Germany, where he also founded, edited, and wrote articles for two magazines. In 1802 he settled permanently in Vienna, becoming successively Councillor, Secretary to the Congress of Vienna, and confidant and adviser to Metternich. Although Goethe called him "a sly fox" and Napoleon "a wretched scribe without honor," his articles were, in fact, impartial and objective; they brought him large stipends from the British and Austrian governments and Louis XVIII, and have endured as "literary monuments and classical examples of German prose." As a gambler and connoisseur of women and wine, too, his reputation almost exceeded his fame as a writer. He was sixty-five, slender, elegant, and youthful for his years when he first saw Fanny Elssler dance at the Kaernthner Thor in 1829 and fell irrevocably in love with her.

The object of his passion was only nineteen, with the beauty and innocent expression of a pre-Raphaelite angel. For all that, she already had led a complicated life, she was (a well-kept secret) the mother of a two-year-old son, and her candid blue eyes and naive manner belied more than enough feminine lore.

Fanny came from a family of Viennese musicians. Her father, two of her maternal uncles, and one of her older brothers were all professionals. During the years when her father was copyist and valet to Haydn, the Elsslers lived in sufficient comfort, but after Haydn died, in 1808,[70] they fell on hard times. They were obliged to settle in rooms over a public laundry, and Frau Elssler did washing to help feed and clothe the five children, all of whom were launched early on their various careers so that they might become self-supporting as soon as possible.

The younger girls, Thérèse, aged nine, and Fanny, aged seven, at the ballet school of the Kaernthner Thor, immediately gave signs of unusual talent, grace, and musicality and were able to profit from the excellent standards set by two distinguished ballet masters— Jean Aumer, who remained until Fanny was eleven, and then Philippe Taglioni. A delightful dance-portrait has survived of Fanny, in 1822, when she was twelve. She is depicted hovering on almost full point (did she not have Brugnoli as an example?), coy and remarkably poised. At this time she already had made her first appearances at the opera house.

Domenico Barbaja, an even more picturesque and spectacular figure than Dr. Véron, had taken over the direction of the Kaernthner Thor in December of the previous year, and continued in charge for seven years, while retaining the same position at the San Carlo Opera in Naples. Having begun his career as a café waiter in Milan and then a circus manager, he was, at forty-three when he came to Vienna, the most outstanding director and impresario in Europe, having discovered or promoted many of the leading composers and choreographers, singers and dancers. His discerning eye was quick to evaluate Fanny Elssler's latent possibilities. Young as she was, he allowed her to appear in several ballets and when he returned to Italy in 1824 he took her along.

The San Carlo at this period was the social center and pride of the Neapolitans, and Stendhal was not the only visitor to be seduced by the splendors of the theatre, its music, and ballet. As the administrator, Barbaja had enormous prestige, besides the advantage of the millions he had amassed as farmer of the gaming tables. With such a protector, Fanny's success was assured, and there is no doubt that she made great artistic progress while in Naples.

Her private life was another matter. King Ferdinand IV's son Leopold, Prince of Salerno, began to solicit her favors. Twenty years her senior, married since 1818 to his own niece, who was a melancholy creature obsessed with the impropriety of her marriage to so close a relative, the Prince was fat, self-indulgent, and the spoiled favorite of his parents. It is difficult to imagine that Fanny could have loved him, but perhaps, after the squalor of her childhood, she was dazzled by his position and ostentation. In any case, she became his mistress and, in spite of the efforts in court circles to separate them, before long she was obviously *enceinte* and had to return to Vienna. As it was a firm rule at the Kaernthner Thor that dancers could not remain there if they were mothers, the birth of Franz, on June 4, 1827, was very much hushed up, and since it was essential for Fanny to continue a promising and remunerative career, the little son of such glamorous parents was placed in a bourgeois foster home.

After an appropriate interval, Fanny returned to the opera with her sister Thérèse, but almost another year passed before Gentz first saw her, sought her out, and began to court her. Gentz was no ordinary lover. Himself an intellectual, he was anxious to teach her as much as possible to make up for her deplorable lack of education. Possibly he had already made up his mind to marry her and wanted her to be able to fill her role as his wife in a fitting manner, though it is more likely, considering the number of his past liaisons, that he thought of marriage only when he became desperate over her impending departure. However it was, he inspired her to perfect her German and learn French, provided her with introductions that advanced her career, and helped her socially, meanwhile overwhelming her with flowers, gifts, love letters, and other delicate attentions. Fanny, who remained shy and unspoiled for many years, was grateful and devoted and became very dependent upon him.

The idyl was interrupted in the autumn of 1830, when Thérèse and Fanny were offered a contract to appear as leading dancers at the Berlin Opera. Gentz attempted to keep Fanny in Vienna by proposing marriage to her at this time, but understood that she wanted to try her wings in the Prussian capital. He commissioned a portrait of her as a keepsake and gave her one of himself which he sent with a touching note in French verse:

> En Remettant mon Portrait à Fanny
>
> Idole de mon coeur, ne te plains pas de moi,
> Si quelqu'air de tristesse obscurcit ce visage.
> Lorsq'un crayon savant dessinait mon image,
> Ton départ approchait, et je pensais à toi.

("On Presenting my Portrait to Fanny

Idol of my heart, do not complain of me,
If an air of sorrow beclouds this face.
While an intuitive pencil traced my portrait,
Your departure drew near, and I was thinking of you.")

When the sisters left in September Gentz hardly guessed that the last of his love affairs was coming to an end.

Later on it became a commonplace to say that Fanny Elssler had no striking success until she was established in Paris. In 1875, a dozen years after he had retired as director of the Opéra, Alphonse Royer wrote that he saw Fanny dance in Vienna in 1831, during one of her return visits from Berlin, and took it upon himself to advise Dr. Véron that she would find favor with the Parisians, a suggestion which the good doctor did not pursue. He added that she was not much appreciated in Vienna and painted a picture of the two sisters returning to their humble abode after the opera performance, trudging through the snow, carrying a basket. Compared with the gaudy luxury enjoyed by French ballerinas, this apparently struck Royer as pathetic, but was certainly nothing unusual under the austere regime of Emperor Franz I. The prejudiced André Levinson went so far as to say quite bluntly: "Fanny owes the greater part of her renown to her rivalry with Taglioni," [71] referring to the time when both of them were appearing in France. In spite of such carping, there is plenty of evidence that Fanny was successful and popular in Berlin. She danced there season after season in a huge repertoire of ballets (many of which originated at the Opéra), was praised by experienced spectators and critics, and received her tribute of jewels from the royal family.

For Thérèse, who was a less gifted dancer and less pretty than her younger sister, Berlin provided the great moments of her very brief career. She had grown immensely tall, and the Germans admired big women in general and statuesque dancers in particular. "According to Castil-Blaze, she was 5 feet 6 inches tall, which was excessive then, though it would be ideal today," [72] says Ivor Guest, while Fanny's biographer Emil Pirchan speaks of Thérèse's extraordinary height of 1 meter 90, or somewhat over 6 feet 2 inches. It is a question which, no doubt, will never be settled; suffice it that she was tall enough to earn such sobriquets as *"la maestosa," "la majestueuse,"* and "the dancing giant," and to be able to appear as Fanny's partner in the type of *pas de deux* called *adagio.* Taglioni, quite in character, derided this style of performance (highly esteemed nowadays) and specified: "We owe the beginning of this bad taste to the Elssler sisters. The elder, Thérèse, who was big, too big, wore male costume. She was extremely deft at turning her sister Fanny. The ensemble produced a great effect; but no one could have called it art." [73]

In June 1832, Friedrich von Gentz succumbed to a final illness. Fanny, in Vienna after her second Berlin season, was at his bedside and tried to comfort him. He had already withdrawn into the detached state of the dying which distressed her deeply, but he admitted, nevertheless, that he was touched by the attentions of "that good child." His friend Count Prokesch-Osten noted in his diary that Fanny wept pitifully over Gentz' death and that her grief confirmed the sincere affection and gratitude she had always felt for him.

Just the same, her love already had been bestowed on someone else. Though Gentz had arranged to have her meet all sorts of influential persons when she first went to Germany, the one who captured her heart was the dancer Anton Stuhlmüller, who was a good-looking young man and her own age. He and Fanny had been fellow students; later, as we have seen, he was Marie Taglioni's preferred partner in Stuttgart. Fanny was happy to find him again as *premier danseur* in Berlin and for once she really fell in love. Soon she found that she was expecting another child, but a scandal was averted because she was able to leave the country. News of her German triumphs had traveled abroad; in Paris false reports were circulating that she was going to appear there, but the contract which she and Thérèse accepted was for the spring-summer season at His Majesty's Theatre. After a farewell performance, in February 1833, they set out for London, where a few months later little Theresa was born.

One of the best things that ever happened to Fanny Elssler, which she sometimes did not appreciate sufficiently, was acquiring the friendship of Mrs. George Grote, whom she met through a friend of Friedrich von Gentz. Married to a man who was a banker, a Member of Parliament, and historian, Harriet Grote was an intellectual in her own right, with an independent character. At a time when "ladies" did not associate with actresses, she had no such silly prejudices and not only welcomed Fanny with warmth and understanding but more or less adopted Fanny's child. Apart from eighteen months in Paris with her mother, Theresa lived with the Grotes until she was nine and perhaps for this reason alone grew into a happy, well-adjusted young woman.

It was no easy matter to stand comparison with Marie Taglioni, who was fanatically admired by the British public, but the Elssler sisters, at first rather coolly received, gradually gained in popularity. Some of the critics were almost too enthusiastic, others overly harsh, but it was generally agreed that Fanny was very pretty, and her shapely legs created a sensation. In July 1833 Thérèse, who had many other talents besides dancing, restaged *La Fée et le Chevalier* (Fanny had appeared in it in Vienna and Berlin) and the following spring she choreographed *Armide*. It is of interest to note that by this time Fanny had already developed her staccato, or *taqueté*, style, which Paris would soon find so exciting in contrast with Taglioni's floating, *ballonné* manner.

One day in May of that year Dr. Véron arrived in London. He had had more than enough of Taglioni's monopoly at the Opéra and her incessant demands, and as soon as he had seen Fanny, he determined to engage her and set her up as a rival *première danseuse*. As usual, his methods were anything but subtle. He gave an extravagant dinner, which terminated with a tray heaped with jewels as a *pièce de résistance*. The unspoiled Elsslers were shocked rather than impressed, but with a little further persuasion were prevailed upon to sign a three-year contract and, in less than two months, they were en route for Paris.

Fanny Elssler's rivalry at the Opéra with La Taglioni, aided and abetted by the audience, the press, and Dr. Véron's flamboyant publicity campaign, has often been compared with the clash between Marie Sallé and Camargo. It was perhaps as violent and, as with the earlier ballerinas, the battle is still being fought. Today's Taglionists and Elsslerists are uncompromising.

On September 15 the first laurels went to Fanny, although the scene added for her in a new ballet, *La Tempête*, in which Mlle Duvernay had the lead, did not provide her with an ideal role. She succeeded because she was beautiful, and Taglioni was not, and because her lively technique seemed novel. There were ecstatic reviews about her speed and point work, which she managed to combine with a seductive, sensuous quality entirely lacking in her rival. Immediately Marie countered with revivals of *La Sylphide* and *La Révolte au sérail*, and the Taglionists felt that their chaste Goddess of the Dance had reestablished her claim.

Later, in *La Presse*, September 11, 1837, the contrasting personalities of the two ballerinas provoked a typical Théophile Gautier effusion, which has been quoted *ad nauseam* in all its details, but it must be admitted that he put it aptly in describing Mlle Taglioni as a "Christian dancer" and Fanny as "quite pagan."

As for Thérèse, the Parisians were as astonished as they had been in 1768, when tall Anna Heinel arrived from Stuttgart. They first saw her in her own choreography of an opera *divertissement* and in male attire as Fanny's partner. As always, Thérèse arranged to have her sister be the center of attention, and her modesty (not a current commodity among French *danseuses*) won her many admiring friends.

After the initial Taglioni-Elssler skirmish, two mediocrities were added to the ballet repertoire: *Brézilia*, April 1835, one of Philippe Taglioni's feeblest efforts, and for Fanny, in August, *L'Ile des Pirates*, Louis Henry's first work for the Opéra in some thirty years. His old enemy, Pierre Gardel, who had caused him to emigrate to Italy, was still living, but at seventy-seven no longer had any say in affairs at the opera house. Unfortunately, his ballet, like Philippe's, was a failure, which deterred neither of the two factions from finding their ballerinas admirable.

Followed a long lull in the hostilities, while Mlle Taglioni was incommoded by her famous "*mal au genou*"; and at last, in June 1836, the Elsslerists were sure that a conclusive victory was theirs. Inspired by the success of Dolores Serral, one of a group of Spanish dancers imported by Dr. Véron, Fanny Elssler had mastered the *cachucha* and, in the role of Florinda, she introduced it in *Le Diable boiteux*. ". . . A feverish activity, the fire of gestures and steps and the whole spirit of sensuality . . . Fanny Elssler understood and expressed this ardent poetry but, remembering that for us there are considerations of grace and beauty, she very tactfully discarded the over-crude acting and too earthy sensuality; she did not accept the *cachucha* of Dolores, she adapted it skillfully and, without weakening it, without lessening or changing it, or removing any of its appealing vitality, she gave it an elegance, grace, and charm which made it doubly pleasing by decking it out delightfully." [74]

In spite of Fanny's modifications, the prudish element of the audience was very shocked, though they kept coming back for more; and even a sophisticate like Charles de Boigne implied that such voluptuous entertainment was unnatural, an acquired taste for jaded palates. Gautier, though he thought Fanny ravishing and devoted a twelve-line paragraph just to the shapeliness of her legs, to begin with was critical of her Spanish dancing. "For Dolores," he said, "the *cachucha* is a kind of faith, a religion: it is obvious that she believes in it; she dances it with her whole heart and with all her mind and all the passion, frankness, and sensuousness possible. Fanny Elssler and Mlle Noblet dance it a bit unbelievingly, more by caprice or to make the public—that bored sultan—raise its opera glass, than from real conviction; so they both are lively, coquettish, and witty in it, but not at all amorous, an unpardonable crime in a Cachucha or Bolero." [75] Soon he was siding with Mlle Elssler to the detriment of Taglioni and, in 1845, he turned out thirty pages on *Le Diable boiteux* for the loveliest of all the Romantic albums, *Les Beautés de l'Opéra*. Meanwhile, he had traveled in Spain; Fanny's suave performance was also enhanced in his memory by her absence of five years. "Fanny Elssler, that German girl who became Spanish; Fanny, the *cachucha* incarnate . . . ," he said, forgetting all his earlier reservations, "the liveliest, the most precise, the most intelligent dancer who ever skimmed the boards with her toe of steel." In 1836 everyone who was not a Taglionist agreed with this, and there was a flood of prints, statuettes (including the famous one by Barre), snuffboxes, fans—all sorts of souvenirs depicting Fanny in her pink and black lace costume and attesting to what had become a craze in Paris.

Although La Taglioni had triumphs of her own in *La Fille du Danube* from September on, while her rival was convalescing from an almost fatal bout of pneumonia, it was clear enough which way the wind was blowing. Véron's successor, Duponchel, with such a drawing card as Fanny, was not at all sure that he wanted to renew the capricious Sylphide's contract; Marie concluded that flight was more dignified than waging a losing battle and wisely accepted an offered engagement in St. Petersburg.

Taglioni's unrenewed contract did not pass without protest from her supporters. As Duponchel emerged from the opera house one afternoon, he was accosted by an employee of a funeral establishment who had been helping to drape the main entrance in black crape and who stopped him to inquire: "Where is the body?" "What body?" "Why, the body of M. Duponchel, the deceased." "Am I deceased?" "No, but . . ." "But I am Duponchel." "Well, if you are M. Duponchel, we have instructions to bury you!" The pranksters had meanwhile plastered the whole city with posters that read THE LATE DUPONCHEL and had delivered hundreds of personal announcements of the funeral service, and the courtyard of the Opéra was soon crowded with "mourners."

However, the departure of Marie Taglioni did not give Fanny all of the hoped-for advantage. There was, to be sure, continued enthusiasm for the *cachucha* but after a while it was no longer a novelty and from the date of its first performance (June 1836), until *La Gipsy* (January 1839), no exciting new role was created for Mlle Elssler. She had been making appearances on the side in Bordeaux, Berlin, Vienna, and London; at the Opéra she was seen in revivals of *La Fille mal gardée, La Muette de Portici,* and *Nina* (and was as much praised for her acting as her dancing); then in a new ballet, *La Chatte métamorphosée en femme,* October 1837 (best forgotten, except for a ravishing print that has survived of Fanny in a feather costume); next, on the occasion of her benefit, in another new work, *La Volière* (May 1838), composed by Thérèse, and which few people liked except for Gautier, and finally in *La Sylphide* and *La Fille du Danube,* unsuitable roles for her, in which she obviously could not compete with the impression left behind by Taglioni.

At last, in *La Gipsy,* she had a first-rate action ballet (it was also Mazilier's first choreography) with a dramatic part in which, according to Gautier, she rose "to the sublimest heights of dramatic art" and with a special *pas,* the *Cracovienne,* in which she was dazzling. The ballet, considered a retort to Taglioni's *La Gitana* in Russia, was held by the latter's partisans to be a mere imitation, a vulgarization, but no such accusation could be made about *La Tarentule*, which followed six months later.[76]

In the meanwhile, Fanny was sharing her successes and consoling herself for her failures with a new love, the Marquis de La Valette. Just past thirty, he was a perfect specimen of the gilded youth of his period. When not abroad on diplomatic assignments, he was a confirmed patron of the *loge infernale*, the box at the Opéra reserved for fashionable young blades, and had already chalked up a number of affairs with dancers, two of them with "les Paulines"—Mlles Guichard and Duvernay—both of whom had children by him. Fanny first met him in London and after becoming his mistress she "scrupulously respected," to quote Mrs. Grote, the liaison, which lasted until she left for the United States.

Since 1838 A. Seguin, a theatrical agent, had been seeking Mlle Elssler's consent to a tour in America. Letters of his still exist which show that he tried to convince Mlle Taglioni to go there, too, promising that she would earn as much as £2,500 in less than a year. By 1840 someone far more persuasive than Seguin made Fanny think of changing her mind. This was Henry Wikoff, an American, more or less permanently settled in Paris and London. Only a few years younger than La Valette,[77] Fanny's new friend presented a striking contrast to her lover, although both were snobs and bluffers, whose ambitions were furthered by their independent incomes. La Valette was the illegitimate son of an actress and had no claim to the title he flaunted; Henry Wikoff, though he made much of his aristocratic connections, was also an illegitimate son, for whom it was more expedient to live abroad. But the resemblances ended there. The Frenchman was sophisticated and astute, whereas Wikoff, in spite of all his travels and the international society he frequented, remained oddly naive and uncosmopolitan, unable to shake off the strictures and prejudices of his Philadelphia background and forever preoccupied with an image of himself as "respectable."

During a London season when he was vaguely posted at the American Embassy as attaché, Wikoff became friendly with Stephen Price, who had tried to run Drury Lane Theatre and failed, and was still one of the directors of the Park Theatre in New York. Now Price turned up in Paris; he informed Wikoff that he was on the verge of bankruptcy, had decided that only Fanny Elssler's appearance in New York could save him from ruin, and begged for help in arranging the matter.

Wikoff had never met anyone as outlandish as an opera dancer, but he was acquainted with La Valette and promised to see him, though he was sure the Marquis would never allow his protégée to make so long a journey. In the event, he was proven wrong. La Valette had just been assigned to a year's diplomatic mission in Persia and, like the Comte de Clermont in 1735, when he had to leave Mlle Camargo and join the army, he was very disturbed at the thought of letting his pretty mistress stay in Paris, unprotected and the prey of any and every temptation. He himself secured the Opéra's agreement to extend her summer holiday to six months and appended his signature to her contract with Price. It was also settled that Fanny would leave for London the first week in March to make a series of appearances at Her Majesty's Theatre and would then sail for New York on the *Great Western* on April 15. La Valette asked Wikoff to look after her until the time of her departure, some six months distant.

"It was flattering enough to have the exclusive charge of such a lovely woman, the idol of Paris," confessed Wikoff in his memoirs, "but might it not involve me in a vortex of demoralising occupations wholly foreign to my life, and in conflict with my aforesaid notions of respectability? . . . I feared I was on an inclined plane and that if I did not look carefully after my foothold I might be launched into unknown perplexities." [78] On meeting Fanny, the anxious young man had been impressed by her low-pitched, harmonious voice, her ladylike manner and modesty, and he was further reassured when he discovered that someone as serious and well connected as Mrs. Grote was really her devoted personal friend; but he might have quailed had he guessed what finally was in store for him.

The particulars of Stephen Price's sudden death, his partner's reluctance to fulfill the contract as Fanny wished, and Wikoff's decision to assume all responsibility for the tour, all these details are too long and complicated for inclusion here, except for one humorous aspect of the affair. "Barely a week had elapsed after Fanny had taken wing [for London, March 4, 1840] when a letter reached me from Philadelphia announcing the sudden death of my guardian, Mr. S. P. Wetherill, and desiring my immediate return to take possession of my property, which had always remained in his hands."[79] Thus Wikoff explained his precipitous return to America. Allison Delarue,[80] however, has found proof that Mr. Wetherill died thirteen months earlier (February 19, 1839), a fact of which Wikoff could not have been ignorant; and it was therefore certainly not his guardian's death which caused him to sail on the *Great Western* but, no doubt, the irresistible charms of the ballerina—a surmise borne out by his remaining constantly at her side for over two years in the United States and Cuba.

With little Theresa safely stowed again at the Grotes', Fanny embarked at Bristol for the eighteen-day voyage. Thérèse had decided to have no part in the perilous sea crossing to a land largely inhabited by illiterates and wild Indians, but Fanny's suite included her devoted cousin Kathi Prinster, her partner and ballet master James Sylvain, her coachman Charles,[81] her maid, and Wikoff, a nervous mother hen, entrusted at the last moment with chaperoning no less than three ladies—"one a bewitching widow, another a fascinating countess, and a third the formidable Fanny Elssler."

The *Great Western* was among the first steamships to navigate the ocean and each time she docked or sailed from New York it was the occasion of a great celebration. With Mlle Elssler on board as a much-heralded passenger, the excitement redoubled, becoming a positive frenzy by the time she began her month's engagement at the theatre. On her first appearance, the whole audience stood up and shouted, bouquets and wreaths heaped the stage, and after the performance huge crowds congregated in the park in front of the American Hotel to catch a last glimpse of her and serenade her until dawn.

Duncan Crow, the British biographer of Henry Wikoff, states: "The cause of all this clamour was not Fanny's ability as a dancer: indeed few of the thousands who saw her dance were competent to judge her as an artiste." She succeeded as "a supreme mistress of the art of sex appeal," he continues, "and into the harsh, cutthroat atmosphere of New York she brought a breath of enchantment which leavened the mediocrity of life."[82] Contrary to Mr. Crow's assertions, the audiences of New York, Philadelphia, Boston, and other major towns were extremely discriminating in theatrical matters. They had a long experience of the finest of foreign and native actors (Stephen Price alone presented Kean, Macready, Charles Mathews and his wife Mme Vestris, Charles and Fanny Kemble, and others, and in London the American Edwin Forrest was found the equal of any local actor); the same public had listened to French and Italian opera, had enjoyed *Der Freischütz* years before Paris or London heard anything but the most distorted versions of it (in London with English ballads added in!), and New Yorkers had also seen plenty of good ballet—Mme Lecomte, Mlle Augusta, Mlle Céleste (later a dramatic actress), Jean and Marius Petipa, Paul and Amalia Taglioni, and many others. In 1838 the Park Theatre even presented a Philadelphia-trained child prodigy, Augusta Maywood, who made a sensation at the Paris Opéra the following year.

Fanny's personal triumph, "the Elssler mania," was greatly enhanced by her newspaper campaign. Wikoff, during his second voyage to Europe, had met James Gordon Bennett, the founder and editor of the *New York Herald*. He kept supplying Bennett with articles and gradually undertook all the public relations and business side of the tour, becoming very efficient. Because of his connections, Fanny also was feted by most of the notabilities of New York society. One of these, Philip Hone, ex-mayor of the city, whose beautiful town house stood only two doors north of the American Hotel, recorded many interesting details of Fanny's visit in his journal. Altogether she performed fifteen times in New York, clearing a profit of $10,000, an impressive sum, especially when compared with Seguin's offer to Taglioni.

"The divine Fanny! the glorious Fanny! the astonishing Fanny! —of the light fantastic toe—who turned the heads of all the ladies and the hearts of all the gentlemen, who produced a perfect mania for dancing, until the citizens of Baltimore danced into the traces of her carriage, proud of the honor of dragging the immortal Fanny from the theatre to her hotel . . ." [83] Twenty-seven years later Wemyss, manager of Philadelphia's Walnut Street Theatre, recorded the excitement of Mlle Elssler's appearances in June 1840, at the rival Chestnut Street Theatre run by Robert Maywood.

After those frenzied weeks came the moment of decision for Fanny: should she accept the proffered engagements in Washington, Baltimore, and elsewhere, with their promise of more ovations and even higher pay, or should she return meekly to Paris to keep to her contract with the Opéra, where younger dancers were, no doubt, supplanting her, and the salary by comparison was insignificant? Perhaps she also weighed the attractions of Wikoff against those of La Valette and favored the former. She was not so naive as to imagine that La Valette would ever consider marrying her, but Bennett later indicated that she believed that Wikoff would. In any case, she opted for America, obtaining successively from Léon Pillet (he had replaced Duponchel at the Opéra) an extension of leave until mid-October, then till January 1841, and finally an ultimatum that if she overstayed she would be fined to the extent of 60,000 francs.

In the meanwhile, regardless of future problems, she went on to Washington, where Congress adjourned in order to see her dance, and she and Wikoff were received at the White House; to Boston; back to Philadelphia and New York; and to Cuba, where the indefatigable Sylvain, who had been dancing, rehearsing a *corps de ballet* in every city, and teaching hopeful young Americans on the side, had a further and very comical task thrust upon him: the ballet girls supplied by the theatre in Havana were so dusky-hued that he was obliged to calcimine their arms and legs before allowing them onstage in their white gauze tutus.

After New Orleans, Fanny and Wikoff went on a long holiday, visiting picturesque and historic places all the way from Louisiana to the Canadian border. It was the sort of excursion that Wikoff loved—in Europe he had been among the rare tourists to venture across Russia from St. Petersburg to Odessa, to Constantinople and Athens—and Fanny, doubtless, was exhausted and in need of a change. The unconventional aspect of their traveling together no longer seemed to bother either of them since, in the meantime, they had weathered all sorts of abusive attacks. The press, so entirely favorable at the start, suddenly began to pry into Mlle Elssler's private life; her relationship with her "impresario" was questioned, discussed, and derided, she was sneeringly referred to as "Mrs. W——," and even the existence of her son Franz leaked out. Her audiences, however, continued to adore her, and, as she was by now legally in disgrace with the Opéra, she chose to stay on in America for another year, even dancing in Havana once more. At last, in July 1842, Fanny, Wikoff, Kathi Prinster (and probably

Sylvain, since he continued appearing with Mlle Elssler in London) sailed back to England.

Had he heard of Fanny's behavior toward him? inquired Wikoff of a friend in New York, in a letter he wrote from Europe the following year. The idyl had ended on a note of bitterness. Fanny even accused Wikoff of mishandling the vast sum of money she had saved—some said it was close to $100,000—and the kind companion who had done so much toward her American success was obliged to make a public statement to defend his reputation. Fanny lost no time in collecting little Theresa—"snatching" her, said Mrs. Grote, who really loved the child—and she also accused the Grotes of embezzling some money she had left for Theresa's care. This was patently absurd as well as ungrateful. The ballerina's head had been turned by the triumphs and the fortune she had made in the United States and, temporarily at least, she was totally unreasonable.

Paris was now a closed book. The Opéra contract was canceled, and the authorities sequestered not only the receipts of Mlle Elssler's last benefit, which she had left on deposit, but also all the personal possessions that remained in her apartment. In any case, she would hardly have enjoyed sharing honors with Carlotta Grisi, who was the new idol of the fickle French public, the critics, and especially of Théophile Gautier. Instead, Fanny revisited old haunts and went on to conquer new territories. She was seen again in Berlin and often in Vienna; in London she made a hit, dressed as a cavalier, in *Un Bal sous Louis XIV*, in 1843 and 1844, and lastly in 1847, when she took over Grisi's role in Perrot's magnificent *La Esmeralda*. During 1843 and 1844 she also danced in Brussels; then in Budapest; and then for three years she made the grand tour of Italy, the high point of which was her appearance at La Scala with Perrot in his *Faust*. It must have been a ballet that she liked particularly, because she was to choose it for her final farewell to the stage.

Pirchan relates an Italian anecdote which is especially interesting considering the attitude the Church always maintained in regard to dancers: Fanny's Roman admirers, after her first appearance at the Argentina Theatre, had a beautiful golden crown made for her, but before bestowing it they prudently asked the Pope for his consent. Pius IX replied: "Give your dancer your beautiful crown; I see nothing in this gift that would offend the dignity of the Church or endanger the security of the State. But it is my thought that the crown be for the head and not for . . . the legs." When Fanny heard of this she sent 6,000 lire for the poor of Rome to show that she had, not only legs, but a heart in the right place.

When eventually she reached St. Petersburg, in 1848, she was no longer young. It seemed to be Russia's fate to receive the greatest ballerinas when they were technically past their prime. Fanny was thirty-eight, but if her point work had diminished in brilliance she was, on the other hand, far more experienced as an actress and she was still a ravishingly beautiful woman. When she opened, in October, in *Giselle,* an ideally dramatic role, the emotional Russian public went absolutely mad, and the fever never abated during the one hundred and three performances she gave during the course of two years. At her suggestion Perrot was engaged to dance with her, and after she left he stayed in St. Petersburg for a further nine years as choreographer and ballet master. Fanny, it must be said, was often very helpful and generous toward other dancers; for instance, she never forgot Augusta Maywood, barely fifteen when she made her debut at the Opéra, where Elssler was the star ballerina, and later her recommendations paved the way for Augusta in Vienna and Milan.

From St. Petersburg Mlle Elssler went on to Moscow. Serge Lifar was mistaken in stating that it was there that "she finished her career as a dancer and said her farewell to the stage." [84] However, the Muscovites' response to her was certainly the most impassioned she ever experienced. She took leave of them in *La Esmeralda;*

in the scene where the heroine traces the name of her beloved Phoebus, Fanny instead spelled out "Moscow" and then knelt down and kissed the word. It was the signal for total delirium. The audience sobbed and shouted, and the ballerina wept; more than three hundred bouquets were thrown onto the stage; for her departure from the theatre the staircase was covered with rare carpets and banked with flowers, and half the audience followed her home.

Compared with such demonstrations, Hamburg (1849–50), could only have been an anti-climax and yet, as we shall see, it may have held some secret and very special significance for Fanny Elssler. And then, in Vienna, on June 21, 1851, in the ballet *Faust*, she made her last appearance on any stage.

Mlle Elssler now had thirty-three years before her as a private citizen. The first three of these she spent in Hamburg—years, says Pirchan, "of quiet happiness that left no history." Other biographers all skip over this mysterious period without query or comment, but can we believe that immediately after all the fanfare Mlle Elssler could simply disappear?

Afterwards she settled in Vienna. Because of the fortune she brought back from America and Russia she lived in luxury, though without ostentation, and her companion was still Kathi Prinster, who shared a lifetime of memories with her. Though Fanny had never married, she now had all the complications of a close family life. Her son Franz always suffered from the insecurity of never having a proper home and he was a careless, unsettled young man. All too late his mother tried her good influence with him and in the end, having gambled away his money on the stock exchange, he committed suicide in 1873, when he was forty-seven. Theresa, happily married to Baron Victor Weber von Webenau, remained a devoted and admiring daughter; she named her child Fanny and called her country house Villa Fanny; but it is nice to note that she also always remembered Mrs. Grote, whose old age was gladdened by visits from the new little Fanny.

As for Thérèse Elssler, Fanny's sister, she grew more handsome and regal with the passing years. In 1848 she was married morganatically to Prince Adalbert of Prussia, at which time the King bestowed upon her the title of Countess von Barnim. Filling her new role with great dignity and charm, she also remained close to her sister's family and was, in fact, staying with Theresa von Webenau when she died in November 1878.

Fanny herself survived her sister by only six years and died of cancer in November 1884. Even in matters of death and burial the Elsslerists must get in their little gibe at the rival ballerina. Pirchan affirms that Marie Taglioni not only died penniless, but that she was buried at the expense of the city in a pauper's grave, and no one accompanied her remains to the cemetery. It will be remembered, however, that she spent her last years with her extremely devoted son, daughter-in-law, and grandson in Marseille where young Gilbert de Voisins had an excellent position. Her remains were later transferred to the family tomb in Paris.

At the present day, Thérèse and Fanny share with Haydn a charming little museum at Eisenstadt near Vienna. The one who is neglected there, as she is in this sketch and most of the Elssler biographies, is the less famous cousin, Hermine Elssler, who, however, was also a beautiful woman and an accomplished dancer.

❧

The legends that sprang up about the "divine Fanny" were even more numerous and extravagant than those that embellished the life story of Marie Sallé. To begin with, it was rumored that both Thérèse and Fanny were daughters of Prince Esterhazy. At least four generations of Elsslers had been in the employ of this autocratic family, from Fanny's grandfather to her unfortunate son Franz. The Prince was supposed to have exercised his *droits du seigneur*, and to this were ascribed the dazzling good looks and distinguished manners of the two ballerinas. It was also bruited about that Napoleon's son, the Duke of Reichstadt, was secretly in love with Fanny, and that he revealed this on his deathbed. Dr. Véron, although he denied it categorically, was accused of spreading the tale in Paris as publicity for his newly engaged star. Later, in London, Fanny's name was coupled improbably with those of Count d'Orsay and other dandies; and in 1844 appeared John Mills' satire *D'Horsay, or the Follies of the Day* by "A Man of Fashion." Because it slandered many well-known persons the book was immediately suppressed, but not before an avid public read that the Earl of "Chesterlane" (Chesterfield) kept, and was the lover of, Mlle Elssler.

Finally, many years ago, when the present author made some inquiries about an American dancer in Spain, no information was forthcoming but, said the correspondent, there was other material of possible interest on the subject of the Viennese dancer, Fanny Elssler. Followed a long, detailed, and perfectly accurate report of the *danseuse*'s life up to 1852, the moment when all her biographers leave her unaccounted for in Hamburg for three years. At that time, said the letter from Spain, Mlle Elssler was "married morganatically to Ferdinand of Saxe-Coburg-Gotha, father of Louis, later King of Portugal. This event caused Mlle Elssler to just miss becoming Queen of Spain. General Juan Prim, dictator of Spain after the overthrow of Isabella II, was seeking a king for Spain through whom he could continue to maintain himself in power. He was making great efforts to obtain the acceptance of Ferdinand of Coburg-Gotha, who was then living in his palace in Cintra. He sent an emissary to Don Fernando de los Rios asking him to beg Coburg-Gotha to accept the crown, but the latter declined. Fernando de los Rios then spoke with Coburg-Gotha's wife, Fanny Elssler, with a view to having her intercede. Fanny Elssler made it a condition —which was accepted—that her marriage be legitimized before she took up residence in the Palacio de Oriente in Madrid. It seemed that Ferdinand was about to accept when, at the last moment, under pressure from the Portuguese, who feared a future union with Spain, he broke off the negotiations. Thus it was that Fanny Elssler was on the verge of occupying the throne of Spain. Prim then directed his efforts elsewhere, until eventually he succeeded with Amadeo of Savoie."

This tale has special savor when we remember that Fanny Elssler always had an affinity for Spain. She was the first to study the traditional and folkloric dances of that country and add them to classical ballet, and should be honored for starting a trend that still endures. Lola Montez, in spite of her reputation, was a fraud as a Spanish dancer. An Irish girl, whose real name was Eliza Gilbert, Lola acquired only the rudiments during a brief sojourn among the Spaniards and never had either talent or technique, though she remains one of the outstanding adventuresses in history. Where Elssler paved the way, many of her contemporaries imitated her with success, and later Maria Guy-Stephan visited Barcelona and Madrid, 1849–52, and became an expert. In Russia, Marius Petipa popularized the Spanish element with his *Don Quixote*, 1869, and Diaghilev's rediscovery of Spain culminated in *Le Tricorne*, 1919, with the collaboration of Picasso and Massine. More recently the scrupulous research of Ana Ricarda as choreographer and dancer produced such authentic and charming ballets for the company of the Marquis de Cuevas as *Del Amor y de la Muerte*, 1949, and *Doña Ines de Castro*, 1952.

CHAPTER 13

Lucile Grahn

1819–1907

IT WAS OFTEN SAID that one of the reasons why Fanny Elssler suddenly agreed to go to America was that she was afraid of competing with Lucile Grahn, who was talented and attractive and nine years younger. Elssler had held her own in her rivalry with Taglioni, not because she was a better dancer, but because she was different and, for the same reason, she could certainly have gone on being popular in Paris after Mlle Grahn was engaged at the Opéra. Lucile, onstage, was a sprite; she was diaphanous, dreamy, and poetical. She excelled in ballets such as *La Sylphide,* in roles which Elssler (Gautier notwithstanding) should never have attempted as, conversely, Mlle Grahn was not at all cut out for the *cachucha* and *jaleo de Xeres.*

Born in Copenhagen, Lucina Alexia Grahn was the daughter of a Norwegian officer who, with his Jutland wife, had settled in Denmark as a customs agent. Lucile was hardly out of the cradle when she began to dance. Along with her first efforts in spelling and arithmetic, she had dancing lessons with a teacher named

Lund, who found her so gifted that at his suggestion she was sent to the Royal Ballet School.

In 1829 Bournonville [85] returned from his own studies and foreign engagements to take up his post as director of the School. There he discovered the ten-year-old Lucile, and then and there began the stormy relationship which was to last for another ten years. Under his personal guidance, the precocious child continued to make astonishing progress; and when she was fifteen he took her to Paris, where she was so inspired by what she saw at the Opéra that she could hardly wait to return and dance there herself.

She was only sixteen when Bournonville created the star role for her in his *Valdemar*, and a year later, with Lucile in mind, he produced his own version of *La Sylphide* to a new score by Løvenskiold, which the Royal Danish Ballet has staged uninterruptedly to the present day, and which the American Ballet Theatre offers at the present time with Carla Fracci as an incomparable Sylphide. When Lucile first danced this role in 1836, the royal family was so pleased with her performance that she was summoned to the palace for afternoon chocolate with the Princesses and was given a gold bracelet.

Though young Mlle Grahn went on from triumph to triumph, hailed in Copenhagen as "the Danish Taglioni," she was dissatisfied and hankering for the greater glories of Paris. She decided to apply for one of the travel grants which the enlightened rulers of Denmark made a practice of bestowing on talented writers and artists, but by now Bournonville was infatuated with his pupil and determined to keep her close by. When he vetoed her petition he had not yet discovered the iron will that motivated his ethereal and seemingly gentle little *danseuse*. She had inherited from her mother, he soon learned, all the proverbial stubbornness of Jutland farm folk, and in due time she would always manage to have her way. In this case, she bypassed him and enlisted the support of

Princess Wilhelmina, the King's daughter, who gave her approval as well as a jewel, and in May 1837 Lucile set out for France.

Her progress under Jean-Baptiste Barrez, director of the Opéra's ballet school, continued to be remarkable, so much so that plans were made for her debut in October in *La Juive*. For this she needed permission to extend her leave but, instead of an affirmative reply to her request, she received a letter instructing her to come home immediately to appear in *Le Postillon de Longjumeau*, which was to be staged as part of the festivities for the Queen's seventieth birthday.

The enforced return to Copenhagen put her in a bitter mood. Spoiled by too much praise in Paris, she was displeased when she was promoted only to solo dancer instead of *première danseuse*, and her quarrels with Bournonville began to take a violent turn. On his part, spurned by Lucile who thought him old (he was fifteen years her senior), dictatorial, and boring, he revenged himself by becoming difficult and cruel. He sneered at the *cachucha* and *jaleo* which she had brought back from France; she made fun of him and flaunted his authority. Turn by turn, they resorted to officialdom; their squabbling involved ministers and came before the King. Bournonville even threatened to resign; and Lucile grew more unreasonable than ever, because she now became entangled in a disappointing romance.

The charged atmosphere, it seemed, was to be at least temporarily relieved when the King granted permission to Lucile for six guest appearances in Hamburg, and her injured feelings were soothed by the response of the new audience. The stolid citizens of Germany found her *cachucha* devastatingly exotic and exciting and they roared their approval. Encouraged by such enthusiasm, she did not wait this time for any further permissions, but proceeded independently to Paris and from there answered the next summons by simply saying that she had another engagement. This was too

much for the conformist Danish authorities; they allowed her a
brief time to reconsider and then ratified her permanent dismissal
without pension. Instead of distressing her, the ruling set her mind at
ease: she was at last free to come and go when and where she wished
and pursue her career wherever it seemed most promising.

So Denmark lost her greatest ballerina and never again saw
Lucile Grahn after her final performance there in February 1839.
Fifteen years later, when a ship taking her from Russia to England
dropped anchor in Danish waters, she refused to land, and her
friends had to go on board to see her.

A sentimental detail of her departure from her country was the
letter of thanks and farewell which she sent to the famous spinner
of fairy tales. At the start of her career, Hans Christian Andersen,
in his naive, gauche way, had written directly to her saying he
would like to meet her to find out if her soul was as valid as her
legs. Later, when she had been in Paris, he sent her this little poem,
which she acknowledged gratefully:

> *Af Laengsel maatte Seinestaden lide,*
> *Sylfiden Taglioni den forlod.*
> *Da sendte Danmark Frankrig sin Sylfide.*
> *En Rosenknop af Nordens Sne fremstod.*[86]

> ("The city on the Seine felt a doleful need,
> When the sylph Taglioni resolved to go.
> Then to France Denmark sent her own sylphide.
> A rosebud blossomed from the northern snow.")

"Mlle Lucile Grahn, the Danish dancer, is tall, slender, small-
jointed, and well made, and would be prettier still if she did not
wear such a persistent smile; a smile should hover about a dancer's
lips in the way that a bird flutters about a rose, but it does not
need to be fixed on those lips under pain of misshaping them. A
smile, which is never found on the marble lips of goddesses of an-

tiquity, produces a disagreeable effect which destroys the harmony of the lines: the cheeks expand, the corners of the nose become creased, the eyes make crows' feet, the lips are drawn back, thinned and lengthened. Nothing is more opposed to beauty. A beautiful woman should keep her features almost motionless; the play of the eyes is sufficient to animate and brighten them," [87] said Théophile Gautier, who often wrote about dancers as if they were so much slave flesh to be analyzed before purchase. Had he not castigated Louise Fitz-James for being as thin as a lizard or silkworm? And a few weeks after his piece on Mlle Grahn he said of poor Taglioni, who was only thirty-four, with some of her great moments still ahead of her, that she had lost much of her lightness and elevation, that "after some bars, signs of fatigue appear, she becomes short of breath, perspiration bedews her brow, her muscles seem to be under a strain, her arms and chest redden. . . ." [88]

Such criticisms were, of course, always painful to an artist. But, after her rather hasty Paris debut in 1838 and her discharge from the Danish company the following June, Lucile was the possessor of a three-year contract with the Opéra, the object of her dreams since the age of fifteen. Besides, there were other important critics who admired her without Gautier's mean little reservations and, after four months of happy and successful appearances, a piece of good luck came her way. Fanny Elssler was unable to dance *La Sylphide* because of illness, and although that ballet, since the departure of Taglioni, was supposed to be exclusively hers, Mlle Grahn was allowed to take the role at the last minute and made a personal triumph of it. Her gossamer, virginal quality, said a number of the reviewers and spectators, was just what that particular role demanded, especially when compared with Mlle Elssler's less suitable verve and sensuality. As a result, Fanny made a tremendous fuss and threatened to leave. Let her go, conceded Duponchel, since she also was becoming too spoiled and difficult; but, no doubt, he could dispense with her, what with having Lucile Grahn under contract and another debutante, the vivacious little Augusta Maywood, as well as Pauline Leroux, a continuing Opéra favorite, and even the possibility of the much-heralded Fanny Cerrito.

What the Parisians could not understand about Mlle Grahn, as was usual in such circumstances, was that she seemed to have no "protector." And indeed she had none. She was still suffering a reaction to her disrupted marriage plans. Before leaving Denmark she had accepted the attentions of a dandified cavalry officer, Count Carl Otto Friedrich von Schulenburg, with the approval of her father, who undoubtedly was impressed by the suitor's social prominence, but should have been a better judge of character. Eighteen years older than Lucile and definitely corpulent, the Count was a more provincial, less elegant, Danish version of Mlle Elssler's Marquis de La Valette and was equally notorious for his many liaisons. This prospective marriage to Lucile, set for 1841, brought on a lot of comment in the press and some wicked caricatures, but one day it became apparent to Lucile and her family that the aristocratic fiancé was not quite disinterested. He was, in fact, far less engrossed in the pretty *danseuse* than he was in the money she was earning as a guest artist in Hamburg, and which would increase as her reputation grew. Lucile was relieved to leave him behind in Copenhagen, but the memory of the affair rankled until late in her life, and in Paris she was in no hurry to become involved in another romance.

Her career at the Opéra came to a sudden end before the 1840 season began because of a knee injury (a real one!) which incapacitated her for a long time. It was a grave blow to Duponchel's hopes, especially as he lost most of his other outstanding *danseuses* as well: Mlle Elssler prepared to leave for New York, Augusta Maywood eloped and never came back, and Mlle Cerrito opted for London. Lucile Grahn's next important engagement was in Russia, in 1843, and she was one of the rare ballerinas to arrive there when she was still young. [She was twenty-four when she made her debut in St. Petersburg, as opposed to Taglioni, who was thirty-three, and Elssler and Cerrito, who were both thirty-eight.]

Although Lifar states that " . . . fear of offending the all-powerful Andreianova [89] made the management abstain from engaging foreign stars," [90] it must be remarked that Russia continued her eighteenth- and early nineteenth-century tradition of importing dancers and that during Andreianova's career (1837–55), the steady succession of foreigners included Taglioni (1837–42), Grahn (1843), Yrca Matthias (1847), Elssler (1848–49), Grisi (1850–53), and others. Lucile Grahn appeared immediately after Taglioni, when the Russian public was beginning to be bored by the aging Sylphide, and was her logical successor since she danced Taglioni's best roles and was fifteen years younger and prettier. On the occasion of her debut, "in the first act of *Giselle* she had no success at all (she did not even get a curtain call), but at the end of the second act she had an ovation which recalled Marie Taglioni in her prime. It is more than likely that Lucile Grahn's success considerably shortened her stay in Russia; nobody had the right to rival Andreianova [who was the mistress of A. Guedeonov, director of the Imperial Theatres], much less to eclipse her." [91]

After provoking the jealousy of St. Petersburg's favorite, Lucile now found herself scheduled to appear with an earlier rival. During the 1844 *carnevale* season in Milan, she made some forty appearances in *Elda ossia Il Patto degli Spiriti* by Bernardo Vestris, while Fanny Elssler was performing in *Armida*. But it was in England, during five years of ever-increasing popularity, that she reached the summit of her career. Beginning rather modestly in *Lady Henrietta*, 1844, at Drury Lane Theatre (Sylvain, settled in London after his American tour with Elssler, was her partner), she starred in Perrot's *Eoline* the following spring and then, in July, was one of the glamorous protagonists of the *Pas de Quatre*. As the youngest of the four, she danced the first variation in this most eventful ballet, charming the audience with her feathery lightness and deft point work; and, as she continued in other Perrot ballets, she also developed very considerable gifts as an actress.

In view of the luster attached to her name from this time on, one wonders why she never returned to the Opéra. However, Hamburg, the scene of her first success abroad, welcomed her back as a mature and world-famous artist, and she found Germany so congenial that she decided to settle there and invested her savings in a house and garden in Munich. In 1849 she danced in Leipzig and gave another seventeen performances in Hamburg, where it was so cold that she wrote to a friend in Munich to forward posthaste three of her fur coats (one of them a satin wrap lined in fox) and two extra pairs of boots.[92]

Having led her life untouched by the usual series of scandals (though rumor briefly had linked her name with Benjamin Lumley, director of Her Majesty's Theatre), Mlle Grahn finally made up her mind to marry when she reached the age of thirty-seven. The marriages of ballerinas are proverbially unfortunate or even tragic, and Lucile's was no exception. In 1856 she became Frau Friederich Young. Her husband was a tenor, of English parentage, who was making his career in Germany, and whose brother Edward was an established painter of alpine landscapes, also residing in Munich. In 1863 Friederich Young fell from a stage platform, injuring his spine, and for the remaining twenty-nine years of his life was condemned to a wheel chair in a nursing home.

Her hopes of a pleasant retirement with a companionable husband suddenly dashed, Lucile Grahn-Young organized her existence courageously to take care of the invalid and herself. She taught privately at first, and later was appointed teacher at the Munich Hoftheater where she also choreographed a number of ballets, including the

divertissements for Richard Wagner operas. In 1869, during a lull
in the seemingly endless Prusso-Danish wars that harassed Denmark
right up to World War II, Bournonville traveled to Munich to
study the production of *Lohengrin,* which was soon to be staged
in Copenhagen. For the first time in thirty years he saw his little
runaway *solodanserinde,* whom he had loved too possessively and
quarreled with too fiercely, but it is recorded that their meeting
was a pleasant one and that they chatted about the past without
bitterness. He was able, too, to give her news of their mutual friend,
Hans Christian Andersen, whom Lucile had seen in London in 1847,
though by that time he had transferred his devotion to Jenny Lind.

   Munich, though a large city, always kept a slightly provincial,
intimate atmosphere, and after the ballerina gave up her work
at the Hoftheater and became widowed nine years later, she continued to be a familiar and revered figure to the people of the town
—a bustling, rather plump lady in a long black dress and mourning
bonnet, greeted affectionately by everyone. One day when she
was seventy-seven, she entered a shop and a chance historic meeting took place when a Danish girl, Adeline Genée, was presented
to her. As Mlle Genée was in Munich to dance *Coppélia* at the
Hoftheater, she was deeply impressed by her encounter with one
of the original four famous soloists of the *Pas de Quatre;* Frau Grahn-
Young had seen the eighteen-year-old *danseuse* perform and com-
plimented her, but she could hardly have guessed that she was
talking to the person who would change the course of modern
ballet in England and become President of the Royal Academy of
Dancing.

   Lucile Grahn survived her husband by twenty-three years and
died in 1907 without heirs. She left all her property to the city,
to be used for helping talented young artists, and the grateful
citizens named a street Lucile Grahn Strasse in her honor.

～

Another retired ballerina was living in Denmark when Mlle Grahn made her debut in Bournonville's *La Sylphide*. Anna Margrethe Schall was only sixty-one at the time, but she belonged to another era. She was born in 1775, the year that marked the arrival of the Florentine dancer-ballet master-teacher-choreographer, the indefatigable Vincenzo Galeotti—indefatigable because he devoted forty years to molding the Royal Danish Ballet during its first great period, was still dancing in public at the age of seventy-eight, and did not resign his post until four years later. His pupil, Mlle Schall, began her career in 1802 with a delightful interpretation of Nina (*Nina eller den Vanvittige af Kaerlighed*, by Galeotti), she continued to be popular until she retired in 1824, and her reputation only paled with the appearance of Lucile Grahn and point dancing.

After Mlle Grahn's abrupt departure from Copenhagen, Bournonville replaced her with Caroline Fjeldsted, 1821–81, and Augusta Nielsen, 1822–1902, both of whom made names for themselves at home and abroad but never attained Mlle Grahn's stature. Juliette Price, 1831–1906, whose family boasted four generations of dancers, was Bournonville's next favorite. An accident on the stage caused her to give up dancing in 1865, though she lived to see the ballet installed in the great new opera house in 1874, Bournonville's retirement in 1877, and much of the decadent period that followed. The decline set in because of the Royal Danish Ballet's stubborn adherence to the master's precepts long after they became outmoded and the too-frequent revivals of his ballets. The resultant stagnation, however, has been the gain of modern audiences, for Bournonville's productions, preserved in ice, so to speak, in Denmark, are today's only valid models of Romantic ballets.

In 1942, when the Royal Danish Ballet was in the midst of its third flourishing period, the rank of *première danseuse*, which Mlle Grahn

coveted and never attained in her own country, was bestowed on
Margot Lander, the only Danish dancer who ever received this distinction.[93] No doubt, Lucile Grahn would have been similarly honored had she stayed in Copenhagen. In any case, her compatriots have
long since forgiven her for running away and honor her as their
greatest ballerina.

CHAPTER 14

Augusta Maywood
1825–1876

Paris, by now, was used to successful debuts, but Augusta Maywood proved to be a truly exciting novelty. To begin with, she was American—the first to arrive from the "land of savages" and dare to enter the lists at the Opéra. She also had a character all her own; even after eighteen months of study with Mazilier and Coralli, she retained a very personal style and, in spite of her extreme youth (she was not yet fifteen), her technique was spectacular if somewhat erratic.

Little Mlle Maywood was introduced on November 11, 1839, in a special *pas de deux* with Charles Mabille, in *Le Diable boiteux*, in which Fanny Elssler danced her *cachucha*. The long article which the debut elicited from the pen of Théophile Gautier was very admiring as well as patronizing. After one of his customary flowery passages all about nothing, he went on to say: "Mlle Augusta Maywood has a quite clear-cut type of talent. It is not the melancholy grace, the dreamy abandon, and carefree lightness of Mlle Grahn

whose eyes reflect Norway's cold, clear blue sky, and who suggests a
Valkyrie dancing in the snow; and it is still less the matchless perfection, the radiant poise and allure of a classic Diana, the sculptural
purity of Fanny Elssler; there is something brusque, unusual, fantastic
about Mlle Maywood, which sets her quite apart. . . . She came to
seek the approval of Paris because what Paris thinks is important
even to the barbarians of the United States in their world of rail-
roads and steamboats. . . . She is of average height, shapely and
very young, eighteen according to her detractors, with dark eyes,
small features, and an eager, untamed expression which verges on
the beautiful; added to this, steely sinews, jaguar legs, and almost the
agility of a clown. Finally, no one could have been less intimidated
by such a formidable test. She came under the fire of footlights and
opera glasses, which shatter the strongest nerves, with all the calm
of an established favorite. One would have thought she simply was
dealing with an audience of her native Yankees. In two or three
leaps she crossed the huge stage from the backdrop to the prompter's
box, performing those almost horizontal *vols penchés* which brought
fame to Perrot *l'aérien*, and then she started to gambol, to revolve in
the air, and to perform *tours de reins* with all the flexibility and
strength of Lawrence and Redisha [popular English clowns at the
Cirque Olympique]. It brought to mind a rubber ball bouncing off
a racquet." Gautier follows this up with a paragraph on the tasteless
American-type costumes worn by Augusta, and he concludes: "Mlle
Maywood will be a good acquisition for the Opéra. She has a style
of her own, a very remarkable touch of originality. . . ." [94]

If Augusta Maywood did not quail under the probing gaze of
the Parisians and their critics, it was because she was already a
seasoned trouper. From infancy she had been surrounded by theatre
folk. Her mother was an English actress, divorced in 1828 from
the actor Henry August Williams, and soon remarried to Robert
Campbell Maywood, who was also an English actor and became the

manager of the Chestnut Street Theatre in Philadelphia. Mrs. May-
wood's two daughters by her first husband, the six-year-old Mary
Elizabeth and Augusta, aged three, took their stepfather's name.
Maywood was determined from the start that Mary Elizabeth was
to be an actress; like her mother, she was exceptionally pretty.
Augusta was sent to M. and Mme Paul Hazard's ballet school,[95] un-
doubtedly because foreign ballerinas were making quite a stir in the
United States, their earning capacity was extraordinary, and Robert
Maywood was unusually money-minded.

Augusta proved to be so astonishingly gifted that in less than
two years her teacher felt that she was ready to appear in public.
Though she was only twelve, her debut was announced for December 30, 1837, as Zelica, the leading role in *The Maid of Cashmere*, an
adaptation of Taglioni's *Le Dieu et la Bayadère* and, because of the
popularity in the United States of the German ballerina Mlle Augusta,[96] the little prodigy was billed as La Petite Augusta. Appearing
with her would be another child wonder, Mary Ann Lee, also a
pupil of the Hazards' school.[97]

Robert Maywood's wildest hopes were more than fulfilled by the
results of this venture. Overnight Augusta became the talk of Philadelphia, the press raved, everyone wanted to see the phenomenon,
and when her benefit performance took place, the receipts were
enormous, and the stage was heaped with flowers as for a grown-up
ballerina, with even a diamond ring attached to one of the bouquets.
Mary Ann Lee also received her deserved share of praise. Alas, the
children immediately were forced into a horrid rivalry by two
factions: those who were pro-Augusta versus those who resented her
as an outsider and favored the Philadelphia-born Miss Lee and became infuriated when manager Maywood at first refused to give a
second benefit for "our Mary Ann." Fortunately for both little
girls, La Petite Augusta soon left town. She was summoned to the
Park Theatre, New York, where she danced in the same ballet (with

the title role changed to Zoloe) and as Dew Drop in *The Mountain Sylph*, an Americanized version of *La Sylphide*. For three months she stirred up even more excitement there than she had in Philadelphia, after which her ambitious stepfather decided to send her to Paris. With training at the Opéra School and perhaps some European appearances, he expected she would be able to command the salaries of foreign ballerinas. She would become, so he thought, a gold mine for him.

No doubt Augusta never forgot May 1, 1838, the day when she and her mother left for France on the *Utica*. The steamer *Sirius* and four sailing vessels all hoisted anchor at the same time, the wharves were crowded with cheering spectators, and the water swarmed with the small craft that accompanied the ships to the outer harbor for a last farewell. Along with six intrepid passengers on board the *Sirius* was Henry Wikoff, setting forth on the journey that would end by linking him to Fanny Elssler and, as he himself admitted, quite uneasy about risking his life on the new steam-powered vessel.

Meanwhile, Robert Maywood stayed behind in a frustrating effort to launch Mary Elizabeth as an actress, first in Philadelphia and New York, later at the Theatre Royal, London, and finally in Dublin, 1840. Augusta's beautiful sister "exhibited no talent for the profession she was to adopt," noted Wemyss after eight years, "nor has a spark been extracted to the present hour." Maywood, however, was able to console himself with continuing splendid news from Paris. Augusta was doing brilliantly in class; her Opéra debut was far more successful than anyone could have foreseen and had resulted in a year's contract; she went on getting excellent reviews for her dancing in *La Tarentule, Nina, La Fille mal gardée, Le Diable amoureux;* she was gaining experience and, of course, profiting by first-hand observation of such stars as Mlles Elssler, Grahn, and Leroux, with even a chance of seeing Marie Taglioni in three of her most famous roles during a brief return engagement. By the end of summer news was drifting back to Europe of the fortune Fanny Elssler was amassing in America, and manager Maywood must have been gloating inwardly over the prospects of his own budding ballerina, when suddenly his expectations collapsed. Augusta, chaperoned day and night by her mother, who had been forewarned of the easy morals of Paris, Augusta, his prize, his promise of a glorious future, had vanished.

For several days there was no word of the missing girl. Her frantic mother rushed to the American Consul for help, the police were called in, the newspapers speculated, and finally it came out that Augusta and Charles Mabille, her first partner at the Opéra, had eloped after outwitting the vigilance of Mrs. Maywood. Charles, in the female disguise of a milliner's assistant and carrying a hatbox, had applied to the *concièrge* of the Maywoods' apartment house at an hour when Augusta knew that her mother would be out. "Mademoiselle is not allowed to come down, and there is no need for you to go up. You can leave her hat with me," the *concièrge* told him. "Not at all," replied Charles. "The hat has to be tried on by Mademoiselle. If it isn't right I shall be scolded." When he came down he stopped to gossip with the *concièrge*, while Augusta crept out unseen behind his ample skirts. Outside he had a hired carriage waiting, and soon the lovers were galloping toward Boulogne, where they hoped to catch the Channel ferry to England and then proceed to Gretna Green to be married. They realized, of course, that their flight would automatically cancel out their contracts with the Opéra, but Charles had danced in London (1837–38), and was confident that they would have no trouble there in getting new engagements.

Unfortunately for the romantic couple, they had forgotten that Augusta, being a minor, had no passport of her own, with the result that they were not permitted to board the ferry. After a series of adventures, which included their being mistaken for the Duc de

Bordeaux, the Bourbon pretender to the throne of France, and his sister, the fugitives were arrested and escorted back to Paris and, on November 10, Charles was jailed at the Concièrgerie. It was then that M. Mabille *père* came to plead with Mrs. Maywood for his son; the penalty for abducting a minor was a long term in prison at hard labor. He prevailed on her to waive the charges and, much against her will, she also gave in and signed her consent to the marriage, though, hoping to postpone it or get out of it altogether, she left immediately for Dublin to join her husband, with the downcast Augusta in tow. Charles followed, and within a few weeks the marriage took place.

Augusta spent the winter months at the house of her father-in-law, 123 rue Saint-Honoré, where for many years he had conducted his fashionable classes in social dancing and which he was neglecting now for a new venture: the Bal Mabille, an open-air amusement park with public dancing, in the Allées des Veuves (nowadays the Avenue Montaigne, near the site of the Théâtre des Champs-Elysées). The Opéra was naturally a closed chapter for the young Mabilles, but in May they started a long engagement in Marseille, where Augusta became a great favorite of the public, and it was there, in October, that they went through a second marriage ceremony to legalize their status in France, because Augusta was expecting a baby, born January 2, 1842, and named Cécile Augusta for Charles' mother and the ballerina.

From January to July of the following year Augusta danced in Lyon while Charles returned to Paris to participate in the great plans that were being drawn up for the redesigning of the Bal Mabille and to help settle the arrangements for running it, and in September they arrived in Lisbon as *primi ballerini* at the São Carlos Opera House. They were in the middle of their second year there when Charles was called back to Paris on account of the death of his father. During his absence a liaison of Augusta's came to a point of no return: she discovered that she was expecting a child which could not possibly be attributed to her husband, since she had been living on purely platonic terms with him for over a year.

Charles was a moody, difficult person, envious of his handsome brother Victor, a successful lawyer, and especially so of his brother Auguste, an outstanding dancer, and perhaps even jealous of his wife's theatre triumphs. She had long since fallen out of love with him, and he was quite aware that only their joint careers kept them together. Nevertheless, he was horribly shocked on coming home one night to discover, instead of his wife, a letter which she had left for him, and which was soon to reappear in the *Gazette des Tribunaux*, the French National Archives, and even in the United States. "M. and Mme Mabille had danced a *pas de deux* at the São Carlos of Lisbon," said the *Gazette*, "and to everyone present the couple had never seemed more charmingly united, more affectionately involved. The theatre rocked with applause, and the happy pair received the tribute of a deluge of flowers. A few minutes after this triumph, Mme Augusta Mabille eloped with one of the artists of the theatre."

"Monsieur Mabille," began Augusta's farewell letter, which was dated Wednesday, February 8 (1845), six o'clock in the evening, "I find myself in a situation which no longer permits me to live in your house. Our characters, as you know, are hardly in accord and, my affections having been bestowed long since on another person, I believe that our mutual happiness requires that I should leave. I am going, therefore, I won't say to be happier, but at least by doing so to escape your justified reproaches. I don't accuse you of anything. Ever since we were married you have fulfilled all the obligations of a good husband. Unfortunately your character has never suited me, and with another, less high-strung woman than myself, I don't doubt that you would have been happy. Forgive me if I have not been able to bring you happiness. I know how much you love our little daughter, so I need not commend her to your care. Only, later on, never let her know the faults of her mother."

Augusta's child was born in July and, with the maternal detachment that seems to have been characteristic of ballerinas in those days, she left it in a foster home. Since divorce had been abolished in France in 1816, Charles had to be satisfied with obtaining a legal separation from his wife; however, there was never any question of his forfeiting a lucrative and prestige-enhancing engagement with her at Vienna's Kaernthner Thor. Augusta's debut there came first, in October, in *Giselle*, with Gustavo Carey as her partner. She had appeared in this role in Lyon and Lisbon and now received laudatory reviews, although it was felt that her performance fell short of Mlle Elssler's. Fanny, who had danced there in the spring, was, to be sure, a greater and far more experienced ballerina and, of course, was a particular favorite in her native Vienna. Mlle Maywood (she had reverted to her maiden name) stayed on until November 1847. Turn by turn, she danced with Charles Mabille (who composed some of the *pas*), Antonio Guerra, Pasquale Borri, and with Eraclito Nikitin from St. Petersburg. Although the repertoire was not very distinguished, she acquired an extremely enthusiastic following, and the two years were very eventful.

The Kaernthner Thor theatre log for August 1846 recorded: "Departed, solo dancer Mabille; re-engaged, Mlle Maywood." A year earlier Auguste Mabille, who was only thirty, had abandoned his flourishing career at the Opéra to become director of the Bal Mabille, which had grown to be such a tremendous enterprise as a tourist attraction and rendezvous for gay Parisians that he now needed his brother Charles to help him run it. Before the fall season began in Vienna, Guerra, who had been ballet master as well as *premier danseur* and Augusta's partner, died suddenly, aged thirty-six, and was a great loss not only to her but to the whole world of ballet. In December Mlle Maywood made such a hit in Bartholomin's

Elina that the Paris *Revue et Gazette des Théâtres* carried a long report which praised her acting as well as her dancing. And in February she had a triumphant benefit. Having made her first attempts at teaching in Lisbon, she also successfully presented a pupil to the Viennese public at this time.

Finally, in March, the Empress let it be known that she wished Mlle Maywood to stop dancing immediately, because the ballerina was too visibly *enceinte*. It was all too true. Only weeks later, Paul Maywood was born. As a father, the most likely candidate would seem to be Pasquale Borri. His sudden mysterious illness was perhaps feigned so that he could leave the theatre briefly and be with Augusta when the child was born; and for many years he continued to take a great personal interest in promoting her career, traveling with her as her partner, from city to city, whenever it could be arranged. The indefatigable Mlle Maywood was back on the program at the Kaernthner Thor in May; and the following month she and Borri journeyed to Budapest for three guest performances.

Augusta Maywood undoubtedly reached the summit of her achievements during the twelve years she danced in Italy. She left Vienna to appear with Nikitin at La Scala, Milan, in 1847. During that *carnevale* season the main attraction was Fanny Elssler in Perrot's *Faust*, but Augusta made such an impression that the star role in this ballet was given to her the year after, and in 1853 La Scala bestowed upon her the signal honor of listing her as *prima ballerina assoluta* when she performed in *L'Araba*. Her progress from Milan to Venice, Trieste, Bologna, Rome, Padua, Ancona, and Viterbo was a sort of triumphal procession. She was hailed as "the incomparable dancer" and "Queen of the Air," and if occasionally a critic remarked that she tended to be more dynamic than lyrically graceful, adoring spectators made no such distinctions. The Italian public has always responded to bravura, and it was more than sufficient for them to be dazzled by her speed, technique, and showmanship. She was constantly booked several years in advance, had to turn down many advantageous engagements, and finally, no longer willing to adapt herself to conditions as she found them in various theatres, she became the first dancer anywhere to have her own traveling company of ballet master, *premier danseur* and other dancers, with all the costumes and props. Most of the business correspondence, written in quite impeccable French, was handled by Augusta; she was also alert to anything which might be new or unusual; shortly after *Uncle Tom's Cabin* was dramatized in the United States, she staged it as a ballet, and when *La Dame aux camélias* was produced in Paris, Augusta immediately converted it into *Rita Gauthier*, which became the most popular ballet in her repertoire.

Although Mlle Maywood never had any intention of returning to America, for a long time her stepfather kept promising the public that she would appear there. Reports of her activities abroad always made good copy and, in 1852, many newspapers reprinted an article about her: "A correspondent of the *Boston Traveller* says the *furore* of the Italians for Miss Maywood's dancing has been most astonishing. She is from Philadelphia, and is really a wonderful dancer, unsurpassed, perhaps, in her vein. If we can credit the newspaper critics here, she excels Cerito, Elssler, and even Taglioni herself. So accurate is her time, that the music seems to emanate from her, and if her grace has been equalled or exceeded by others, her activity and endurance are unrivalled. . . . All the while she was in Florence the excitement continued unabated . . . and on the occasion of her benefit it took three carriages to carry away the bouquets. We have a few words to say upon this subject. The above person is an adopted daughter of Robert Campbell Maywood, some years since distinguished as the Lessee and Manager of the Chestnut Street Theatre in this city. He expended thousands upon this child Augusta, who since her European residence has fallen from that position of respectability adorning virtue and integrity, and in their declining days left Mr. and Mrs. Maywood neglected and in abject poverty. 'How sharper than a serpent's tooth it is to have a thankless child.' " [98]

Augusta preferred to forget that unsavory character Robert Maywood, whose main preoccupation had always been money and more money, who had embittered her own childhood, and had cheated or quarreled with most of the fine actors who attempted to work with him; and, in view of the place she had made for herself in Europe, she could also afford to ignore the sniping of petty American journalists.

Writing to the directors of a north Italian opera house, in 1855, Mlle Maywood thanked them courteously for their interest and regretted that prior engagements prevented her accepting the one they offered her. She could manage, she told them, two or three appearances in the spring of the following year after her scheduled season in Turin, always with the proviso that she would have her own ballet master and *premier danseur* and would choose her own ballets. "I hope to hear from you here in Vienna where I shall be detained for another six weeks by a legal matter which is of utmost importance to me," [99] she concluded.

The legal matter concerned Paul Maywood. It was only now, when the boy was seven years old, that Charles Mabille learned of his existence and embarked on proceedings involving lawyers, embassy officials, and even the Foreign Office in order to deny his paternity of the child. No bastard offspring of Augusta's was to inherit any part of the very considerable estate which the Bal Mabille was bringing in. The affair dragged on from end of summer, 1854, until the next spring. By then, Augusta had been in Austria off and on for more than a year, at the beginning of which she renewed contact with her public in such major ballets as *Faust* and *Esmeralda*, and with the faithful Borri as her partner. Perhaps it was the friendly reception tendered her at this time which made her decide that eventually she would make her home in Vienna.

Charles Mabille died February 18, 1858, and Augusta, who had avoided Paris for fifteen years, was called there for the settling of the estate, and had a glimpse of her daughter, Cécile Augusta, who was being brought up by the Mabilles and was one of the legal heirs. A month later, when she returned to Italy, Carlo Gardini applied for their marriage license.

Could there ever have been a more curious personality than the man who was to become Mlle Maywood's second husband? Six years her junior, he was a native of Bologna and, to mention but a few aspects of his checkered career, he was a graduate doctor of medicine from the University of Bologna, but did not practice his profession; he was editor-in-chief of *L'Arpa*, a newspaper devoted to the arts; he was an impresario; at a time when foreigners were still permitted to hold such posts, he was American consul in Italy; he was a professor of literature and also the author of a number of books on a wide variety of subjects; in Vienna he became a land-owner; and finally, after Augusta's death, he founded and directed a ballet and music school in Sasso-Marconi. At first sight of Augusta Maywood, he fell in love with her, dropped everything he was doing and followed her from town to town; and as soon as she had honored her remaining obligations at half a dozen opera houses, he married her, and she decided to retire. Or was it perhaps Gardini's possessiveness, rather than her own decision, which caused her to withdraw from the stage?

"The celebrated dancer Augusta Maywood has arrived in Vienna, and will spend the winter here," reported the *Neue Wiener Musik-Zeitung* on October 8, 1859. Augusta, however, was a mere thirty-four and, with her restless temperament and energy, found it quite impossible simply "to spend the winter." A few months later the newspapers announced that the famous Frau Maywood-Gardini had settled in Vienna, and was opening a ballet school. Nor was it any ordinary school. The program embraced not only classes in ballet and acting for the training of competent dancers, but also instruction in French and Italian, in world history, art history, and mythology "so that the students might become true artists." It is nice to imagine that Carlo Gardini taught the Italian classes at the beginning and that at least some of the young Viennese *danseuses* thought him very dashing. Though he must have been a stimulating companion in contrast with the morose Charles Mabille, his wife grew bored with him in less than three years and lost no time in seeking consolation with another lover. The city records show that on June 26, 1864, she gave birth to a son, father unknown, and that the child died the same day, half an hour after a hurried baptism had been performed in the neighborhood church. All this was too much for Carlo Gardini, and he packed up and left the fickle Augusta and Vienna forever.

The ballet school prospered and twice had to be moved to larger quarters. Its directress not only taught, but worked at choreography and, in 1869, was ballet mistress for a popular revue. Interested in everything, as she was, we must suppose that in May of the same year she attended the opening of the new Hofoper (later the Staatsoper), which replaced the Kaernthner Thor, where ballet had been flourishing for over a hundred years. Her name, she knew, had added its own special luster to the roll of those who had made history in that theatre: Mme Angiolini, Maria Medina, Heberle, Taglioni, and Elssler.

It is difficult to believe that, during the last years of her life, busy Frau Maywood-Gardini was ever troubled with loneliness or boredom, though she was saddened, no doubt, when she learned, in 1870, that her granddaughter and namesake had died at the age of seventeen months. Cécile Augusta, when she was twenty, was married in Paris to a young architect from Amsterdam, Johan Othon van Soolen; her mother had not left Vienna to attend the wedding, which had also taken place without the consent of the bride's uncle and guardian, Auguste Mabille.

In the course of her picturesque career, Augusta Maywood had survived all sorts of accidents, conflagrations in theatres, and even a cholera epidemic in Viterbo, which caused the death of one of her ballet girls, but while she was in Leopoldville (then part of Austria and later the Polish city of Lvov) she contracted smallpox, and it proved fatal. She died, aged only fifty-one, on November 3, 1876. Her death attracted no notice even in those cities where, not long since, she had been the idol of the public; and more than two years after she died American newspapers, which had been so eager to report that she had forsaken her husband and neglected her aging parents, stated that she was still living in retirement in Italy, enjoying the advantages of a purely imaginary fortune.

❧

In spite of the fact that people were terrified of the long voyage in sailing vessels and later equally afraid of steamships (they sometimes caught fire or ran out of fuel), a surprising succession of dancers kept crossing the Atlantic for appearances in the United States. First arrivals in the mid-eighteenth century were dancers from England, then the Placides who came in 1793 and stayed. From the 1820s to the 1870s the list included Mlle Celeste, Madame Lecomte, née Martin, Mlle Augusta, née Fuchs, Jean and Marius Petipa, Paul and Amalia Taglioni, Fanny Elssler and Sylvain, the Monplaisirs, Giovanna Ciocca, Giuseppina Morlachi, Marie Bonfanti, Rita Sangalli, and many others.

America owed them a debt of gratitude, because their performances set the standards for good ballet, and a number of them stayed long enough to teach and even to establish schools. Only in the twentieth century would the United States begin to repay the debt through Isadora Duncan, Ruth St. Denis, Martha Graham, the American Ballet Theatre, and the young dance companies, which have had and continue to have an important role in modernizing the ballet in Europe.

In the meanwhile, for well over a hundred years, American dancers were satisfied to perform at home. Augusta Maywood is to be remembered as the first who went abroad and competed on equal terms with the best dancers of her period.

CHAPTER 15

Carlotta Grisi

1819–1899

In the windy stretches of Théophile Gautier's dance reviews the contradictions seem to have been overlooked by the balletomanes who are his undiscriminating devotees. "We shall conclude this portrait [of Fanny Elssler] with a few comments," said Gautier. "All too often Mlle Elssler's smile is not expansive enough; it is sometimes taut and constrained." But, as we have seen, he was soon berating Mlle Grahn: "A smile produces a disagreeable effect; nothing is more opposed to beauty; a beautiful woman should keep her features almost immobile." Again, after stating Madrid's Dolores Serral to be the foremost dancer of the *cachucha* and accusing Mlle Elssler of the "unpardonable crime" of not being at all amorous in her rendition of this dance, he then called Elssler "the *cachucha* incarnate" and added "we have seen the best dancers of Spain but nothing approaches the *cachucha* danced by Elssler."

Of Carlotta Grisi he wrote: "She has fire, but not enough originality; her dancing lacks distinction," and exactly a year later (although

Gautier said it was two years) he declared that "she is possessed of a strength, lightness, suppleness, and originality which at once places her between Elssler and Taglioni." [100] The interval of twelve months between his stated opinions had not made all that difference in the ability and originality of Carlotta, who had been dancing for fourteen years, half a dozen of which she had spent with Perrot, who loved her and concentrated all his efforts on making her into a finished ballerina. But, in the case of Mlle Grisi, perhaps Gautier should be pardoned for changing his mind, because when he met her he, too, fell in love with her, and it was a love which, forever unfulfilled, nevertheless endured until the day he died.

The enchanting ballerina who was to make history as the first Giselle might never have become a dancer at all, although she began her ballet classes in Milan when she was only seven, and had made such progress within three years that she was singled out from among the *corps de ballet* children at La Scala and given individual roles to perform. Though her parents were not musicians, nearly all the other members of the family had operatic careers. Carlotta's maternal aunt was Josephina Grassini, 1773–1830, one of the celebrated singers of her day; Carlotta's cousins, the sisters Giuditta and Giulia Grisi, were also outstanding. Giulia, who sang for sixteen years in Paris, twenty-seven years in London, and finally toured in America, was acknowledged as a great beauty and one of the most splendid voices of the nineteenth century. Carlotta's own sister, Marina, retired from the opera prematurely when she married an Italian nobleman, and a second sister, Ernesta, who gave promise of an extraordinary career, stopped singing in public to bring up the two children she had by Théophile Gautier, to whom, however, she was never married.

It was rather surprising, then, that Carlotta Grisi did not make singing her profession, especially as she was encouraged to do so when she was a child by La Pasta and later by Malibran, both of them more than competent to evaluate her future possibilities. Actually Carlotta did sing in theatres on several occasions, Perrot always encouraged her to go on with her voice lessons, and for many years she continued singing at home for her own pleasure, but dancing was her first love, and she was wise, no doubt, not to try to compete with her famous cousins.

When she was fourteen her parents allowed a tour of Italy to be arranged for her, and it was in Naples that Perrot met her and immediately succumbed to the double charm of her personality and her dancing. Only the most cynical, among them Serge Lifar, could suggest that Perrot's attachment to her from this moment was motivated by his ambition to get back his place at the Opéra. Quite the opposite is true, for he was later offered a renewal of his old contract, which he turned down because it did not include Carlotta, who was by then his mistress. Besides, Perrot, both as dancer and choreographer, was a genius who could stand on his own merits.

Perrot began by being Carlotta Grisi's teacher, soon he was her lover, and for a long time he aspired to become her husband.[101] As a teacher he was a true follower of Philippe Taglioni's relentless tactics with Marie. Determined to have Carlotta rival or even excel Mlles Taglioni and Elssler, he was an indefatigable taskmaster, meanwhile helping her to gain experience and stage presence in appearances with him in London, Vienna, Munich, and Milan.

The performance which elicited her first review by Gautier was at the Théâtre de la Renaissance, February 1840, in *Le Zingaro*, a sort of gypsy comedy-ballet. Teacher and pupil were still living together, and were billed as M. and Mme Perrot. Carlotta danced and sang, but it was Perrot who triumphed this time. Although Gautier despised male dancers and couldn't resist saying: "Perrot is not handsome; he is extremely ugly," he had only the highest praise for his accomplishments as a dancer, and the Paris public, which hadn't seen him since 1834, welcomed him back with an outburst of enthusiastic clapping, stamping, and shouting.

In view of this reception, it was odd that he was not engaged along with Carlotta when she received her first modest contract at the Opéra the following year, though he did succeed in making an arrangement to choreograph her dances. For her debut, February 1841, he produced a *pas de deux*, which she performed with Lucien Petipa in Donizetti's recently staged opera *La Favorite;* this was followed by *pas* in several other operas; and then, a mere eighteen weeks after the debut, she emerged in the greatest role of her career—one of the greatest roles, in fact, of all time for any ballerina: Giselle.

With the galaxy of talents at work together to produce the new ballet, it was small wonder that it turned out to be such an extraordinary success. Inspired by a piece in Heine's *De l'Allemagne*, which describes the elfin creatures known in German folklore as "wilis," Gautier had begun to write the libretto but, being dissatisfied with the results, he consulted Vernoy de Saint-Georges. This friend of his, apart from figuring as one of the most eccentric and picturesque persons on the Paris scene, was the ablest and most imaginative of all the librettists. He had written the book of *La Gipsy*, 1839, for Fanny Elssler, and more than twenty years later, in 1860, was to collaborate with Marie Taglioni when she created *Le Papillon* for Emma Livry. It took him only three days to prepare the script for *Giselle*. Adolphe Adam, equally knowledgeable in ballet matters, was commissioned to write the music; the stage magician, Ciceri, was to design the sets; Coralli was announced as the choreographer, with Lucien Petipa as Grisi's partner, and the beautiful Adèle Dumilâtre as Queen of the Wilis.

In all this, the unfortunate Perrot was the forgotten man. Carlotta had left him, and was settled in an apartment with her mother and sister; and from the start of her Opéra career she was no longer Mme Perrot but Mlle Grisi. Also, although posterity has since given Perrot his due, his name did not even appear on the program of the original *Giselle;* no attention was paid to the fact that he had trained the sensational new *danseuse* nor that it was he who had choreographed most of the dances that were bringing fame to both the ballet and the ballerina. Only here and there a lonely voice was raised in his behalf: "It is well to add, out of fairness, since the billing does not mention it," said the *Moniteur des Théâtres*, on June 30, "that M. Perrot himself has arranged all his wife's *pas*, in other words he is the author of a good part of the new ballet." *La France Musicale*, on July 4, made a similar defense: ". . . There is a fifth collaborator, unmentioned—Perrot, Carlotta's husband and teacher, who has arranged all the *pas* in the scenes for his wife."

On the subject of *Giselle* and its main protagonist, a flood of Gautieresque prose swamped the newspapers; the style of Mlle Grisi's enamored critic seemed to be contagious, and other journalists began to load their articles with superlatives, flowery comparisons, tears and sighs, and romantic digressions. The following year, when Carlotta danced (rather reluctantly, because she did not want her own popularity to deprive another, older dancer, Pauline Leroux, of a promised role) in *La Jolie Fille de Gand*, Gautier's reviews became more hyperbolic than ever. "How she flies, how she rises, how she soars! How at home she is in the air! When, from time to time, the tip of her little white foot skims the ground, it is easy to see that it is out of pure good nature, so as not to drive to despair those who have no wings." [102] Is this dance criticism? If it is, then we, too, should like to leap straight from the eighteenth century into the arms of the twentieth. After reading thirty pages of one of Gautier's books, André Gide commented: "I know of nothing more inane," and he added later: "Gautier, one of the most useless haranguers who ever encumbered any literature." [103] Among today's balletomanes, only Clive Barnes of *The New York Times* seems to have brought his perceptive faculties to bear on this silly rambling, calling him "a positively rotten ballet critic."

What was indeed rather extraordinary in connection with *La Jolie*

Fille de Gand, June 1842, was the reappearance of Albert as the choreographer and performer of one of the roles, Albert, who was first seen at the Opéra in 1803, and who had been Mlle Bigottini's partner in such long-forgotten ballets as Gardel's *Paul et Virginie* and Milon's *Clari*. Almost all of the collaborators of *Giselle* joined forces again in staging Albert's ballet, and he must have felt gratified too by the lavish production accorded it, which rose to almost double the sum spent on *Giselle*, as he must also have been delighted with the sparkling performance of Mlle Grisi, though the part he wrote for her was less suited to her talents than *Giselle* or others which were to follow.

Over another year went by before a new role was created for Carlotta, and toward the end of that time she seemed to be languishing. Even the press remarked on it. As a child, when she had first begun to dance at La Scala, she had gone through a period of such nervous exhaustion that it had been necessary to interrupt her studies and her appearances. Now, with her delicate, quiet, very feminine personality, lacking both Taglioni's iron dedication and Elssler's buoyant physique, perhaps she was suffering again from the demands of too much work and excitement. Or was she perhaps pining for Lucien Petipa, with whose name gossip had linked hers? It is more likely that what she missed was the constant support of Perrot. He and Gautier both had accompanied her to England in the spring of 1842 for the staging of *Giselle* and her first season there as a star soloist. It now seemed certain that Perrot would settle there permanently, and it was, in fact, the moment when he was about to begin his long and prolific association with the composer Pugni and all the visiting dancers who were to make London into a new mecca for balletomanes.

The announcement, on December 7, that *La Péri* would be the next opus to feature Carlotta Grisi coincided with the obituaries of Auguste Vestris, who had died two days before at the age

of eighty-two. For some of the older members of the Opéra staff
who had known him well it was astonishing to think that he, who
had appeared with Mlles Heinel and Guimard before the Revolution,
had survived to dance with La Taglioni and see Mlle Elssler. Perrot
was one of his pupils, so even Carlotta Grisi inherited quite directly details of his classicism and elegance, which enhanced the
Romantic aspects of her dancing.

La Péri, July 1843, was the invention of Théophile Gautier. He
intended it to be not only a vehicle for his beloved Carlotta but
also, in an exotic Egyptian setting, a version of the theme which
inspired *La Sylphide:* physical man in search of the ideal. The hero,
Achmet, first sees the Péri in a dream—"it is only when the eyes of
the body are asleep that those of the soul are awakened"— and at
the end of the dance which she performs for him, the *pas de songe*,
she falls from the clouds into his arms. In this terrifying leap,
variously reported to be from six to twenty feet, Carlotta each
time risked her life. Her partner, Lucien Petipa, was very adept
at catching her and holding her aloft in a graceful pose, but sometimes this feat didn't come off. It was interesting then to contrast
the reactions of the public in London and Paris. When she missed,
the British, true sportsmen, implored her not to endanger her life
a second time in the course of a single evening, and when voluntarily she tried and succeeded, they rewarded her with a deafening
round of applause; the Opéra audience, on the other hand, waited
in stubborn silence on one occasion, forcing her to do it three times
over before they were satisfied.

It was old Coralli who did the choreography, and for a man of
his age (he was sixty-four) the dances were very novel and
daring, not only the famous leap but also, in the second act, the
pas de l'abeille, when the Péri plucked a flower, and a bee flew out
and into her garments, which she tossed aside in her fright. "If
you only knew with what modest embarrassment Carlotta removes
her long white veil," confided Gautier to his friend the poet

Gérard de Nerval, " . . . how well she expresses the hopes, the anxieties, all the phases of the struggle, as the bodice and scarf, and the skirt which the bee tries to penetrate, fly off to right and left and vanish in the whirl of the dance." [104] No doubt, a first, and very Victorian, balletic version of the modern strip tease!

As the Péri, Carlotta achieved all the popularity of the early *Giselle,* and six months later the Opéra renewed her contract for three years at more than four times her original salary. There followed an eventful period during which Marie Taglioni, weary and looking older than her forty years, gave her series of Paris farewell performances and profited by her stay to see Mlle Grisi in *La Péri*; Auguste, the famous Opéra *claqueur* died; two new luminaries, Sofia Fuoco and Flora Fabbri, made their debuts; and the thirty-six Viennese Children, five to twelve years old, demonstrated to adult dancers that discipline (little known at the Opéra) could produce extraordinary results. Carlotta herself starred in two new admirable ballets, both by Mazilier: *Le Diable à quatre,* August 1845, and *Paquita,* April 1846.

In the meanwhile, her *Giselle,* in many varied versions, had traveled all over the world—to St. Petersburg with Andreianova, to Vienna with Augusta Maywood, Milan with Fanny Cerrito, and even to the United States with Mary Ann Lee and Mlle Augusta. During this time, too, Mlle Grisi had become a great favorite in London, where she never failed to appear for nine consecutive years. There she was reunited (in theatre matters, at least) with Perrot. She danced in one after another of the masterpieces which he turned out for Benjamin Lumley, the inspiring manager of Her Majesty's Theatre: she created the role (soon appropriated by Fanny Elssler) in *La Esmeralda,* 1844; had her share of glory in the *Pas de Quatre,* 1845; rose out of the flames in the role of Fire in *Les Eléments,* 1847; and interpreted Summer in *Les Quatre saisons,* 1848.

In *La Esmeralda* Mlle Grisi was said to combine all the best

qualities of her rival ballerinas, and there were many of them assembled in London then—Taglioni, Elssler, Grahn, Cerrito, and
others. It was, besides, one of Perrot's major works (Ivor Guest
calls it, along with *Giselle*, one of the two greatest ballets to be
produced during the Romantic period), and it was actually Perrot's
only ballet to survive into modern times, since today's versions of the
Pas de Quatre are not revivals but reconstructions based on what
modern choreographers imagine the original might have been. *La
Esmeralda* was Mlle Elssler's *pièce de resistance* in Russia, where it
continued as the preferred ballet of Mathilda Kchessinska who, at
the time of writing, is still living in Paris at the age of ninety-eight.
There have been other twentieth-century productions with Touma-
nova, Krassovska, and Violette Verdy.

Already the death knell of the Romantic ballet had sounded
with the last of Perrot's London productions. Mlle Grisi alluded
to one of the main causes of the decline when she said, rather de-
fensively, in regard to *Les Eléments:* " . . . Even without Lind,
we have had two magnificent houses, and the Queen has honored
us with her presence." [105] Jenny Lind, in fact, had become the new
craze in London; on her account, singing regained its former as-
cendancy over the dance, and furthermore the great personalities
of ballet all were drifting away now from England and France
toward Russia. When Perrot departed his place was taken by Marie
Taglioni's brother, Paul, who had made his reputation in Berlin,
and who brought with him his daughter, Marie Taglioni II,
a delightful, accomplished dancer. He presented a long series of
revivals and new works, two of which featured Carlotta Grisi:
Electra, ou la Pléiade perdue, 1849, about which Cyril Beaumont
remarks that "it has a particular interest in that it is presumably
the first ballet in which the new invention of electric light was
used," and *Les Métamorphoses,* 1850, the last ballet in which Western Europe had the privilege and pleasure of seeing Carlotta.

Perrot himself, in the interim, was participating in a great final conjunction of the masterminds in Paris. With a book by Vernoy de Saint-Georges, music mainly by Adolphe Adam, Perrot's choreography, sets by the Opéra's best team of stage designers, and Mlle Grisi as *première danseuse*, *La Filleule des fées* was staged in the autumn of 1849. Perrot then settled in Russia. Fanny Elssler was there, she admired him enormously and had persuaded the Director of the Imperial Theatres to send for him the year before. And so it came about that he was on hand when Carlotta arrived in St. Petersburg and, after a lapse of ten years, became her dancing partner again.

Mlle Elssler had made her Russian debut in *Giselle*. It was, to be sure, Carlotta's ballet, but Fanny had left such a deep impression, especially as a dramatic actress in Act I, that it was a mistake for Carlotta to appear for the first time before the same audience in the same ballet. Her reception was lukewarm, and for a while she did not succeed in evoking the enthusiasm shown to her predecessors from the Opéra. She fared better when Perrot was appointed ballet master, 1851, and, among other works of his, revived *Ondine* for her. Renamed *The Naiad and the Fisherman*, it was staged by him in the theatre and also, for a gala, on a specially constructed platform built across a lake. The naiads arriving at the scene in little shell-shaped skiffs and Mlle Grisi performing in real moonlight the *pas de l'ombre*, a dance in which she pursues her own moon-shadow, must have created a magical effect, the essence of which was preserved for posterity in one of the most ravishing of all scenic ballet prints.

After three years in Russia, with over one hundred and fifty appearances and ever-increasing popularity, Mlle Grisi went to Warsaw in 1854. From there she might have returned to London or to the Opéra, where a ballerina of her caliber was much needed —Cerrito was adored, but it was known that she would soon leave

Paris for St. Petersburg; Rosati had a following, but was somehow lacking in glamour; and it had become all too obvious that pretty Adeline Plunkett did not have the makings of an outstanding dancer.

However, for the time being, Carlotta was in no position to accept an engagement, because she was soon to bear a child. The father, Prince Radziwiłł, possessor of a distinguished ancient name and immense wealth, had known Carlotta almost as long as had Théophile Gautier and in his attitude toward her seemed more like a kindly husband than a demanding lover. He had given her a splendid property at Saint-Jean, not far from Geneva, and now tried to prevail upon her to retire. Had she not enjoyed the life of a great star in Vienna, Milan, London, Paris, and St. Petersburg? And what more could she look forward to except the inevitable decline in her abilities, saddened perhaps by the sort of cruel comments that were cast at even the peerless Taglioni when she last appeared in Milan and Paris? Carlotta allowed herself to be persuaded and, like Augusta Maywood, withdrew from the stage when she was only thirty-four.

The remainder of her life ran out "sans histoire" says one of Mlle Grisi's biographers; nevertheless she lived on at Saint-Jean for forty-six more years, and she herself certainly would not have described that long span as uneventful. A conscientious mother with a profound sense of family, she was busy bringing up her daughter, Ernestine Grisi. Her property included a large manor house, cottage, and park, all of which required her attention, and the house, besides, was invaded by a steady stream of visitors. A frequent guest was Théophile Gautier. It had never been any secret that Carlotta was the love of his life, though he lived *en ménage* with her sister Ernesta, and their two daughters, Judith and Estelle, both used the name of Gautier. "Do you like Carlotta Grisi?" wrote Albéric Second in 1844. "I am mad about her. There is perhaps only M. Théophile Gautier who loves her more than I do." [106] Although Carlotta had never reciprocated this passion, she had grown very fond of him and dependent on him over the years, and their friendship had settled into the platonic relationship so delightfully qualified by the French as *une amitié amoureuse*.

After his second trip to Russia, in 1861, a journey he made with the twenty-five-year-old son born of his early liaison with Eugénie Fort, he stayed for some time at Saint-Jean; he was there for two months in 1864, and for as long again the following year. With all his travels and activities, journalism, the writing of novels, plays, poems, and libretti, he was a stimulating visitor who also brought the latest gossip about Paris and the ballet.

My dear Théophile:
  I received your adorable little letter with infinite pleasure [wrote Carlotta in November 1864] and I was happy to know that you had arrived safely. . . . Come back when and for as long as you wish. Everyone's arms (and mine in particular) will be stretched wide to welcome you.
  I am very happy at what you tell me about things at your house and hope very much that they will continue that way.
  The *kilométrage* [she refers to the endless hours of talk] ended with you, my friend. You were the main pillar of our family life around whom we all liked to gather. Now you are so far away! And the weather has been like our hearts, somber and sad and weeping. Those tears are dried already, but I can't say the same of the tears that spring from our hearts. However, since it's better not to think of oneself alone but also of beloved friends, I wish to share your happiness, my sister's, and that of all those whom you love and who now have their turn at being with you.

After giving him detailed news of the other house guests, she continues:

As for the worthy, tattered Duchasul, I managed to sew up the sleeves of his overcoat, but it would be more difficult to mend the distorted notions of his mind. . . .

Embrace your daughters for me, tell Ernesta that I love her and send you both a kiss which comes straight from my heart. . . ." [107]

At Gautier's house the happy state of affairs to which Carlotta alluded did not last long. In the spring of 1866, while he was away on one of his frequent trips, Judith, in opposition to her father's wishes but abetted by her mother, married the writer Catulle Mendès. The ensuing reproaches and strife never quieted down, and finally Gautier moved out of the villa in Neuilly and settled alone in a Paris flat. In the meanwhile, he went more often than ever to visit Carlotta and wrote some of his finest poems for her, as well as the novel *Spirite*. He lived long enough to see his daughter, Estelle, married to Emile Bergerat, in May 1872, and then his heart ailment worsened. In October, when Carlotta heard he was dying, she hastened to see him, but arrived too late. She was told that the last word he uttered was her name.

Ernestine Grisi married a gifted young French painter, Emile-Auguste Pichart, in 1875. Carlotta was pleased when he won a prize in Paris that same year and soon was delighted to have grand-children. Gradually she subsided into the quiet, routine existence of old age, absorbed in her family and household details, her lifelong hobby of embroidering, and compulsive shopping for trifles. She outlived Prince Radziwill and she survived her romantic friend Théophile by twenty-seven years. A month before her eightieth birthday she died and, as happened with almost every other great ballerina, her death went entirely unnoticed by the public. By 1899 almost nothing was left of the ballet world she had known. Fanny Cerrito, eighty-two and with failing eyesight, lingered on in Paris, and there remained Lucile Grahn, aged eighty, in Munich. The others—Taglioni, the Elsslers, Carlotta's partners Perrot, Petipa, Saint-Léon, and Paul Taglioni—had all preceded her to the grave, and even the opera house which saw the first *Giselle* had burned to the ground. No one remembered the exquisite Wili, the Péri, or "the charming archness and twinkling steps" of Mlle Grisi in the *Pas de Quatre*.

❧

Carlotta Grisi has her special place in ballet history as the creator of the role of Giselle. Appraised when first staged as the greatest ballet since *La Sylphide*, *Giselle* has come down to modern audiences with Adolphe Adam music and in versions based on the one Marius Petipa produced in Russia, and as such it is a work of much greater scope than the *Sylphide* we see today with Bournonville choreography and Danish music. Apart from the fact that the leading male role in *Giselle* is also more challenging than that of James Reuben in *La Sylphide*, an uninterrupted tradition of one hundred and thirty years has made of *Giselle* a sort of test piece for the world's leading ballerinas, in which they can display their dramatic powers in the first act (innocent gaiety followed by madness and death) and their technical capacities and a special poetry in the second. Although Pavlova is conceded to be "the incomparable dancer" of the early twentieth century, most experts feel that the finest Giselle of modern times was Olga Spessivtzeva and also have said that, at present, Carla Fracci is her uncontested successor.

It is the concensus of opinion, too, that Carlotta Grisi was the first ballerina to dance in a boxed slipper. Taglioni, who made such a stir with her early dancing on point, is known to have worn a soft ballet slipper, padded inside with cotton batting for comfort and reinforced outside, at the toe, with stitching or darning. Slippers of Taglioni and her contemporaries can be seen nowadays in a number of public and private collections and especially at the Musée de l'Opéra, Paris.

CHAPTER 16

Fanny Cerrito
1817–1909

THE BRITISH PASSION FOR BALLET rose to its highest pitch in the 1840s, when London was the world center of dance activities. The audience was divided among those who still preferred the airy refinement of Taglioni, those who felt that her laurels now belonged to Mlle Grahn, the faithful who welcomed Elssler back from America, partisans of Carlotta Grisi, and a host of wild enthusiasts in the throes of "Cerritomania."

Enthusiasm for ballet was nothing new in England; it dated back to the seventeenth century, though it had gone through its ups and downs, as was indeed the case in other countries. We find it most astonishing, therefore, to read in André Levinson's *Marie Taglioni:* "It [the ballet] had no roots in British soil, but had been grafted on the English stage by artists such as Albert and Noblet whom the Restoration had loaned to 'perfidious Albion.' " [108] No one would deny the contributions of the French to ballet in England, but it is well to remember that as early as 1665 *The Queen's Ballet*

28. Marie Taglioni, 1842

29. *Marie Taglioni, 1845*   30. *Marie Taglioni*   31. *Marie Taglioni, 1879*

32. *Fanny Elssler in* La Chatte métamorphosée en femme

33. *Lucile Grahn*

34. *Augusta Maywood, Ancona, 1853*   35. *Fanny Elssler*

36. *Carlotta Grisi and Lucien Petipa in* La Péri *(The Leap)*

Mon cher Théophile,

C'est avec un plaisir infini que j'ai reçu votre adorable petite lettre, et heureuse de savoir que vous êtes arrivé en bonne santé. Puisqu'il a fallu que vous nous quittiez il m'est doux une fois de plus d'entendre que votre séjour à St Jean, vous a été agréable et qu'il vous en restera un beau souvenir. Revenez quand et tant qu'il vous fera plaisir, tous les bras [et] les miens en particulier seront ouverts pour vous recevoir.

Je suis bien contente de ce que vous me dites de chez-nous et je désire beaucoup que cela continue ce que j'espère.

De Vilancbourg a cessé avec vous mon franc ami, vous étiez la colonne du centre de notre vie intime où chacun de nous aimait à se réunir autour

qui vient tout droit de mon cœur.

Toute à vous

Carlotta Grisi

ce 22 9bre 1862

Mes bons souvenirs à Tata et à
vos sœurs

37. *Letter to Théophile Gautier from Carlotta Grisi*   38. *Jules Perrot*

39. *Le Foyer de la Danse*   40. *"Rats" of the Opéra*   41. *Théophile Gautier*

42. *Fanny Cerrito and Arthur Saint-Léon*

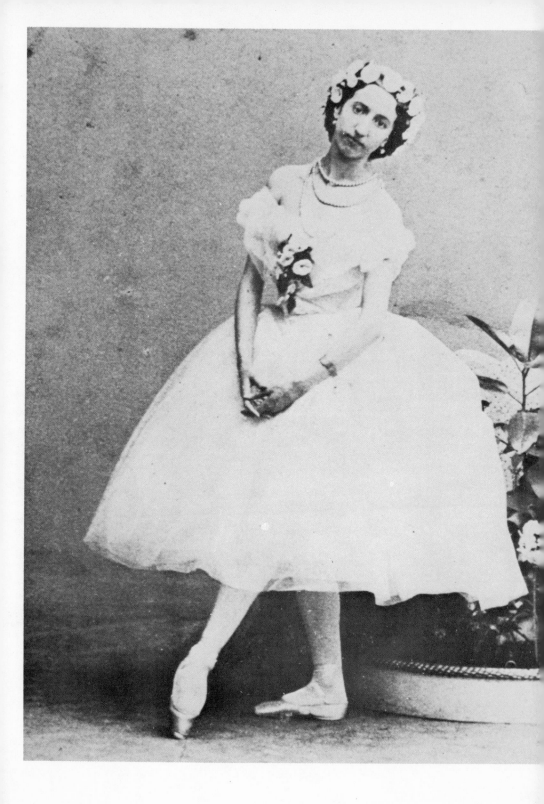

43. *Emma Livry, 1860*

44. *Pauline Leroux*   45. *Amalia Ferraris*   46. *Giuseppina Bozzacchi, 1870*

47. *Martha Mouravieva*   48. *Elena Andreianova*

49. *Students at the Imperial Ballet School, St. Petersburg*

50. *Mathilda Kschessinska*　　51. *Anna Pavlova as a student*

was staged, that by 1690 the manager of Lincoln's Inn Fields, Thomas Betterton, had made two trips to France with a view to examining the theatres there and engaging some French dancers to augment his own troupe. He took back Mlle Subligny and, in 1699, the Opéra idol, Jean Balon, who found the English far more critical than the Parisians concerning the court ballet type of formality which the Opéra had not yet outgrown. John Weaver complained that Balon ". . . pretended to nothing more than a graceful motion, with strong and nimble risings, and the casting of his body into several (perhaps) agreeable postures. But for expressing anything in Nature but modulated Motion, it was never in his head." It was Weaver, too, who, in 1717, presented the English Hester Santlow in the leading role of *Mars and Venus*, a new sort of action ballet which preceded Noverre's *ballets d'action* by nearly half a century. Not long afterward the London public went mad about Marie Sallé's anti-traditional ballets, which she was never permitted to stage in her native Paris, and later there was just as great a response to Noverre, who had also been coolly received in France.

The most brilliant *étoiles* of the Romantic ballet also favored London. Mlles Elssler, Cerrito, Rosati, and Ferraris all chose to dance there before they were ever seen in France, and during the Golden Era it was to England that the Opéra directors went to look for new *premières danseuses*. Of all of these none was a greater object of adoration in London than Fanny Cerrito, who first appeared at Her Majesty's Theatre in 1840.

Francesca Cerrito radiated the assured charm and flirtatiousness of young women who have been the center of attention since childhood, but have escaped becoming too spoiled. She was the daughter of simple Neapolitans who doted on her; what they lacked in money they lavished on her in love and admiration, and when she showed an early inclination to dance they were the first to encourage her. As a little girl she was plump, less tall than average, with a face that was rather too round—characteristics that she never outgrew—and to begin with she gave little evidence of outstanding talent. But she was endowed with unusual strength and vitality, and once she had entered the Ballet School of the Royal Theatres, she worked so tirelessly at improving her technique and even her physical appearance that when she was only fifteen she had skipped through all the intervening grades to the rank of solo dancer and made her debut in *L'Oroscopo*, in July 1832, in a *pas de deux*.

The audience at the San Carlo had been exposed to a lot of first-rate dancing; actually they preferred singing, but little Francesca, in spite of her immaturity, kindled new excitement among them. She was lively and lovable, and had grown very pretty; even her faults seemed endearing because they added somehow to her individuality; and was she not a child of Naples? Her triumphs there launched her on a brief engagement in Rome. Then, as she journeyed north to Florence, she crossed paths with Carlotta Grisi, who was on her way south from Milan. They were to meet soon again in Naples, where Perrot would discover and fall in love with Carlotta, and the two young *danseuses* would be rivals later in Vienna, Milan, and London.

After two seasons in Turin (1835–36), Mlle Cerrito embarked on her first major engagement abroad, some eighteen months at the Kaernthner Thor in Vienna. There, too, an enlightened public found her delightful. They did not pretend to compare her to Mlle Elssler, a frequent and idolized visitor in her native city, but they applauded her warmly, subscribed to her glowing reviews, and, with the true Germanic fondness for diminutives, they showed their affection by converting her from Francesca to Fanny, the name she always used from then on.

From Vienna the good news traveled quickly to Milan, all the more so because this was one of the regions of Italy still under the Austrian yoke, and from 1838 to 1840 Fanny was prima ballerina and the acknowledged darling of the audiences at La Scala. Though none of the ballets in which she appeared was remarkable per se, her poise and skill and her reputation at home and abroad all benefited from her stay in Milan. For these two years she had the opportunity to observe and work with many accomplished performers—Antonia Pallerini, the great actress-dancer who had created roles for Viganò, now long past her prime, but still an imposing personality in mime parts; the "Perrot Conjugi" (Carlotta Grisi and her teacher-partner-lover), who came for fourteen guest appearances; Louis Bretin and Francesco Rosati, Fanny's partner at her debut in Naples; Ronzani, Borri, and other Italians, many of whom were soon to add luster to London's theatres and, on the 1838 program, even Luigi Mabille, who could have been none other than Charles Louis Mabille, future husband of Augusta Maywood.

Equally important for Fanny was her contact with Carlo Blasis, one of the ablest teachers of the nineteenth century. Insufferably arrogant, vain, and snobbish, he was nevertheless very perceptive about art and music as well as ballet, was the author of many valuable books on these subjects, and an extraordinary number of prominent dancers were indebted to him for their style and technique. He was obliged to give up dancing because of an injury and, shortly before Fanny arrived in Milan, was appointed director of the ballet school at La Scala. Later, through Maestro Cecchetti, many of his precepts were handed down from generation to generation, and influence the teaching of today's classic ballet.

Fanny had grown up accustomed to the noise and turmoil of the San Carlo, where audiences were apt to behave more as if they were at a sidewalk café than in a luxurious opera house, but nothing she had ever seen in Naples could have prepared her for the fracas on the evening scheduled for her debut in London. A hundred years earlier there had been rowdy demonstrations in the theatre against Handel when he failed to re-engage Senesino, the favorite singer of a group of influential aristocrats. Now, on April 30, 1840, at Her Majesty's Theatre, when the manager Laporte did not produce the tenor Tamburini, there was an even wilder riot, instigated mainly by the patrons of the omnibus box which was the equivalent in London of the *loge infernale* at the Opéra. These spoiled dandies were used to having their own way about everything, and when their chosen singer was not forthcoming they started a violent hullabaloo of shouting and whistling and finally swarmed onto the stage and stopped the performance altogether.

On May 2, with the troublemakers pacified by Queen Victoria's presence and by promises that Tamburini would soon appear, the postponed debut took place. Fanny's conquest of London was instantaneous, and her opulent figure was almost as great a factor of her success as her dancing. Nowadays, when the ideal ballerina is as slim as a willow wand and embarks on a strenuous diet if she gains a pound or two, it is comical to visualize the buxom dancers admired during the nineteenth century. Their engraved portraits look slender enough to our eyes, since the artists tended to etherealize them, but after the 1840s, when the first photographs began to be popular, we get a truer picture of the ample bosom, wide hips, and sturdy legs which today would be laughed off the stage.

Gautier, who never seemed to mind the hurt feelings that were bound to result from his gibes, had his say on this subject, too: "We are grieved," he protests, "to utter unpleasant truths about Mlle Fitzjames." Then why did he utter them? However, he continues: " . . . The sight of her abnormally thin body is quite painful. . . . Mlle Louise Fitzjames has no body at all; she is not even substantial enough to play the part of a shadow; she is as

transparent as a lantern pane, so that the *corps de ballet* girls who
hover behind her are quite visible through her. Dancing is essentially
pagan, materialistic, and sensual; [what about the revered Taglioni?]
Mlle Louise Fitzjames' arms are truly too ghostly, and her legs are
aesthetic. . . ."

His remarks on Mlle Elssler's shortcomings were tempered with
flattery: ". . . Her hips are but little developed, her breast is not
more rounded out than that of an antique hermaphrodite; but just
as she is a very charming woman, so might she also be the hand-
somest young man in the world." [109]

As in Milan, the ballets staged in London for Mlle Cerrito were
mediocre, but it hardly mattered because by this time her dancing
could only be described as spectacular. She took peoples' breath
away with her soaring leaps, speed, and dashing point work, and
Guerra, who was also the choreographer, was a more than adequate
partner. Such flamboyance, combined with Fanny's beguiling manner and her very feminine figure, had so entrenched her in the hearts
of the Londoners that her assurance was hardly shaken when Marie
Taglioni arrived for her annual summer engagement. La Taglioni,
it must be added, having none too happily reached the age of
thirty-six, was a less frightening rival than she might have been in
years past.

In 1841 a long and very curious letter, dated Milan, June 1,
was printed in the *Revue de Paris* under the heading: "A Dance
Revolution in Italy." After reading the opening paragraphs and
bearing in mind that Italy had just been presenting such native
and foreign marvels as Brugnoli, Heberle, Elssler, Grisi, and Cerrito,
we come upon the following: "To appreciate properly the significance of this new sort of Revolution, to understand the importance which the whole of Italy attaches to it, one must realize that
the most famous Italian theatres such as the San Carlo of Naples,
La Fenice in Venice, and La Scala in Milan are well supplied with

music but not with ballet. . . . In all of them, there are excellent
singers, but as for dancers that's another matter. There isn't a sign
of one." Follows another long digression and then: ". . . We come
now to Mlle Fanny Cerrito, whose fragile scepter was shattered
like glass by a single wingbeat of Mlle Taglioni. The total lack of
good dancers in Italy, and consequently the profound ignorance
here of anything relating to the dance, explains furthermore the
success which La Cerrito has enjoyed for the past two or three
years." The poor creature, continues the writer, was taught, no
doubt, by some Neapolitan yokel, who told her that all that
was necessary was to jump high and ogle the audience. Whereas
La Taglioni . . . ! Needless to say, the letter was written by a
Frenchman, and it was addressed to the editor of a paper to which
Gautier was also a contributor.[110] And, to be sure, once Mlle Cerrito had performed in Paris and had received the stamp of approval
there, she too would be considered as much of a wonder as other
Opéra stars; but that was still in the distant future.

By now she had indeed returned to La Scala, and there, in
January 1841, she was, in French eyes, guilty of another crime.
She dared to dance *La Silfide!* To add to the sacrilege, it was in
a version rechoreographed by Antonio Cortesi and, to make matters worse yet, she usurped the role before the original Sylphide
had a chance to appear in Milan. *"Ottimo"* success, reported the year-
book of La Scala, announcing at the same time that Marie Taglioni would make eight guest appearances in the spring, in Philippe
Taglioni's *La Sylphide*, as well as in *La Gitana*. La Taglioni's reception turned out to be *"buonissimo"*—her style of dancing was as
surprising to the Milanese as it had been to the Parisians when they
first saw her.

But the real clash took place two years later, when both ballerinas were engaged for the same season, Cerrito starring in Cortesi's dismal staging of the Coralli-Perrot *Giselle* and Taglioni in

her father's equally dreary rendition of Coralli's *La Péri*. Since she was thirteen years younger and very appealing, Fanny clearly had a certain advantage; she was also, so to speak, on home territory. But the Italians are hotheaded, and there was violent partisanship for both contenders. For the final double appearance the theatre was packed, and the piazza in front was milling with people who could not get in and crowds that had gathered simply for the excitement. Inside, on the stage, cheered on by continuous bravos, clapping, and stamping, a contest was fought out which ended, in point of fact, by being a battle of flowers, tens of thousands of flowers. Both sides, of course, claimed a decisive victory.

The same year was filled with important happenings in Cerrito's life. She had a series of successes in many Italian cities. Oddly enough, in connection with her visit to the Aliberti Theatre in Rome, the same story was circulated about her that had been told about Mlle Elssler. Pope Gregory XVI was reported as saying that he supposed that properly it was heads that were crowned rather than feet. The confusion of heroines resulted, of course, from both dancers being called Fanny.

The year 1843 was also a turning point for Cerrito in London. It marked the moment when she began to dance in ballets by Perrot, works which not only captivated the public, but brought out all of Fanny's best qualities. The year before she had delighted the audience in *Alma;* now she positively dazzled them in *Ondine*, especially in the *pas de l'ombre*, in which Grisi would later triumph in St. Petersburg. This was the year, too, when her own choreography achieved a new maturity. Ever since the first of her visits to Vienna she had been arranging *pas* for herself or for small groups in various ballets. In *Ondine* some of the loveliest dances were credited to her, and eventually she would produce two complete ballets entirely on her own. It was most unusual for women to embark on this sort of activity; Marie Sallé and Marie Allard in the eighteenth century and Fanny Elssler's sister Thérèse were among the exceptional cases. It was in 1843 that Fanny began to dance regularly with Arthur Saint-Léon, who was briefly her partner in Vienna, in November 1841, and was destined to become her husband; and the same year saw her pitched rivalry with Mlle Elssler, culminating in their performing a sensational *pas de deux* together at the request of Queen Victoria. Finally it was at this time that Mlle Cerrito began to be not merely adorably plump but, alas, something considerably more than that. It did not interfere with her remarkable *ballon* and verve, but it was noticeable even in her portrait prints; it made her look far more matronly than her twenty-six years and caused a few carpers to hint that she was a marvelous dancer now "in spite" of her figure.

During seventeen years, from 1840 to 1857, Mlle Cerrito missed only five London seasons. It is not possible in this curtailed account to enumerate all her conquests, not only of the public but also of the infatuated young gallants who were offering her anything and everything in exchange for her favors, while her doting father (he called her *la divinità*) kept a watchful eye on her honor and reputation. In London Fanny spent the happiest part of her brief marriage with Saint-Léon, who was in many ways an extraordinary individual. Born Charles Victor Arthur Michel, he began by performing in concerts as a child-prodigy violinist; when he decided to become a dancer he outshone everyone except Perrot in feats that were almost acrobatic; he composed music; and afterward in London, Paris, and Russia he was a prolific choreographer, his greatest claim to fame being *Coppélia*, 1870, which today is still one of the most appreciated ballets in Europe and America. Four years younger than Fanny, he was not a suitor welcomed by her parents, who obviously hoped for a son-in-law with an important fortune or at least a title, but Fanny persisted, and they were married in Paris, April 17, 1845.

Less than a month after the wedding, they had created and danced in *Rosida,* and in July Cerrito shared honors with Taglioni, Grisi, and Grahn in the *Pas de Quatre.* Her other notable roles, all in Perrot's ballets, included *Lalla Rookh* and a goddess in *Le Jugement de Pâris,* 1846; Air in *Les Eléments,* 1847; and Spring in *Les Quatre saisons,* 1848. The *Pas de Quatre* had set the trend of presenting star performers together, and all of the ballets that followed it boasted various combinations of the original four ballerinas besides Carolina Rosati and two new members of an illustrious family—Paul's daughter Marie Taglioni II and Salvator Taglioni's daughter Louise. What a feast of dancing and choreography! There would be nothing like it again until Diaghilev brought his Ballets Russes.

Review in *La Presse,* October 25, 1847: "Although still young, Fanny Cerrito has long enjoyed a reputation abroad which sooner or later was bound to bring her to Paris, that modern Athens and center of the arts and elegant manners. In fact, it is odd that a dancer who participated in the famous *Pas de Quatre* . . . should have remained unknown in France; all certificates of merit which are not endorsed by Paris are somewhat irregular; they lack a certain authenticity. The approval of Italy, Germany, and England does not satisfy an artist . . . for, in matters of art, all other capitals compared with Paris are merely provincial towns. . . ." It was the opening shot of Gautier's article on Mlle Cerrito's debut in *La Fille de Marbre.* Poor, chauvinistic Gautier! However, now that Fanny had been engaged at the Opéra, she belonged to the inner circle, and everybody was ready to admire her. She was compared to the proverbial leaping doe or gazelle, praised by all for her happy vivacious temperament and, added Gautier: "Saint-Léon amazed everyone with the daring energy of his dancing and the ease with which he soared in the air; he knew how to win applause, which is not easy at a time when male dancing is out of favor."

And so, after an interlude in Venice and another London season, they were back at the Opéra. Saint-Léon was now choreographing their ballets. Although he had neither the taste nor inventive gift of Perrot, he understood exactly what would set off to best advantage Fanny's talents and his own, and every scene was crammed with fireworks, often to the detriment of the ballet as a whole. Their repertoire included revivals of *La Vivandière* (London, 1844), and *Le Violon du Diable* (Venice, 1848, as *Tartini il Violinista*), in which Saint-Léon's violin-playing excited the Parisians as much as his dancing, and the novelties were *Stella*, 1850, and *Paquerette*, 1851.

But, in spite of the fact that they appeared together as late as October 1852, their marriage had already deteriorated to a point of no return. Fanny, spoiled since childhood, could not put up with the constraints of being a wife; Saint-Léon quite naturally resented the men who flirted with her and offered her jewels and luxuries which he could not afford. Besides, Fanny, who had no competition to fear in Paris from such dancers as Elssler, Grisi, and Grahn, was not at all pleased to find that the multiple accomplishments of her husband made him just as much of a rival as any ballerina. It was no secret that they had violent quarrels, while Fanny obstinately went on encouraging the admirers who infuriated Saint-Léon.

They left together for Spain, nevertheless, in the spring of 1851, and conquered Madrid as they had conquered Paris. It was the last engagement they shared. While Fanny returned to London, and then to Spain and her greatest adventure, Saint-Léon went on to a varied and fruitful career in Paris and afterwards in Portugal, Russia, and elsewhere.

It is not unlikely that Fanny first met the Marqués de Bedmar in Paris and that this was one of the reasons which tempted her to accept a contract in Madrid. The distinguished young Spanish nobleman was well known in the coterie of those fashionable French dandies who prided themselves on frequenting ballet dancers. In any case, his liaison with Mlle Cerrito only became public when she went back to Spain without Saint-Léon. The escapades of the Marqués had taken him as far as the arms of the unfortunate Isabella II. Declared of age and placed on the throne at the age of thirteen, the child-queen then became a political pawn in a sinister game played by her mother, the Regent, her uncle and his Carlist party, the British, and the French. Among them they contrived to marry her three years later to a cousin, Don Francisco d'Assis, believed by them to be incapable of producing heirs. Isabella made up for her dreary marriage in a manner which caused her court to become a scandal in all of Europe, and one of her consolations, a favorite in fact, was the Marqués de Bedmar. Although he was married, and others also claimed his affections, his relationship with Mlle Cerrito was not merely a passing whim. Their daughter Matilde was born in October 1853; the Marqués became a devoted and generous father, and his love affair with Fanny evolved into a lifelong friendship.

Fanny was thirty-six when her child was born, but it never occurred to her to retire from the stage after the event as Carlotta Grisi had done. She was, if anything, busier than ever, and twenty months later had collaborated with Gautier on the libretto, had done all the choreography, and was dancing the lead in a successful and unusual ballet at the Opéra. *Gemma*, set in Cerrito's native Naples, was the first ballet to make use of hypnotism as its theme. Everything relating to mesmerism, magnetism, and spiritualism had a special fascination for the nineteenth-century public. In the 1830s Dr. Alexandre Bertrand had revived French interest in the experiments of Mesmer. His efforts, apart from their scientific consequences, were taken up by fashionable and artistic circles as a fad, and ushered in a craze for spiritualism that spread like an epidemic during the fifties. *Gemma*, therefore, was bound to stir up a certain excitement, the joint authorship of Gautier and Cerrito gave it added luster, and it was only a pity that a considerable part of this ballet was made up of "borrowed" bits and pieces, especially one entire scene lifted from *Le Délire d'un peintre*, which Perrot had staged in London eleven years earlier. These defects did not escape the notice of the experts, many of whom had already fixed on a new ballerina as their idol.

Alphonse Royer states categorically that Mlle Cerrito retired after *Gemma* and never went to Russia. She was vanquished, he said, by the extraordinary dramatic ability of Carolina Rosati who, besides, was nine years younger, and had seduced the fickle Paris audiences while Fanny was convalescing after the birth of Matilde. But, in 1855, Cerrito did, in fact, go to St. Petersburg, and one wonders why she waited to make her first appearance there until she was nearly thirty-nine and no longer at the top of her form either technically or in physique.

Russia, with the oncoming decline of ballet in the West, was more than ever the golden goal that beckoned to European *danseuses*, but the latest arrivals found that they had to contend with a wave of chauvinism. Because of the Crimean War, the national spirit was high in 1855. Tolstoy, arriving in St. Petersburg on November 19, the day before Cerrito's debut, discovered the intelligentsia divided into "Westerners," middle-of-the-road liberals, and a preponderance of "Slavophiles" who worshiped the Czar and everything Russian and enjoyed government protection. Fanny's former collaborators, the London team of Perrot and Pugni, were on hand to welcome and encourage her, and Perrot as ballet master introduced her in a major ballet, *Armida*, but nothing could offset the Slavophiles' determination to play down anything foreign.

The favored ballerina of this group was Nadezhda Bogdanova. Only twenty-two, she had been Saint-Léon's pupil and protégée in Paris after his wife abandoned him. Her Russian debut three months after Fanny's caused a frenzy. The excitement was short-lived. This public sensed very soon that Bogdanova was vain and superficial and they opted for the more vital qualities of Mouravieva, Marie Petipa, and Radina; and when Saint-Léon also turned cool and thwarted her hope of being a star at the Opéra again, her career petered out prematurely. The dazzling first impression had been enough, however, to distract attention from other dancers, and it was a disillusioned Cerrito who removed to England in the spring of 1857 with her mind made up to retire.

This was a painful decision, but one which was well taken, because her final reviews were very condescending. As Covent Garden was destroyed by fire while she was gaining her first meager laurels in Russia, she had danced during the 1856 season at the Lyceum, and now at this same theatre she was seen for the last time, a fading exponent of an art which had ceased to be popular in London.

The longevity of ballerinas has often been noticed. Mlle Augusta lived to be ninety-five, Lucile Grahn eighty-eight, Mlle Plunkett eighty-six, Taglioni and Grisi eighty. In our day one can cite Kschessinska, who died in 1971 at age ninety-nine. Others still living as this is written are Egorova age ninety-two, Karsavina eighty-seven, and that perennial *jeune esprit*, Marie Rambert, who at eighty-four can't wait to show off her *pliés* and *arabesques*.

Of such stuff was Cerrito. From childhood on, her vitality was proverbial, and it carried her through more than another half-century after her retirement. As with Grisi, her greatest joy was educating and bringing up her daughter, and in this Matilde's father never failed to be helpful. Material ease freed her of the obligation of most retired dancers, which is to teach, but for a long time she remained involved with the ballet world. She kept in contact with former associates and followed the progress of the younger generation, especially Taglioni's pupil Emma Livry. But, as time went by, she outlived them all, and at last was remembered by no one except the members of her immediate family, their friends, and the persons who cast a passing glance at her portrait in the Foyer de la Danse at the Opéra.

Mlle Cerrito died May 6, 1909, less than a week before her ninety-second birthday. Even if she had lived a few weeks longer she would have been too frail, too feeble-sighted to witness a new miracle in Paris—the appearance of Anna Pavlova, greatest dancer of modern times.

∾

Although Fanny Cerrito did not contribute anything as novel and startling as Taglioni's point dancing or Elssler's exploitation of the Spanish dance, she was nevertheless one of the great ornaments of the Romantic ballet. Furthermore, she handed down her talent in a more personal way: Mme Egorova, a Diaghilev ballerina and celebrated teacher in Paris, recently pointed out one of her most promising pupils, Muriel Belmondo, who stated with pride that she and her brother, the popular cinema actor Jean-Paul Belmondo, are descended from Fanny Cerrito.

Part V
POST-ROMANTIC BALLET

CHAPTER 17

Postscript to the Romantic Ballet

WHILE THE GREATEST of the Romantic ballerinas were holding the center of the stage, a pleiad of slightly lesser stars shone bravely in the ballet firmament. Some were true luminaries; others achieved an effective if transient popularity only because they were promoted by their teachers, by partial critics, patrons, or lovers. Therese Heberle and Amalia Brugnoli, idolized in Vienna and Italy during the 1820s and '30s, might have joined the first rank had they added Paris to their conquests, and if Marie Taglioni had not eclipsed them.

Dr. Véron reported in his *Mémoires* that Vestris, at this time past seventy years of age, "devoted himself to his two favorite pupils, those two charming young women: the wild and witty Pauline Leroux and the melancholic Pauline Duvernay. Mademoiselle Leroux was always laughing. Mademoiselle Duvernay often wept; Vestris was pained by her sadness and, in order to enlist my sympathy, he would point at drops of water on the floor, spilled there by the little sprinkler [used instead of rosin to make the floor less slippery]. 'Look,' he would say, 'look at her tears.' " [111] Mlle Duvernay's sorrows, however, were imaginary or self-created, and it was the gay Pauline who might have grieved over a career interrupted by calamities. Although five years younger than Taglioni, she made a promising start at the Opéra a year earlier than this rival, in 1826. Then, after a long convalescence from rheumatism and injuries, and fourteen years after her debut, her heroic efforts enabled her to make an astounding comeback in *Le Diable amoureux* in September 1840. For a short while she enjoyed the adoration of the audience and critics, but her moment of triumph had come too late: Carlotta Grisi appeared on the scene, and by the following June the fickle public had eyes only for *Giselle*.

Pauline Duvernay was the first dancer to be picked out and launched by Dr. Véron, who was so entranced by her that she bypassed the *corps de ballet* and subsequent grades and went straight from class to a stellar role. "She was twenty, with lovely eyes, shapely legs, and a svelte figure," said Charles de Boigne. She also knew how to make effective use of her tears and, in addition to her gift for dancing, had a natural aptitude for scandal. During her brief five years at the Opéra excitement was never lacking. Shortly after her debut as Miranda, the diabolical seductress in the ballet *divertissement* of the opera *La Tentation*, in June 1832, Mlle Duvernay disappeared. A search of the morgue and other more likely places all proved fruitless, until she was discovered, hidden away in a convent, through an anonymous letter (written by herself). Thoroughly bored after her escapade had lasted a few days, she was impatient to return to her public.

Among this ballerina's host of suitors was one at whom she jeered when he backed up his entreaties with a coffer containing 100,000 livres in gold, but the most extraordinary was a youth who pleaded poverty, but swore he would sacrifice his life for her. "Men are always making idle boasts," she told him, "but you may offer me one of your teeth, the middle one." Undaunted, the young man rushed out and returned within the hour, clutching his mutilated jaw while tendering the demanded gift. But his ardor suddenly cooled. "Poor wretch," Mlle Duvernay taunted him, "I asked you for a lower tooth, and you've brought me an upper one."

More successful, because he bribed her mother, was the Marquis de La Valette. He became the father of Pauline's child, and when she thought he might leave her she staged one of her several attempts at suicide. But he, too, was supplanted by an Englishman who persuaded the venal Mme Duvernay *mère*, by means of a far more impressive bribe for herself and the promise of a large independent income for her daughter. The immensely rich Stephen Lyne-Stephens had fallen in love with Mlle Duvernay when he saw her in London where she performed in 1833, '34, '36, and '37, retiring from the stage when she became his mistress. For a number of years they lived happily together (while La Valette consoled himself with Fanny Elssler), until suddenly Pauline fell ill and seemed to be pining away. When it came out that the cause was a lady's maid who refused to continue in Pauline's employ on discovering her unmarried status, Lyne-Stephens was anxious to repair the slight. "Hurry and get well, my dear," he said, "for tomorrow we'll have the banns published and in a fortnight we'll be married."

"It was unthinkable that Mlle Duvernay should fall from glory," commented Charles de Boigne. "The position she once held in the theatre she has achieved in English society, where she is now one of its brightest stars." She had, in fact, grown into a very respectable, even prudish, person. Ivor Guest notes that when her husband died in 1860 she inherited over £1,000,000, which she devoted to charity and good works. The ballet's loss was the gain of the community she graced.

The stories about Mlle Duvernay and a profusion of others are to be found in a little book entitled *Petits Mémoires de l'Opéra* which came out in 1857. Its author, Comte Charles de Boigne, editor of *Le Constitutionnel*, wealthy man-about-town and balletomane (he was the lover of Mlle Nathalie Fitz-James) bore a name which was to become celebrated when the four-volume, posthumously published *Récits d'une Tante* appeared, in 1907, and made an indelible impression on Marcel Proust. During the Romantic Era the eighteenth-century penchant for historical memoirs was turning into a craze for printed gossip and scandal, with ballerinas as a favorite subject. Not only Gautier himself, but also Balzac, Dumas, Janin, Second, and many other well-known writers contributed to these frivolous books, often anonymously. But they should be pardoned, no doubt, for such literary lapses. As assiduous in their ferreting as the secret police of M. de Sartine under Louis XV, they have furnished to-day's readers with a colorful if sometimes biased picture of the greater and less great dancers.

Duvernay, in spite of the brevity of her career, was enshrined in Boulanger's mural at the Paris Opéra, an honor not achieved by the Fitz-James sisters (emaciated Louise and too-modest Nathalie), the Dumilâtre sisters (pretty Adèle and plain Sophie, both excellent dancers), nor by the Belgian-born Mlle Adeline Plunkett who was ravishingly beautiful, but surely was more engrossed in acquiring lovers than in dance technique and who, after several turbulent seasons in London, appeared in Paris in 1845.

By this time, the Romantic ballet had nearly run its course, and it would not be right to conclude the story of this epoch without mentioning two of its most picturesque personalities, Mme Crosnier, guardian of the stage door at the Opéra, and Auguste, leader of the claque. Charles de Boigne, who devoted an entire chapter to Mme Crosnier, said: "She was, after the director, the greatest power at the Opéra." Throughout her forty years of service as *concièrge*, during which she never missed a day nor asked for a holiday, it was not only her job to pass in and out the hundreds of people employed by the institution—the singers and dancers and their dressers, relatives and friends, the musicians, designers, authors, machinists, stage crews, firemen, and scrubwomen—but it was also she who admitted or detained the throng of notables and nonentities, rich and poor, who came to pay court to the artistes in their dressing rooms or the foyers. Mme Crosnier took it upon herself to promote or obstruct the intrigues and liaisons, she advised the lovelorn, consoled neglected ballet girls, fed those who were all too often half-starved, and made herself indispensable as well as feared, respected, and loved. And Mme Crosnier would have liked nothing better than to remain at her post until she died, but it was felt that dignity required that she retire when her son was appointed director of the Opéra in 1854.

In his own way, Auguste had as much prestige as Mme Crosnier. With his contingent of hired applauders, it was in his power to make or break the reputation of any artist, none of whom dared to ignore him. Each afternoon he conferred with the management as to how to direct the applause and received his daily allotment of forty-five tickets or, for more crucial occasions, as many as two or three hundred. Eventually he knew every passage of all the operas and ballets better than anyone and took enormous pride in his profession. Once, because of a run-in with Fanny Elssler, he was replaced by another *claqueur*, but the results were so disastrous that he was soon called back. And one day Mme Duvernay, misled by her daughter's popularity and the knowledge that she was Dr. Véron's special pet, announced arrogantly that Pauline needed no protection. As a lesson to her, Dr. Véron instructed Auguste to withhold all applause and after her *pas* Mlle Duvernay was received in a deathly silence. In lieu of salary Auguste received money from almost all the performers and often their own complimentary tickets, which he sold. Charles de Boigne calculated that from Lise Noblet alone he received the equivalent of $11,000, which in today's currency would amount to more than double that sum. By the time of his death in November 1844, he had become a man of means, owned several houses, and was able to bequeath a substantial fortune to his daughter, Mme Cogniard. Furthermore, besides the pages devoted to him in the *Petits Mémoires de l'Opéra*, he achieved an immortality of his own in Balzac's *Lost Illusions*, Berlioz' *Evenings with the Orchestra*, Bouteron's *Danse et Musique Romantiques*, and other serious works.

Long before its overtones reached Paris, the passing bell of the Romantic ballet had sounded in England. The promise of a new generation of native *danseuses* was to remain unfulfilled after the most gifted of them, Clara Webster, died in 1844, as the result of burns sustained when her costume caught fire from a gas lamp; and although Perrot's masterpieces were produced during the following seasons, by 1847 even Carlotta Grisi seemed surprised that the ballet at Her Majesty's Theatre was playing to a full house. In alluding to Jenny Lind, Carlotta touched on the chief cause of the decline, for the British public en masse had fallen in love with "the Swedish Nightingale," and from then on opera was the top attraction. For a dwindling group of faithful adherents, first-rate dancing would continue to be available for another dozen years or so: Flora Fabbri, dynamic and flaunting unusual speed and *ballon;* the fiery Sofia Fuoco, whose point work became legendary; Marie Taglioni the younger; Mlles Plunkett and Dumilâtre; Carolina Rosati, who had replaced Lucile Grahn in the revival of the *Pas de Quatre*, 1847, and starred in one of the last grand, spectacular ballets, *Le Corsaire*, 1856; and the elfin Amalia Ferraris; all of them were appearing in London during this period. But the spirit, the drive, the glamour of the Romantic Era had departed. Ballet in England was to survive mainly in a more popular form, in pantomimes and music halls, at the Alhambra and Empire theatres, and through the efforts of Katti Lanner and Adeline Genée [117] and occasional visitors. Not until the twentieth century would there be a rebirth, a new ballet.

Meanwhile, across the Channel in Paris, balletomania was still very much alive. Nearly all of the old guard was on hand, most of them, though none would have admitted it, producing their weary second-best—Vernoy de Saint-Georges, inexhaustible librettist; the same teams of stage designers; Mazilier and Saint-Léon as choreographers; Adolphe Adam, who since *Giselle* had composed the music of such hits as *La Jolie Fille de Gand*, 1842, *Le Diable à quatre*, 1845, and *La Filleule des fées*, 1849; and, of course, Théophile Gautier, ever-present at performances, busy as a beaver with his reviews, novels, poetry, and essays, his collaboration with Cerrito, his other ballets, his journeys, and his love affairs; and the same gaggle of critics always clacking up their friends and favorites.

Flora Fabbri and Sofia Fuoco, *la pointue*, had come and gone when Carolina Rosati, fresh from her London conquests, arrived in 1853 and dethroned Fanny Cerrito. She was already as plump as Cerrito, and her technique was far less striking, but she was nine years younger, her acting ability was exceptional and, above all, she was new to the fashion-minded Opéra public. She managed to pro-long her sway for more than five years, and during her third season everyone joined forces to produce a major ballet for her. This was *Le Corsaire* and the final opus of Adam, who died that year, aged fifty-three.

Staged in Paris, in January 1856, six months before the London production, *Le Corsaire* was a real blood-and-thunder drama, complete with pashas and slave girls, pirates and a sinking ship, fantastic stage effects, a music-hall-style peacock-feather fan dance, and La Rosati bounding about and bringing down shouts of approval and mountains of flowers. In the chorus of superlative reviews an impressed critic reported that, instead of the usual paper frill, a bertha of rare lace worth more than $1,000 encircled one of the bouquets. And the audience, including Emperor Napoleon III and his Eugénie, adored not only the ballerina but the ballet itself, which continued popular into the present century.

A year later, in *Marco Spada*, Rosati was paired with Amalia

Ferraris, who recently had made a glittering Paris debut in spite of the absurd ballet in which she was presented, *Les Elfes*, by Mazilier, now completely played-out as a choreographer. Then, in 1859, leaving the honors of the Opéra stage to Ferraris, Russian guest stars, and local talent, Rosati joined the migration to St. Petersburg. "Like her illustrious predecessors, starting with Marie Taglioni," said Lifar, "Rosati had come to Russia toward the end of her career when she was heavy and stout and quite incapable of moving the audience by the lightness of her dancing. In any case, even at her zenith she had never been an outstanding dancer, but more a mime, and a very gifted dramatic artist. This was precisely what was most appreciated in her by the Russians," [113] as indeed had been the case when Fanny Elssler arrived there at the age of thirty-eight. Rosati was thirty-three. According to today's standards, this would be considered young enough, but when she had spent only three seasons in St. Petersburg she was impatient to retire for good. Happily for her, she went out in a burst of glory, though it was less due to her dancing than to the ballet which Marius Petipa created for her. *La Fille du Pharaon*, January 1862, completed in a record six weeks, was a huge success; it launched its choreographer as ballet master at the Maryinsky Theatre and lasted into the twentieth-century repertoire.

Always a delightful, warm-hearted creature, Rosati returned to become a beloved figure on the Paris scene, especially in the entourage of the ballet. It was her pride to remember that during her term at the Opéra she was, with her salary of 60,000 francs, the most highly paid of all the ballerinas (Taglioni received 36,000; Elssler, 46,000; Grisi, 42,000; and Cerrito, 45,000); she was also the last of the twenty ballerinas to be portrayed by Boulanger for the new opera house. After forty-two years of retirement, she died, aged seventy-nine, in 1905.

A new impetus was given to ballet in France by the emergence in 1858 of the prodigious, but ill-fated, Emma Livry—though perhaps prodigious is too sturdy an adjective to apply to the gossamer being which materialized before the astonished gaze of the Paris public, and so soon was wafted away forever.

It will have been noticed that for some fifteen years the majority of outstanding ballerinas at the Opéra were importations; apart from the Danish Caroline Fjeldsted in 1843, the English Caroline Forster who stayed till 1844, and the Russians, Smirnova (1844), Andreianova (1845), and Bogdanova (1851-55), most of the foreigners were Italians of the bravura school. Mlle Livry was French—by heritage, by training, and in spirit—which, however, was not an advantage but an obstacle to be overcome. "Maybe you believe in French *danseuses?*" one critic challenged his readers, a bias which was to be echoed later by Théodore de Banville in connection with one of Emma Livry's fellow students. "She is, it must be admitted, a French *danseuse*," he lamented, "but I doubt if one can seriously reproach her with anything worse than that."

Emma's mother, also a French dancer, was Mlle Célestine (Marguerite Adélaïde) Emarot who, at the time of her daughter's debut, had been appearing in very minor roles briefly in London and then for more than fourteen years at the Opéra. Charles de Boigne described her as "rococo" in its derisive sense of old-fashioned or antiquated; and she was not only a dancer devoid of artistry or sufficient technique, but was also so plain that one wonders how she was able to captivate not merely one lover but, in rapid succession, two, both of whom were aristocrats, men of means, and Jockey Club members, and who might have had their pick of the prettiest little *coryphées*. Perhaps her secret was a gentle nature, a sweet character, or some special feminine wisdom, because it is known that she also had distinguished friends in all circles who remained devoted throughout her life. Among the dancers, Mlle Cerrito was her constant companion. At seventeen, Mlle Emarot was already the mistress of Baron Charles de Chassiron. Emma was born the following year.

By the time Emma was eleven, Mme Dominique, an ace in the

Opéra's long line of inspired teachers, was launched on the career (1853-79) which would produce the last *étoiles* of French nineteenth-century ballet. Under the name of Caroline Lassiat, Mme Dominique had a none too exciting past as a dancer, but as a teacher she obtained far more extraordinary results than even Gosselin, who was nominally the head of the professional staff. Her star pupils included Mlles Livry and Bozzacchi, both marked out for premature death; Mlle Beaugrand, also ill-starred, because she had no protector powerful enough to offset the handicap of her being French; and, later on, Rosita Mauri, an energetic Spaniard, who held the stage until she was fifty-eight, in 1907, and then taught for another dozen years.

Beyond question the most brilliant of Mme Dominique's students, Emma was a mere sixteen when it was decided that she was ready to appear in public. Her mother's new lover, Vicomte Ferdinand de Montguyon, taking the attitude that Emma was his protégée and a sort of adopted child, exerted all his influence at court, with the minister, and with Opéra director Royer to arrange a most unusual debut. The young girl was to start out with the rank of *première danseuse* and in the title role of *La Sylphide*. Revived often at the Opéra since its creation in 1832 with Mlle Taglioni, *La Sylphide* had been interpreted by an imposing series of experienced and beloved ballerinas: Elssler in 1838; Grahn, 1839; Blangy, 1840; Adèle Dumilâtre, 1841; Fabbri, 1844. Could a novice hope to compete with memories of such performances? Though she obviously would feel sure of faring better than poor Olimpia Priora of recent fame. As if Mlle Priora's failure to understand the nuances of *La Sylphide* had not been humbling enough, M. de Boigne finished her off with a few of his typical pungent phrases: "Daughter of Italy and of Signor Priora, *maestro di ballo*. A dancer of the *grande école*; very black hair; very black eyes; very black moustache; very black eyebrows; four details of black which ordinarily give some sort of expression to a face and which give none at all to hers." [114]

On October 20, 1858, newly baptized with the stage name of Emma Livry (it would hardly have helped to start a career with the dusty name of a dancer as unsuccessful as her mother), the youngest Sylphide came forth before an audience infused with advance publicity, but totally unprepared for what they were to see. There were some who had vivid recollections of La Taglioni and Lucile Grahn. For the others, long accustomed to the flashy ostentation of the Italians, it came as something novel, a wonderful surprise, when Emma Livry gave a display of the gentle grace, the airiness, and poetry of the classic dance in the tradition of Marie Taglioni, supported besides by a more than adequate technique.

Though the debutante had an exquisite slender figure, she was, like her mother, far from pretty. Perhaps no dancer ever had such unpleasing features—a long, very prominent nose, a receding chin, and a mouth that drooped at the corners, all of which soon made her a tempting butt for caricaturists—but these defects not only failed to detract from the general impression and grace, but were hardly noticed at all. "Two beautiful eyes, filled with fire and tenderness, illumine that small ethereal face. . . . ," observed Jules Janin, who had championed the first Sylphide twenty-six years earlier, and now plunged into one of his typical rhapsodies.

The rest of the press found nothing to censure except youth and the want of experience, which time would overcome. Many of the critics also were quick to link Mlle Livry's name with Taglioni's, and it was news of these comparisons which lured the retired ballerina from Lake Como and propelled her into a new life in Paris. Before long, Madame Taglioni, as we have seen, was appointed *Inspectrice de la danse* at the Opéra and then *Professeur de la classe de perfectionnement.*

In the meanwhile, Emma was gaining assurance as she appeared in various roles, then Madame Taglioni began to coach her, and the mounting paeans of public approval established her reputation. With M. de Montguyon still guarding her interests, it was settled that by

1862 she would be paid triple the amount of her original salary. Preparations began, too, for a new ballet intended to feature her.

For this work, eventually presented as *Le Papillon*, on November 26, 1860, a ridiculous, complicated script was furnished by Marie Taglioni and Vernoy de Saint-Georges, utterly unworthy of the latter, who had a long history of writing libretti for ballets and operas; no less than six artists concocted the pretentious decors; and Offenbach produced his first ballet music, some of it lilting and charming, but much of it banal. It was also the only ballet for which Marie Taglioni composed the choreography, and her contribution redeemed all its other shortcomings and was a triumph. She loved Emma Livry as a mother might love a daughter, a teacher her favorite pupil, and especially as being the one person capable of perpetuating the Romantic image which Taglioni herself had been the first to create. As she had once been the ideal Sylphide, Emma was now to become the ideal *papillon;* and Emma did not fail her. "Mlle Emma Livry, wafted by Madame Taglioni into the rarefied air of the ideal dance, has risen up among the stars," declared *La Presse* a week after the première of *Le Papillon.*

Alas, the ephemeral butterfly was destined not to enjoy for long her reputation, the benefits of her increased salary, and the world of friends and admirers who had gathered around her. As she continued dancing in the many performances of *Le Papillon* and in other ballets, there were, it seemed, all sorts of omens and forebodings prior to her needless and avoidable death. And for a long, long time there had been no lack of warnings and advice on the dangers of fire. From Saint-Germain-en-Laye, where he retired during the French Revolution, Noverre, aged eighty, had sent forth his views together with practical suggestions for safeguarding the lives of both public and performers (Letter XVI in *Lettres sur les Arts Imitateurs*). In the course of nineteen years the Opéra had burned down twice, he said, and during the same span there had been conflagrations in the theatres of Vienna, Milan, Venice, Mantua, Stockholm, Amsterdam, and Warsaw. Soon after, the opera houses in London, Berlin, and Naples also burned to the ground. Individual dancers ran equally terrible risks from exposed gas lamps. While Augusta Maywood was performing in *Giselle* in Lyon (1843), the *tutu* of a *corps de ballet* girl caught fire from the footlights; Clara Webster died at the age of twenty-one after a similar accident in London; and as lately as a rehearsal of *Le Papillon*, a young dancer's skirt burst into flames, and she was lucky to escape with only minor burns. Finally, at a dress rehearsal of a revival of *La Muette de Portici*, a similar fate overtook Emma Livry.

In people's minds Emma had come to personify the *papillon*, and it seemed that, like a moth, she almost invited death, drawn into the flames after deliberately rejecting the protection that would have prevented the catastrophe. A recent regulation at the Opéra that made it compulsory for costumes to be dipped in a fireproof solution had raised an outcry among the performers. The process, known as carteronizing (after Jean Adolphe Carteron who invented it), made the diaphanous skirts look dingy and rigid, and the dancers felt that it defeated all the efforts they had made to acquire an air of lightness and *ballon*. Emma Livry signed a release absolving the authorities of any responsibility, stating that she refused categorically to dance in a treated costume. And on that dire November 15, 1862, when her skirt brushed too close to a gas light, it was only a matter of seconds before towering flames were swirling around her. Two dancers risked their own lives in a vain attempt to save her, and in their *Journal* the Goncourt brothers noted: "Under the soaking blanket which the fireman had thrown over her, Emma Livry, the poor *danseuse* so horribly burned yesterday, had struggled to her knees and was praying." For Clara Webster the end came mercifully on the third day after the disaster. Emma Livry's frightful suffering lasted for more than eight months. Only extraordinary courage and deep religious faith enabled her to endure it, and while she fought to live, silent and uncomplaining, the whole of Paris grieved for her. When at last she died, on July 26, 1863, the last vestige of the Romantic ballet died with her.

There was no one of any stature to fill the void left by Emma Livry's death, apart from a few transient guest stars. Amalia Ferraris, having inaugurated with great éclat Lucien Petipa's *Gracioza* and Borri's *L'Etoile de Messine* in March and November of 1861, became so spoiled and difficult that the management was glad to see her go. As stopgaps, three dancers were imported from Russia. During the summer months Parisians briefly enjoyed the various styles of Marie Petipa (1861–62), Martha Mouravieva (1863–64), and Adèle Grantzow (1866–68), who was German-born and a special protégée of Saint-Léon.

Otherwise, a dreary falling-off characterized the steady fare at the Opéra. Should we name fat Amina Boschetti; Louise Marquet, a fixture for eighteen years and a Sunday painter; Laura Fonta, also faithful for eighteen years, but better qualified as a ballet historian than as a performer; the shapely Eugénie Fiocre, of whom a critic remarked: "There is positively no one who would say anything against her except partridges, because shooting is the passion of this charming artist," but then neither could anyone say anything for her in regard to her dancing; Mlles Sanlaville, Salvioni, Fioretti, Vernon, and Dor; Mlle Annette Mérante, part of a prolific dynasty of dancers such as the Vestris family and the Taglionis (there were Mérantes at the Opéra dating back to the time of Napoleon); Zina Richard, married to Louis Mérante, *premier danseur*, ballet master, and choreographer; the unlucky Léontine Beaugrand; and even Rita Sangalli? All of them had pretty faces or figures or nimble legs or temperament, but in no case did their combined or separate qualities add up to a single great ballerina.

Nor was one new ballet staged at the Opéra for nearly two years, from *L'Etoile de Messine* until Saint-Léon created *Diavolina* (July 1863). Saint-Léon was now traveling like a shuttlecock back and forth between Russia, where he was ballet master, and Paris. After *Diavolina*, with its hurdy-gurdy music by Pugni, he produced *Néméa, ou l'Amour vengé* in July 1864 (abridged from his four-act *Fiammetta*, staged at St. Petersburg the previous February), and then back in Russia, in December of the same year, he turned out *The Little Humpbacked Horse*, which was still popular nearly a hundred years later under the Soviet regime. All of these works were choreographed especially for Mouravieva.

In 1866 a newcomer collaborated with Léon Minkus, composer of *Fiammetta/Néméa*, in producing a score for Saint-Léon's *La Source*. Léo Delibes was thirty, and for the past three years had filled the rather tiresome post of accompanist at the Opéra. In his spare time he was organist at the Eglise de Saint-Jean-Saint-François and also composed operettas. The ballet airs for *La Source* were so sprightly and danceable that he was entrusted with the entire score of *Coppélia* and eventually *Sylvia*. "My own *Swan Lake* is simply trash in comparison with *Sylvia*," admitted Tchaikovsky in a letter to his friend and patron Nadejda von Meck.

However, after another three and a half years had passed without a single new ballet to follow *La Source*, it was *Coppélia* that turned into a "smash hit" of music, choreography, and dancing. Season after season, the preparations and rehearsals had dragged on, but *Coppélia* was to prove worth waiting for, and indeed has become a perennial favorite with modern audiences all over the world. Finding a heroine was one of the complicated problems. Saint-Léon, impressed by Adèle Grantzow's Russian triumphs and far more admiring of her than most of the Paris critics, at first persuaded Opéra director Perrin to engage her for the leading role. When she fell ill and had to remain in Russia, Mlle Beaugrand was sure that at last her chance had come. But Léontine, although a skilled dancer and a preferred pupil of Mme Dominique, had grown up in the *coulisses* of the Opéra, and therefore could never be considered glamorous. "One can't make a star of the heavens out of a garden firefly," sympathized Gautier, and another critic added: "Her only fault, the one which has hindered her reputation, is that her name doesn't end in *off* or *ski.*" [115]

When Perrin had searched Europe in vain for a new ballerina, he made a bold decision, and from within the very precincts of the Opéra he chose a naive, wide-eyed girl of fifteen, who had no stage experience at all. Giuseppina Bozzacchi was a native of Milan who, at the age of eleven, had been taken to Paris so that she might study with Mme Dominique. Her astonishing facility, her natural verve, tempered by Mme Dominique's emphasis on the French style of *danse noble*, her technical strength and endurance, all indicated that she might become a very exceptional dancer. Physically very appealing, she presented a vivid contrast to the impression left by Emma Livry. Whereas Mlle Livry was slender and ethereal, with sorrowful eyes that seemed almost to hold a premonition of the fate that was in store for her, Mlle Bozzacchi was warm and earthy and, in spite of the many privations in her home life, was spontaneously gay and lively. Her eyes sparkled, she had the instinctive Latin gift of gesture, and Mme Dominique, herself very short, had known how to teach her to compensate for her lack of height.

As the long drawn-out rehearsals came to an end, the collaborators of *Coppélia* were more and more convinced that they had found the right dancer to interpret the mischievous character of the heroine, Swanilda, and when the ballet was presented at last (May 25, 1870), Giuseppina even surpassed their hopes. At each successive performance, public enthusiasm mounted; the critics promised a brilliant future for the young girl, and Gautier went so far as to say that she would become a second Carlotta Grisi.

Alas, any might-have-beens were going to remain forever unrealized. The Franco-Prussian War, which began in mid-July with such brave cries of "To Berlin!" "To Berlin!" was to end, before the French citizenry could grasp what was happening, with the siege, the capitulation, and the humiliation of seeing the Prussians parade down the Champs-Elysées.

Long before the national calamity had been played out, tragedy also struck at the Opéra. By the end of August, when Giuseppina had gamboled her way through *Coppélia* less than twenty times, the Opéra closed its doors for the duration of the war. A day or so later, on September 2, Saint-Léon, who was only forty-nine, died suddenly of a stroke. He was overworked as well as depleted by several previous illnesses, and had gained too much weight, which put a strain on his heart. Besides being a great loss to the Opéra, his death was a dreadful blow to the circle of friends who loved and depended on him.

By the time another two weeks had passed the Germans had surrounded Paris and, on September 18, the siege began, with all the horrors of the bombardment, starvation, lack of fuel, and the resultant sickness and death. It was at this point that Théophile Gautier redeemed all or any of his past lapses. He had been away, first in Switzerland with his old love Carlotta Grisi, and then in Neuilly, but the moment he learned of the impending blockade he rushed back to the city in order to share the misery and dangers with his fellow Parisians. Among the Opéra personnel were dancers who still hopefully tried to continue taking class, though some of them, like the rest of the population, were growing weak from a diet of putrid horsemeat, dogs and cats, and finally rats. Léontine Beaugrand organized groups to collect food and money for the neediest and she also managed to have a sloping floor installed in her apartment so that she could practice every day against the time when her services might be wanted. Delphine Marquet, who had long since laid aside her ballet slippers, was discovered by Gautier rolling bandages in the basement of the Comédie-Française, which had become an improvised hospital for wounded soldiers.

Gautier was everywhere, trying to help and writing up reports. In October he watched the launching of the mail balloon, the only means of sending news of the besieged city to the outer world, and he went to inspect the sandbagged ramparts, where the famished defenders were dying more often from exposure than from bullets. Toward the end of November he learned that death had also taken the little dancer for whom he had foreseen such a sunny future. Over-fatigued from the intensive preparations for *Coppélia*, heartbroken at having her career at a standstill, worn out by the rigors of the siege, and finally stricken by fever—was it typhus or smallpox?—Giuseppina Bozzacchi died on the very day she might have celebrated her seventeenth birthday.

Famine forced Paris to surrender in January, and it might have been thought then that the calamities were ending. But far worse was yet to come. Spring saw the beginning of the terrible events which have gone down in history as the Commune, a second and more dreadful siege, when the rebellious elements in the city resisted the troops sent from Versailles to establish order. As Frenchmen fought each other, the streets became an inferno of fire and slaughter, the bloodiest battles raging back and forth in the glare of walls of flame. The insurgents not only set fire to the public buildings—the ministries, palaces, museums, and even the Cathedral of Nôtre-Dame—but had the further fiendish idea of filling the firewagons with petrol instead of water.

It is strange to think that before the end of the year, when the ruins had hardly stopped smoking, the Opéra reopened its doors, and Léontine Beaugrand at long last had her chance to appear in *Coppélia*. She was highly praised, but it must be admitted that by now there was simply no one else to take the role.

Théophile Gautier died in October 1872, age sixty-one, and, in spite of his redundancies and fatuity, it should be said that he had been almost as much a part of the Romantic ballet as its dancers. He did not live long enough to see the end of the Opéra in the rue Le Peletier. Having escaped the holocaust of the Commune, the opera house nevertheless burned down on October 28, 1873, and with it vanished the last splendors of the French ballet. Performances were held temporarily in the Salle Ventadour. Then, after fourteen years under construction, at a cost of 35,400,000 gold francs, the huge new Palais Garnier, the thirteenth Opéra, was inaugurated in 1875 with a program of assorted scraps unworthy of either the edifice or the occasion.

Part VI
BALLET IN RUSSIA: TERPSICHORE REBORN

CHAPTER 18

St. Petersburg and Moscow: A Brief Survey

As THE LIFE SPARK OF BALLET flickered out in England and France, the same decline was apparent elsewhere in Europe. In Denmark, after Galeotti's early achievements, the ballet fostered by August Bournonville prospered for forty-five golden years, only to have stagnation set in. All creative spirit seemed lost when Bournonville retired in 1877, leaving the Royal Danish Ballet to go on and on monotonously in the pattern he had laid out. Vienna and Berlin, too, had extended a warm welcome for over a hundred years to most of the leading dancers and choreographers, but then the enthusiasm waned. As for Italy, birthplace of the earliest ballet, it was the country which had sent out into the world Lully, La Barbarina, the Vestris family, Angiolini, Viganò, the Taglionis, Cerrito, Rosati, and Ferraris. During the late 1800s notable dancers such as Rita Sangalli, Virginia Zucchi, and Pierina Legnani were still being trained in the Blasis tradition, but the actual production of ballet was at its lowest ebb. The rivalry of opera houses in many large and small cities that formerly stimulated the best Italian efforts was gradually petering out. Milan remained a center, and too much admired at La Scala were vulgar spectacular ballets no doubt resembling those which are staged nowadays in New York's Radio City Music Hall. In fact, all the Italian public frankly preferred any bombastic opera to ballet, a bias which still prevails. Confronted by such a falling off in Western Europe, serious balletomanes now had to turn their eyes toward St. Petersburg and Moscow, where the art of dance was rising to a state of perfection never seen before.

Ballet made its appearance in Russia much later than in Italy, France, or England. Michel Florinsky, in his *History of Russia*, speaks of the "capricious, unpredictable and stringent" censorship which hampered the development of literature and the theatre. "Until the late 1830s," he says, "Russia had no national opera or concert music worthy of the name. . . . Ballet did not take firm root until 1779, when Catherine founded in St. Petersburg a ballet school modeled on that of Paris." This choice of dates, however, is somewhat dismissive, if not altogether inaccurate. Perhaps Russian ballet history should be said to begin with the arrival of Jean-Baptiste Landé, in 1734. A Frenchman by birth, who had danced in Paris and Dresden before becoming ballet master in Stockholm, Landé was engaged by the Empress Anna of Russia to teach deportment and dancing to the cadets of the Military School for Nobles. He then, on his own initiative, started a ballet academy, and in 1738 the Empress granted him the privilege of founding the institution which evolved into the famous Imperial Theatre School.

Landé was followed by a succession of the most celebrated ballet figures in Europe who variously danced, taught, choreographed, directed, and set the standards: the great Hilferding from Vienna in 1758; Angiolini, a few years later; Charles Le Picq for twelve years beginning 1786; Didelot, 1801–11 and 1816–36; [116] Perrot, 1848–58;

Saint-Léon, 1859–70, and Marius Petipa, who arrived as a dancer in
1847 and staged his last ballet in 1903, at the age of eighty-one.

For a long time, people in Western Europe remained in ignorance
of these developments and, in fact, knew hardly anything about
the remote mysterious land of steppes and snows. Tourists were
not encouraged, and Russia was always as closed to the outside
world as it has been during much of the twentieth century. The
same Henry Wikoff who would later escort Elssler to the United
States, did something quite unusual in going there as a private
citizen in 1835. "The formalities were innumerable, and it was
plain that foreigners were not wanted in Russia," he noted in his
memoirs. "We were catechized over and over again as to our
motives in visiting Russia," and exactly the same complaints were
made four years later by the Marquis de Custine, in *La Russie en
1839*. If theatre circles in the West were better informed than the
average public, it was because of the continual *va et vient* of foreign
performers who brought home reports of what they had seen. They
had tales to tell about the luxury of the glittering gilded theatres,[117]
reserved almost exclusively for the Czar and nobles and their guests,
themselves aglitter in their extravagant dress, but constrained by
the most inflexible court etiquette. Listeners were amazed at accounts
of the salaries, the jewels, and furs lavished on visiting artists; and
not less impressive were stories about the absolute tyranny of the
emperors.

At various periods, interested in promoting the theatre or utterly
indifferent to it, some of them quite insane or beset by notions
(Paul I dismissed all male dancers and replaced them with women
en travesti), some unfairly prejudiced by the *danseuses* whom they
favored as mistresses, all of the succeeding czars were feared and
revered as gods whose slightest whim held the threat of banishment
or death. In general, their influence on the ballet was perhaps more
beneficial than detrimental. The czars themselves always appointed

the Director of the Imperial Theatres and, even at times when the czars and their delegates imposed their antiquated ideas and bad taste, at least the Imperial Treasury provided unstinted funds for the Theatres and the School.

Never before or since has stricter discipline been maintained than at the Imperial Theatre School. At the age of eight or nine the pupils went to live there, a cloistered life devoted to study which ended only when, like butterflies emerging from drab cocoons, they graduated and appeared on the stage. Eventually, as the curriculum widened, languages, music, art history, and other subjects were added to the stringent and meticulous ballet training. While Didelot, the so-called "father of Russian ballet," presided in St. Petersburg, the School was producing ballerinas who were equal or superior to any in Paris, "but people claimed," said one writer, "that our Russian dancers learned by blood and tears to become real artists under Didelot, for he was always armed with a horrible whip which he used as his most forceful argument," and the dancer Karatyguine declared that "the greater his [Didelot's] interest in one particular pupil, the more 'attention' was lavished on him. Often one could pick out a coming star by the bruises she had. The slightest mistake was rewarded by a blow, a slap, or a thump." Among the many outstanding graduates of this harsh routine, two whose fame first traveled westward were Danilova, born in 1793, and Istomina, who was six years younger.

Maria Danilova was to become a sort of poetic tragic legend. Consigned to the School at the age of eight, she left in 1809, but long before then her phenomenal talent was recognized by Didelot. She was only nine when she was presented in the role of Cupid. At fifteen she was permitted to interpret stellar roles partnered by one of France's greatest dancers, the obstreperous Louis Duport,[118] who had recently escaped the strictures of his Opéra contract by disguising himself as a woman and fleeing to Russia, accompanied by Napoleon's former mistress, the actress Mlle George. Duport was now twenty-six and at the peak of his dancing career. Noverre once had said of him that "credulous people took him for a spirit of the air," and Danilova, in her own way, created a similar illusion. Critics tried to define her rare lightness; poets attempted to capture her elusive grace in a web of words; and suddenly she was gone. Like Giuseppina Bozzacchi at a later date, she was too frail to withstand overwork, the strain of public appearances which perhaps were premature, as well as the humid midwinter climate. Before she had even made her official debut, she contracted consumption and, like Bozzacchi, she, too, died at the age of seventeen.

Eugénie Kolossova was another favorite pupil of Didelot, who declared that her abilities were limitless but, after Danilova, the ballerina who most stirred the public imagination was Avdotia Istomina. As had happened with Danilova, she was already performing as a soloist in advance of her graduation at the age of sixteen. By the time she was twenty-one, her exceptional technique and acting ability had won her the rank of *première danseuse-mime*, and her striking appearance was causing havoc among the spectators. Perfectly proportioned with the raven-haired, sloe-eyed beauty of Latin or gypsy women, she was the very type to inspire sensational dramas.

Duels, at this time, were frequent. Pushkin introduced a fatal affair of the kind in *Eugene Onégin* in 1823, and he too died in a similar affray five years later when he was only thirty-eight. When Count Scheremetyev and Alexander Griboyedov fought over Istomina it provoked a scandal. The duel caused the death of Scheremetyev, who was an officer in the Imperial Guard and the scion of an immensely rich family, the owners of vast landed estates, armies of servants, three hundred serfs, whom they were free to barter or sell, and who kept a table lavishly set each night for thirty persons whether anyone was expected or not. Griboyedov, a rising young diplomat already celebrated as a playwright, was merely wounded in the hand, though he also met a violent end soon afterwards when he was sent as Minister to Teheran and was murdered there by fanatical Moslems. Oddly enough, his mutilated body could be identified only by his scarred hand.

Pushkin himself did not escape Istomina's fascination. He admitted to being infatuated with her, and the verses he wrote for her have been often translated, often quoted:

> By nymphs accompanied on every side
> We Istomina then descried
> Who on the solid earth scarce seemed to glide.

or more literally:

> Dazzling, ethereal,
> Responsive to the magic bow,
> Encircled by a group of nymphs,
> Stands Istomina. With one foot
> She barely skims the stage
> And slowly turns upon the other.
> Suddenly she leaps, suddenly flies away
> Like some light down under the West Wind's sway.
> She draws herself up straight, turns,
> And lightly beats one foot against the other.

The rhythm and color of the original may be missing, but the poet's keen observation of the dancer is clear. It has been said that his "barely skims the stage" suggests that Istomina, at this early date, may have been dancing on point, and that one of the ballet masters affirms that he saw her dance "on the tip of her toe," but without further proof this would seem an over-interpretation. Pushkin, whose works were to provide the themes of many ballets over the years for Didelot and Diaghilev and the

Soviets, had the pleasure during his lifetime of having Istomina dance the role of the Circassian woman in his *Prisoner of the Caucasus,* 1823, at the Imperial Theatre.

Spurning all the jealous rivals who were courting her, Istomina married the actor Ekounine. In 1829 she sustained a foot injury and from then on she danced seldom and finally gave up the stage in 1836. Serge Lifar cites a cruel description of her after her retirement, when she had grown stout but, in an effort to look young, "made herself up terribly. Her hair was black as pitch, and people said she dyed it. Her eyes were enormous, black, and brilliant." In 1848, aged forty-nine, she succumbed to a fatal siege of cholera.

Only a year after Istomina retired, Marie Taglioni arrived in St. Petersburg for what was to become her five-year reign. She was the forerunner of the invasion of Romantic ballerinas: Grahn, the adored Elssler, Grisi, Cerrito, and finally Ferraris and Rosati. However, although the craze for foreigners would last until the 1860s, the Imperial Theatre School went right on producing Russian dancers who were every bit as gifted as the guest stars, even if they seemed to be less appreciated. Tatiana Smirnova and Elena Andreianova, recent graduates, were both dancing during the whole of Taglioni's sojourn and had the advantage of observing at first hand every aspect of her style and especially her technique at a time when point dancing was still comparatively new. In 1844, when Smirnova had accumulated seven years of stage experience, she was the first Russian dancer to travel to Paris and appear at the Opéra. Taglioni's example had added to her own natural deftness and delicacy, but she was too self-effacing for the sophisticated Parisians. After all, even the modest air affected by Taglioni concealed an iron will and a jealous intolerance of any rival. Apart from some sarcastic comments by Gautier, Smirnova's passage at the Opéra hardly created a ripple. One can readily imagine with what feelings of excitement and anticipation she had departed from

Russia as her country's first representative abroad and what dashed hopes she must have suffered from the patronizing attitude of the French. A happier tour to Brussels assuaged the disappointments, and then she returned to St. Petersburg to round out her career in peace and quiet.

On December 18, 1842, a year and a half after Grisi had introduced the original in Paris, Andreianova had the honor of being the first Russian Giselle, though by temperament she probably was less suited for the role than Smirnova. She was a more energetic, impetuous dancer and had a much more worldly character than her gentle rival, who was relegated to the role of Myrtha. Andreianova was also the mistress of Alexandre Guedeonov, then in the middle of his long, inept dictatorship as Director of the Imperial Theatres, a bad influence which did not end with his retirement, since he refused to stop meddling and obstructing. Once Taglioni was out of the way, Guedeonov was determined that nothing should interfere with his favorite's monopoly of stellar parts, but it was never easy to force a star on the Russian public. Grahn, Grisi, and Cerrito were all to meet with a sort of sullen indifference at the beginning of their St. Petersburg engagements. And so, when Andreianova had recovered from the inconvenience of a pregnancy, Guedeonov shipped her off to Paris with enough publicity to launch her for the winter season of 1845. All the reservations about Smirnova were forgotten when the Opéra presented this very different product of the Russian School, the type Parisians adored, technically showy, fiery, and self-assured.

On the way home Andreianova stopped for a few performances in La Scala, but it had been a disastrous season there, with one bad ballet after another creating an unreceptive mood. She was not invited to return, which mattered little once she was reinstated as Guedeonov's protégée. For three years she reigned supreme and might have continued so had Elssler not arrived to snatch away her laurels and to be the unwitting cause of perhaps the worst humiliation suffered by any ballerina. Temporarily transferred to Moscow to avoid conflict with the new guest dancer, Andreianova was received not merely with apathy, but with actual hostility and, instead of flowers, a dead black cat was hurled onto the stage. Tied to its tail was a card that read: "To the *première danseuse étoile.*" Andreianova fainted and had to be carried offstage by her partner, and the public was so affected that their mood changed. They called her out and gave her an ovation. The aftermath of the affair was typically Russian in its severity. The Moscow postal chief who instigated the affront to the ballerina was sent into exile for several years by Czar Nicholas I; Guedeonov issued an order that in future no ballet could be staged unless Andreianova took part in it; and whenever she danced he assigned plainclothesmen to the front row seats to prevent any further incidents.

Upon her return from a second foreign tour (she danced at Covent Garden in 1852), she discovered that Guedeonov no longer cared for her, her star began to wane and, though she was only thirty-four, she was told bluntly that it was time for her to retire. To remain in St. Petersburg unwanted must have seemed bitter, and perhaps her remembered triumphs at the Opéra were what lured her back to France, where she died three years later.

Although infatuated czars and directors were more than likely to impose their chosen dancers, generally speaking it was the ballet master-choreographer who was in a position to promote careers. Perrot, in the 1850s, had mainly ready-made stars in Andreianova, Elssler, Grisi, Bogdanova, and Cerrito; but Saint-Léon, engaged in 1859 to restage some of his early works and create new ones, might be said to have specialized in protégées. He was already bored with Bogdanova, whom he had trained and presented in Paris after the breakup of his marriage with Cerrito. Soon he would concentrate his energies on Martha Mouravieva and later still launch Adèle Grantzow.

In the meanwhile, Marius Petipa was patiently climbing toward that eminence from which he would one day dominate the entire ballet scene. After his debut as Andreianova's partner, in 1847, he persevered as a dancer, teacher, and minor choreographer for a dozen years before his triumphant staging of *La Fille du Pharaon* won him the post of second ballet master under Saint-Léon. Petipa also had his candidate whom he would pit against Mouravieva. "In 1854 I married Marie Sourovschikova, a very graceful dancer whose figure rivaled that of Venus," he recalled in the memoirs he wrote at the age of eighty-six, and added: "for her I created and staged the following ballets: *The Parisian Market, The Blue Dahlia, A Wedding in the Time of the Regency, The Traveling Dancer, The Beauty of Lebanon, Florida*, and many others."

The figure so admiringly mentioned by Petipa, the slenderest of legs and ankles (a rarity in those days), and a contagious gaiety made up for the rather plebeian features of Marie, who was a milliner's daughter. Besides, she was no mere technician, but a dancer with her own brand of fantasy. Petipa married her when she was eighteen, a few months after her graduation, but already for several seasons he had been pushing her to the fore and arranging appearances for her at the theatre. They had their first joint success as choreographer and leading dancer in *The Parisian Market*, 1859, and by that time they were also the parents of Marie II, a daughter who quite literally was to follow in her mother's footsteps.

Emma Livry was dispensing the magic of her Papillon, and Ferraris had just been described by the press as "a whirling feather, a floating scarf, a hovering butterfly" (shades of Gautier!), when the Petipas descended on Paris. They had been granted a summer leave by the "grumbler-benefactor," as Guedeonov was called behind his back, and after brief, profitable stops in Riga and Berlin, they were to try their luck at the Opéra. Not an easy challenge, but since *The Parisian Market* had proven very popular in Russia and Germany (Kaiser Wilhelm rewarded Marie with a diamond bracelet and Petipa with a diamond-studded snuffbox), there was reason to hope it would also find favor with the critical Parisians. Petipa, as an old man, was pleased to remember: "The Emperor Napoleon III, the Empress Eugénie, the Duke and Duchess de Morny, and the entire court attended the first performance [May 1861, with the ballet renamed *Le Marché des Innocents*]. My wife's grace and talent captivated everyone, and following the example of Their Majesties, the public gave her an enthusiastic ovation and innumerable curtain calls." Reengaged the next summer, Mme Petipa added to her repertoire a Polish mazurka inserted specially for her in a revival of *Le Diable à quatre*. The celebrated character dancer Felix Kschessinski came all the way from Russia in order to be her partner in this number, whose frenzied climax affected the French public in much the same way that the Diaghilev Company's wild *Polovtsian Dances* would rouse them in 1909.

These were successes to be savored and remembered, for when Marie went home it was already the beginning of the end for her. Backed by Saint-Léon, Mouravieva was in the ascendant, and it would seem that even Petipa's interest in Marie was on the wane. When they separated, in 1867, perhaps the faithless husband was already showing too much interest in his next protégée, the nineteen-year-old Ekaterina Vazem, soon to be famous for her cold, flawless technique and later for creating the role of Nikia in *La Bayadère*. Marie Petipa retired from the stage in 1869. She lived long enough to see Marie II make her debut in *The Blue Dahlia*, in which she herself had starred fifteen years before, but not long enough to see her daughter give the first interpretation of the enchanting Lilac Fairy in *The Sleeping Beauty*.

Martha Mouravieva's career began early and ended all too soon. She was one of the children from the Imperial School who took part in *Le Délire d'un peintre*, first staged by Perrot in London, 1843, and revived by Elssler in St. Petersburg, 1848. At the time,

Mouravieva was ten years old. Mlle Elssler singled her out from among the others and kissed her, and when she paid a visit to the School she saw the gifted child again and predicted a splendid future for her. Mouravieva grew up to be a striking young woman, not at all pretty, since she had a long aquiline nose, but favored with jet black hair and eyes and the ideal dancer's figure, petite and willowy. She was still a student when the press also spoke of her as a coming star.

In 1857, the year she graduated, she was featured, along with Mme Petipa and Mlle Madaieva in an out-of-door performance of *The Butterfly, the Rose, and the Violet*, at the estate of Prince Oldenburg. The Prince himself composed the music for this ballet by Petipa, a happy association that later on procured a Berlin engagement for the Petipas when the Prince gave them a letter of recommendation to Kaiser Wilhelm. Here, too, on this gala evening, began the rivalry between the two ballerinas which smoldered through several St. Petersburg seasons and flared up when the Opéra invited Mouravieva to follow the Paris appearances of Marie Petipa. When all Mme Petipa's machinations failed to obtain a third engagement for herself, Mouravieva made her debut in a lavishly mounted *Giselle*, in May 1863.

Lucien Petipa, the svelte, elegant dancer who had partnered Grisi in the original *Giselle*, was now ballet master at the Opéra. What must he have thought of Mouravieva's partner as his successor in the role, Louis Mérante with his pudding face and fat legs? And what, for that matter, could he have thought of Mouravieva when he compared her with "the Divine Carlotta"? In spite of her sparkling technique, the Russian *danseuse* had neither the acting ability required for the first part nor the wistful poetry needed as a Wili in the forest scene. The public and critics were divided in their opinions and were more lenient, no doubt because the last Giselle they had seen was a disastrous attempt by the Italian Regina Forli.

Mouravieva was appreciated more and had many curtain calls that summer in lively *Diavolina*, a ballet better suited to her talents because Saint-Léon composed it especially for her.

Saint-Léon in person escorted her to Paris in July 1864 to present her in *Néméa, ou l'Amour vengé*, a condensed version of their shared St. Petersburg triumph, the four-act *Fiammetta* (the Russians always had more patience than Western Europeans for full-length productions).[119] Mouravieva had matured to the top of her form, and the Opéra public wanted, expected even, to have her back the following year, but they never saw her again. That December, in St. Petersburg, at the age of twenty-seven, she created her last role, achieving a special immortality, along with Saint-Léon, in *The Little Humpbacked Horse*, the first ballet to be based on the folklore of Russia and a perennial favorite among balletomanes of that country.

In *The Little Humpbacked Horse*, Ivanoushka, the peasant's son, marries the Czar-Maiden; in real life, Mouravieva, a serf's daughter,[120] married her prince, but she did not "live happily ever after." It was said that she pined for the stage life she had abandoned and, in 1879, she succumbed to a lung ailment.

Martha Mouravieva's early death brings us to a curious observation. Whereas most of the Romantic ballerinas in Paris survived in excellent health to an extraordinarily advanced age—Cerrito to ninety-two and Mlle Augusta to ninety-five—nearly all of the Russian dancers of the same period died very young. Smirnova, who lived longest, died at fifty, Danilova at seventeen, Andreianova at thirty-seven, and Istomina, Marie Petipa, and Mouravieva in their forties.

Petipa, at last a veritable dictator in the ballet world of the Imperial School and Theatres, produced his first *Don Quixote* in Moscow in 1869. It was not his initial venture in that city, where the Bolshoi Theatre opened its doors in 1825 and was jealously proud of its own traditions. It was, in fact, to guard the interests of local

dancers that Andreianova had been so ungraciously received on the
occasion of the dead cat, at which time Petipa also staged several
ballets there. The crowning point of Elssler's Russian tour, as we
have seen, was in Moscow, where the reigning deities included Mlles
Yrca Matthias, Sankovskaia, then Lebedeva and, for *Don Quixote*,
Mlle Sobeshanskaia.[121] And though the Moscow public may have
seemed provincial, with many in street dress and kerchiefs, compared
with St. Petersburg, where formal attire was not compulsory, but
a sort of voluntary etiquette in emulation of the court, nevertheless
dance standards were very high, if somewhat unsophisticated, vigorous rather than refined.

Don Quixote was to become a vehicle for leading dancers all
over the world, and an amusing sidelight on these many productions
concerns the problem that always arose in trying to obtain a scraggy-
looking steed for the hero. Pavlova's husband said that for her company's London season the available healthy horses had to be "made
up" to look lean and miserable, and with such effect that the
R.S.P.C.A. officials came backstage to lodge protests.

Don Quixote was also a turning point in Petipa's choreographic
career. Although he was nearing fifty, his best work still lay ahead
of him. One after another, along with mediocre ballets and even
failures, he would be turning out some first-rate productions, mainly
with Russians as chief protagonists, and finally, toward the end of
the century, his masterpieces. Are we to believe those authors who
speak of the sad state of ballet during the sixties and seventies which,
according to them, was only remedied during the following decade
by an influx of Italian dancers? We read of the "decadence" of this
period; we are told that, in 1869, public enthusiasm had dwindled,
ballet had reached a "low ebb," and that for the next dozen years
little of interest would be forthcoming. All of these writers like
to quote August Bournonville who, at the time of his visit to St.
Petersburg, was almost seventy, a relic of the creative force he once

had been, and narrow-minded because of the limitations imposed by ultra-traditional Denmark.

Bournonville had no qualms about commiserating with his old friend Petipa, who politely pretended to agree with him. He remarked that the wildest dreams of any Dane were exceeded by the money lavished on the Russian theatre where *ballet now held undisputed sway* (author's italics). "I did my best," he said, "to forget the principles which I have followed in my own compositions for more than forty years." (The same old routine repeated for forty years! No wonder ballet was turning sterile in Copenhagen, while in Russia it was on the upgrade.) "I looked in vain for action, dramatic interest, some sanity; occasionally I was lucky enough to find a part in which reason prevailed. . . ." (But who has to look for sanity and reason in the ballet, or in any art for that matter?) As for the costumes, "the skirts were shortened out of all proportion, queer fashions originating in Paris theatres and naturally enough copied abroad and exaggerated still further with added details in the worst possible taste." He suffered, poor Bournonville, over the short *tutu*, which today is *de rigueur* for classical ballet, since it reveals what the dancer is doing.

Fortunately there was other testimony. A group came to the fore during the 1860s, exerting considerable influence then and later on, the balletomanes for whom ballet was the main interest in life, and at least one foreigner must have found himself very much at home among them. This was the indefatigable Théophile Gautier. He arrived for the first time at the end of 1858 in search of material for a publication to be called *Art Treasures of Ancient and Modern Russia* and, in 1861, he went on a second trip accompanied by his son. Although only a fragment of the art history ever materialized, eventually he brought out *Le Voyage en Russie* and a number of articles. Who could have been a better observer than Gautier, who had seen hundreds of the best European dancers come and go in

Paris? He was not only impressed by the remarkable soloists trained in the Imperial School, but was particularly struck by the straight lines, neat groups, and precision of the *corps de ballet*. He also unconsciously cast a reflection on the undisciplined behavior of the Paris Opéra *corps* when he remarked that among the young dancers in Russia there was "no chattering, no laughter, nor even a glance toward the loges or the parterre."

Indeed, the much denigrated sixties and seventies were witness to Saint-Léon's best ballets for Martha Mouravieva; splendid productions by Petipa for Caroline Rosati and Henriette Dor; Petipa's Moscow *Don Quixote* and the revised and lengthened version for St. Petersburg two years later; his very successful *Camargo* for Adèle Grantzow; not to mention *La Bayadère* for Ekaterina Vazem, and nineteen lesser works. And all the while, year after year, those touching young girls in their sober uniforms and ample pinafores were issuing forth from the Imperial School to sparkle before the public: Mlles Vergina and Radina; the beautiful Eugenia Sokolova, who would create many roles for Petipa; Marie Petipa II, who made her debut in 1875; then Mlle Nikitina; and the airy Gorschenkova a year later—too many of them to crowd into the confines of a single book, though one might wish to linger over each of their names, their aspirations, dreams, and loves, their triumphs and disappointments, with old age and death at last dealing transient fame or oblivion to all of them.

The earliest invasion of Italian dancers had taken place during the eighteenth century. A second one began with Marie Taglioni [122] in 1837, and was over even before Rosati left, because the Russians were going through a period of intense chauvinism. The last influx came at the end of the nineteenth century and was perhaps the most important, because the Italians did not merely arrive as guest artists, to set a dazzling example and then depart, but they also left behind some extraordinary teachers, who influenced the whole subsequent course of ballet in Russia, and whose effect is still felt everywhere at the present time.

A precursor of the third group was Caterina Beretta, in 1877, and, if she went down in Russian annals less stressed as a star performer than some of her compatriots who came later, it was partly because no important ballet was choreographed specially for her (she was, in any case, already thirty-seven and too plump for Russian taste), but mainly because her fame as a teacher overshadowed everything else. Nevertheless, she had already enjoyed a long, full life on the stage. At sixteen she appeared briefly at the Paris Opéra; in 1858 she was on the program of La Scala as *prima ballerina assoluta di rango francese* and danced there off and on during the next eighteen years, after which she went to St. Petersburg. In 1902 Signora Beretta was once again in Milan, this time instated for a period of six years as ballet mistress. She was now as celebrated a teacher as Mme Dominique had been in Paris, and dancers who afterwards became the glory of the Diaghilev Company traveled all the way from Russia to study with her—Trefilova and Pavlova, and then Karsavina, who described her as "a ludicrous little figure . . . fat and short, her pyramidal shape emphasized by a very small head with a meagre blob of hair on top." The little old lady survived for only three years after resigning her post as ballet mistress, in which she did more for other ballerinas than she had ever done for herself.

Nearly all of the Italian prima ballerinas who danced at La Scala during the fifteen years from 1874 to 1889 [123] eventually found their way to Russia to appear variously at summer theatres, at the so-called "café concerts" in the amusement park, or at the Imperial Theatres. The phenomenon among them, Virginia Zucchi, came on the scene in midsummer, 1885. All St. Petersburg heard about her immediately and hurried to the park to see her for themselves. What they found was a dancer already thirty-eight years old, not remarkably beautiful, and deficient in any sort of sensational technique except for a curious ability to flash across the stage on the tips of her steely pointed toes. Her attraction was her gift for acting, which bordered on genius and held people spellbound. The conventional ballet public, satiated with *pirouettes* and *entrechats* and the chill perfection of Mlle Vazem, finally had the excitement of having her at their own Imperial Theatre that winter in revivals of *La Fille du Pharaon* and *La Fille mal gardée*, and in *L'Ordre du Roi*, created for her by Petipa. There the narrow-minded traditionalists engaged in a losing battle with Mlle Zucchi's army of partisans. Blasé patrons were shaken out of their apathy; elderly balletomanes sat up and gazed with relish at her pretty legs—"the legs of Diana"—and high above the parterre the little girls craned over the rim of the loge that belonged to the School, spilling tears over their idol's impassioned portrayal of La Esmeralda and marveling at the skill and assurance which this ballerina had reaped from twenty years of trouping in Italy, Spain, Germany, France, and England.

After two seasons, in spite of all the adulation, Mlle Zucchi yearned to revisit the theatres of other foreign capitals before she gave up the stage for good. And since she was verging on middle age, perhaps she was wise not to incur the danger of outstaying her welcome in Russia, as many people felt Taglioni had done. So she set out on another tour and, at last, following the course of most retired dancers, she resigned herself to teaching. She opened a school in Monte Carlo and stayed there until her death in 1930.

The void left by Virginia Zucchi was filled by Antonietta Dell'Era, still very young, fragile, and exquisite, and by Emma Bessone, who stayed only a few months before settling in Moscow for several years. Mlle Bessone made her debut in *Giselle* (always popular in Russia in contrast with the Paris Opéra, where, after Grantzow's last performance, in 1868, in Lucien Petipa's version, it was never shown again until after World War I). La Bessone clinched her success by dashing off fourteen *fouettés* in *The Tulip of Haarlem*, 1887, produced for her by Petipa before he went on to two more ballets for another Italian contender, Elena Cornalba.

Marius Petipa was now entering upon the final and best period of his creative output. In the space of a mere six months after Mlle Zucchi came to the theatre, he had turned out three ballets, a revival which was practically a new work, and an opera interlude, but all of this was very minor compared with the masterworks he was going to bring forth during the next ten years. Much of this productivity Petipa magnanimously attributed to Ivan Alexandrovich Vsevolojsky, Director of the Imperial Theatres, 1881–99. In 1905, when he was suffering under a totally unsympathetic director, Petipa would recall with nostalgia "those never-to-be-forgotten seventeen years of Vsevolojsky's management, during which every one of my ballets was successful, and I staged many. [More than thirty, in fact.] All the artists, without exception, adored their noble, kind, cultured director," and so Petipa, who had never before wanted to lend himself to any kind of collaboration, was pleased to accept Vsevolojsky's proposal for a libretto and other suggestions for *La Belle au bois dormant* (*The Sleeping Beauty*). Pugni had long since been consigned to the dust heap where he belonged (by the time he died he had composed three hundred and twelve ballets, and his music sounded as if it had been ground out by formula); Minkus would soon be dropped by the Director, and in his place there would be Tchaikovsky, followed by other composers of stature. This alone was a great forward step for Russian ballet.

Everything combined to make *The Sleeping Beauty* into an extraordinary event when it was first presented, on January 3, 1890, preceded by a gala preview for the Czar. The St. Petersburg Bolshoi having been recently condemned as unsafe, the Imperial Theatre was now permanently settled at the Maryinsky which, though architecturally less distinguished, was spacious and glamorous, with its two thousand five hundred seats, pale blue decorations, and the most elegant audience in Europe. On the stage everything was equally sumptuous. A group of artists produced decors worthy of the occasion. Vsevolojsky himself designed the costumes, and Petipa's choreography surpassed by far anything he had done previously. Bournonville (he had died ten years before) surely would never have approved the lack of dramatic action, the episodes and *pas* all loosely strung together on the thread of a fairy tale. Petipa used Perrault's story mainly as a pretext for a series of interludes and show pieces for soloists, many of which remain models of classic dance. The admirable last-act variations are often revived separately as *Aurora's Wedding* or *Princess Aurora*, and the Blue Bird *pas de deux*, also staged separately, is a constant favorite of leading dancers. Of all the ballet music Tchaikovsky wrote, *The Sleeping Beauty* was what he himself liked best, and with reason. Without any false pride, he collaborated closely with Petipa, accepting the hundred and one detailed instructions that resulted in a perfect harmony of music and dance. Kschessinska, who had the leading role three years later, remembers Tchaikovsky as a charming man who was pleased to sit down at the piano to accompany the dancers at rehearsals.

The original performers of *The Sleeping Beauty* were also an unparalleled combination of talent and grace: Carlotta Brianza as Princess Aurora; Paul Gerdt as her partner, Prince Charming; Enrico Cecchetti [124] in the character role of the wicked fairy Carabosse and also in a spectacular exhibition of leaps, *pirouettes*, and *entrechats* with Nikitina in the Blue Bird; Marie Petipa II as the Lilac Fairy (whose beauty, the historian André Levinson admitted thirty years later, haunted all his boyhood dreams).

Carlotta Brianza, like Cecchetti, was first seen in St. Petersburg at a popular theatre, in 1887, but unlike Cecchetti, who made a career in Russia, she departed four years later. Although nearly all ballet dictionaries refer to Brianza as a pupil of Blasis, he can hardly have done much toward forming her style since she was only eleven when he died. Typically Italian of her period, all feminine curves and effervescence, Mlle Brianza made a dazzling Princess Aurora. She then created the roles in two more Petipa ballets before leaving on tour and finally settling in Paris to teach. There is a sentimental postscript to her connection with *The Sleeping Beauty*. When Diaghilev assembled his galaxy of stars for the revival of this ballet in London, November 1921, Carlotta Brianza, then fifty-four, took the role of the wicked Carabosse. Moreover, just two months later, to celebrate his fifty years on the stage, Maestro Cecchetti himself, aged seventy-one, took over the role of Carabosse, which he had first played in the original production.

Casse-Noisette (*The Nutcracker*), drafted under the supervision of Petipa, but choreographed by his able second ballet master, Lev Ivanov, is today one of the most beloved of all ballets. Restaged every year by numerous companies as a traditional Christmas offering, it is a source of joy to grownups and children alike, but when it was first produced in 1892 it was received only halfheartedly. Tchaikovsky himself embarked on the work without enthusiasm, and the lovely, haunting melodies that accompany the dances of the Snow Flakes and the Sugar Plum Fairy were hardly appreciated. Even as late as the 1930s, Cyril Beaumont dismissed *The Nutcracker* as having only two or three good numbers to compensate for its general mediocrity. On the night of the première the Sugar Plum Fairy was danced by Antonietta Dell'Era. She had matured into an accomplished ballerina, but was almost immediately cast into the shade by the feats of the last and the most astonishing of the visiting Italians.[125]

Pierina Legnani's career, which included appearances in Italy, Spain, France, England, and even the United States, was very similar to that of other stars borrowed by Russia from La Scala, except that whatever anyone else may have done, Mlle Legnani did more and did it better. Born in 1863, she had attained to no exalted rank by the time she was twenty. La Scala's schedule of programs for 1883 listed Virginia Zucchi as prima ballerina; the main attraction was Manzotti's *Excelsior*, and Pierina Legnani was merely among the one hundred and thirty-six members of the Scuola di Ballo who took part in that monster extravaganza, which before long, with Elena Cornalba in the role of Electricity, was to jolt the jaded Paris public.

Mlle Legnani's triumph, when it came, was in Russia and was worth waiting for, and Fokine, in his *Memoirs of a Ballet Master*, has left us a vivid impression of it. "In 1893, during my fifth year in the School, the Italian ballerina Pierina Legnani came to St. Petersburg to make her debut in the ballet *Cinderella*. Much about this ballet has been forgotten, but not the fact that in it Legnani executed a series of thirty-two *fouettés*, a technical feat which had never before been seen on our stage. She turned with an amazing force and assurance, standing on one toe in the center of the stage without moving an inch from the spot. The artists were awestruck by her virtuosity and expressed their approval with thunderous applause at each rehearsal. . . . At the first performance, playing the role of a pageboy and standing way back on the stage, I became so excited at her execution of the *fouettés* that when she finished I began to applaud madly, forgetting that I was a member of the cast. I was severely reprimanded." [126]

The excitement generated by the novelty at the Maryinsky brought about some unheard-of changes. At the School the masters met and decided that along with classes in the French-Russian tradition there should be one in the Italian method; and the huge closed "bus," which was hauled by four horses and resembled an antiquated Black Maria, delivered the students to the theatre so that they might observe and learn at first hand. Karsavina, who entered the School in 1894, remembered that Legnani's exploit suggested acrobatics and the circus: while the music stopped the dancer advanced to the center of the stage and slowly, deliberately took her preparation, and then a "string of vertiginous *pirouettes*, marvelous in their precision and brilliant as diamond facets, roused the audience to ecstasies." But the ballerina was not merely sensational. Karsavina added that though she was far from beautiful, with rather short legs, she was nevertheless graceful and charming and endeared herself to everyone.

Legnani went on to even greater triumphs in *Swan Lake*. A first, poorly staged version had been shown in Moscow in 1877, and was a failure; a second showing of only Act II, with Mlle Legnani as the Swan Queen, took place in 1894, at a concert in memory of Tchaikovsky, who had died of cholera the previous year; and at last, when Petipa and Ivanov staged the final complete version at the Maryinsky in 1895, it was a resounding success, perhaps the apotheosis of Petipa's long reign as ballet master. The famous thirty-two *fouettés* were seen again in the coda of the *grand pas de deux*, Act III, and today are a specialty in performances in Russia and England.

Other ballets in which Mlle Legnani created new roles were: *The Pearl*, at the Gala in Moscow for the coronation of Czar Nicholas II, 1896; *Bluebeard*, the same year; *Raymonda*, 1898; *Ruses d'Amour*, 1900; and she appeared in revivals of *Caterina, Coppélia, The Talisman, The Halt of the Cavalry, Camargo*, and many more. As *prima ballerina assoluta* (a rarely conferred rank), she monopolized so many stellar roles coveted by rising young Russians that it was with an almost audible sigh of relief that they saw her take her farewell benefit in January 1901.

Fired by the example of the Italians, the splendid dancers of the Imperial School became *fabulous* dancers. Virginia Zucchi had taught them to combine "motion and emotion"; Pierina Legnani had shown them that technique could be carried further than anything previously imagined. With Cecchetti adding his special wisdom to a staff which was already thoroughly competent and often inspired, the School, during the last decade of the nineteenth century, graduated a series of paragons. Olga Preobrajenska, Mathilde Kschessinska, Vera Trefilova, Serafina Astafieva, Agrippina Vaganova, Julia Sedova, Lubov Egorova, Anna Pavlova, and others, not forgetting the Moscow *danseuses*, Roslavleva, Geltzer, and Fedorova II. Although a number of them made names for themselves before 1900, they belong mainly to the twentieth century and a second volume in the history of great ballerinas.

However, among all these dancers, two must be mentioned in a category quite apart. Mathilde Kschessinska, born 1872, graduated 1890, took over Brianza's role as Aurora and Dell'Era's Sugar Plum Fairy in 1893; she had to wait a long time before she inherited the roles of Legnani, but in the meanwhile she had mastered Legnani's *tour de force*. During an audience with Baron Frederiks, Minister of the Imperial Court, she thanked him for enabling her to perform perfectly the famous thirty-two *fouettés*. "I am delighted to hear of it," he replied, "but I confess I am at a loss to understand. . . ." "It's very simple," said Kschessinska. "In doing these *fouettés* it is essential with each revolution to have a very visible fixed point before one's eyes. Well then, you are always seated in the very center of the first row and, in the semi-darkness, the decorations you wear shine out in the glow of the footlights." [127]

Everything was "very simple" for Kschessinska. Technical difficulties were no problem to her; she was beautiful, with a perfect figure and a waist so tiny that a man's two hands could span it; she had inherent style no matter what costume she wore; she had acting ability that ranged from the frivolous to the tragic, and an enchanting personality. The author-critic Adamovitch called her the very prototype of the great star, the *prima ballerina assoluta* of the Imperial Ballet. "The Star," he said, "is recognized by the way she comes onstage; it is up to the Star to eclipse everyone else immediately," [128] and the special gift of Kschessinska was that she caught hold of the public the moment she came in view. He added that even Isadora Duncan, who despised classic ballet, could not remain unmoved by Kschessinska's magical presence.

Kschessinska might be thought of as the last great czarist dancer, doubly so because she married the Grand Duke André Wladimirovitch. He was a cousin of Czar Nicholas II, who had also been in love with her, and another cousin, the Grand Duke Cyril, bestowed on her, at the time of her marriage, the title of Princess Romanovsky-Krassinsky. But she must be remembered as the "flawless ballerina."

And finally there was Pavlova. In 1900 she had only recently emerged from the School, but everyone—her fellow students, the dancers, the public, and the critics—sensed immediately that she was unique. It was her destiny to become even more than a flawless dancer, to transcend the dance itself and attain the quality of genius. "She was first and last a great individual artist," says the often-quoted passage by Cyril Beaumont, "a complete unity in herself, who had the supreme power of not only being able to breathe into a dance her own flame-like spirit, but, no matter how many times she had danced it before, to invest it with an air of spontaneity, novelty, and freshness, as though it had but just been born. She was something more than a great artist-dancer. She made her features speak and her body sing."

Others may have been "great ballerinas," but Pavlova was to be the ideal toward which all future dancers might aspire.

With the passing of the nineteenth century, it was obvious that many of the old traditions were beginning to disappear. In the offing were the upheavals of the Russo-Japanese War and the stirrings of the great mass of Russian people, passive for centuries and now about to explode and establish a new order. An advance wave of rebellion on the part of young intellectuals was reflected in the world of arts and letters, and inevitably included the ballet. Serge Diaghilev had arrived in St. Petersburg, was briefly associated with the Maryinsky Theatre and, with a group of similarly inclined friends and enthusiasts, had founded the magazine *Mir Isskoustva* (The World of Art) though he was soon to concentrate his efforts on producing ballets. The object, of course, was to dispense with the old, to promote the new.

It is sad to think that Petipa, who had done so much for Russian ballet was to die in 1910, an embittered old man, close to his ninetieth birthday. Teliakowsky, appointed Director of the Imperial Theatres in 1901, was impatient to rid himself of Petipa and his outmoded ideas and, unfortunately, also seemed to enjoy humiliating him. Certainly the Director was largely responsible for the organized hissing, catcalls, and jeers that greeted the curtain rise of Petipa's last ballet, *The Magic Mirror* (1903), and caused the old ballet master to resign. Nor could Petipa forget that, on the occasion of his jubilee benefit, he was not allowed to accept in public the wreath presented to him by the dancers. As a final affront, instructions were given forbidding him to visit the stage, and the theatre he had served faithfully for fifty-six years was shut to him.

Marius Petipa's era had come to an end; however, many of the dancers who had grown under his guidance and had performed in his ballets would soon go on to another life in the West. Led by Diaghilev, in a company that numbered the dancer-choreographer Fokine, the artists Bakst and Benois, the male stars Bolm and Nijinsky, the ballerinas would shine again in new settings in Europe and in North and South America. For nearly two hundred years Russian ballet had been receiving its inspiration from Western countries. Now Russia would give back all that it had received, and more, and would light the way for the rebirth of ballet in the twentieth century.

Notes

---

1. For the Foyer de la Danse in the Académie de Musique et de Danse (generally known as the Opéra), designed by Charles Garnier and inaugurated January 5, 1875, the mural painted by Gustave Boulanger depicts the following dancers with these dates:

   1. Mlle de la Fontaine—1681
   2. Subligny—1690
   3. Prévost—1705
   4. Camargo—1726
   5. Sallé—1740
   6. Vestris—1751
   7. Guimard—1760
   8. Heinel—1766
   9. Miller dite Gardel—1786
   10. Clotilde—1792
   11. Bigottini—1807
   12. Noblet—1817
   13. Montessu—1821
   14. Julia—1823
   15. Taglioni—1828
   16. Duvernay—1832
   17. Elssler—1834
   18. Grisi—1841
   19. Cerrito—1847
   20. Rosati—1854

   Also in the foyer are four sculpted heads representing Opéra dancers of 1875: Mlles Mérante, Fiocre, Montaubry, and Beaugrand; and elsewhere busts of Marie Taglioni, Carlotta Grisi, and Emma Livry.

2. This work on dance notation was never published, but it is known that later authors made use of the ms., and in the engraving by Chéreau from the portrait by Tournière we see Pécourt holding the manuscript.

3. At the Paris Opéra, the categories still in effect after only minor changes since the first *école*, are: *élève*, "*rat*," or student and beginner; *second quadrille*, *premier quadrille* or ballet girls; *coryphée*, *petit sujet*, *grand sujet*, or varying degrees of soloist; *première danseuse* and *premier danseur* or leading dancer;

and *étoile*, or star. The *étoile* may be prima ballerina and after that the supreme rank is *prima ballerina assoluta*.

4. Not the Abbé DuBois, the statesman-priest, as is often stated, but Jean-Baptiste Dubos, author, 1670–1742. Fontenelle lived to be 100 years old and later also gave a letter of introduction to the eighteenth-century ballerina Marie Sallé, addressed to M. de Montesquieu in 1730.

5. This school was established at the Paris Opéra in 1713, and under various forms has continued to the present day.

6. Celebrated at the Opéra, the eldest was known as "*le Diable*," the devil, because he specialized in demon roles; the second Malter called "*l'Oiseau*," the bird, because of his elevation; and the youngest, Malter III, called "*l'Anglais*," because of his long sojourn in England.

7. Quoted by Selma Jeanne Cohen in *Famed for Dance*, New York Public Library, 1960, p. 53.

8. Cahusac, Louis de: *La Danse ancienne et moderne*, La Haye, Paris, 1754, Vol. III, p. 154.

9. The same omission has been perpetuated by Cyril Beaumont and others.

10. Not the Marquis d'Argenson (who was a police commissioner), as stated by Deryck Lynham in *The Chevalier Noverre*, Sylvan Press, London, 1950, p. 17 and note 7.

11. Noverre, Jean-Georges: *Lettres sur les Arts Imitateurs*, Paris, 1807, Vol. I, p. 294.

12. Capon, Gaston: *Les Vestris*, Soc. du Mercure de France, Paris, 1908, p. 58.

13. Grimm, Frederic Melchior: *Correspondance de Grimm et de Diderot*, Furne, Paris, 1829, Vol. VI, p. 142.

14. *Fermier général*, or farmer general, was a title held by many French aristocrats allowing them to be "farmers," or collectors of taxes. They kept a percentage of the money they collected and amassed enormous fortunes.

15. Douglas, Robert B.: *Sophie Arnould, Actress and Wit*, Charles Carrington, Paris, 1898, p. 134.

16. When Jean-Baptiste Vestris was watching Gaëtan dance one evening, he exclaimed with brotherly admiration, in his strong Italian accent: "*C'est le diou (dieu) de la danse.*"

17. Douglas: *Op. cit.*, p. 82.

18. Goncourt, Edmond de: *La Guimard*, Flammarion, Paris, 1893, p. 51. M. de Goncourt in making this remark forgot that Marie Sallé composed her own *entrées* to Rameau's music.

19. Capon: *Op. cit.*, p. 83.

20. Grimm: *Op. cit.*, Vol. VIII, p. 61.

21. It has been mistakenly said that *pirouettes* were an innovation at the turn of the century, *i.e.*, about 1800, and Blasis is quoted in order to justify the statement. "Pirouettes," wrote Blasis, "were unknown to Noverre." However, Noverre actually speaks of *pirouettes* frequently. In *Lettres sur les Arts Imitateurs*, p. 128, he even says that Vestris *père* who danced at the Opéra from 1749 to 1782, performed them better than his son, Auguste.

22. Although Vestris and Anna Heinel retired on May 12, 1782, they were seen from time to time as guest performers and Vestris, at seventy-one, made a touching appearance with his son, Auguste, and grandson, Armand. Auguste, too, when

he was in his seventies, appeared once with the Romantic ballerina Marie Taglioni.

23. Grimm: *Op. cit.*, Vol. VII, p. 418 (February 1772). ". . . *et vera incessu patuit dea*" ["in her step she was revealed a very goddess"]. Virgil: *Aeneid*, I, line 409.

24. Not *"un chanteur de l'Opéra,"* as we read on p. 176 of Adolphe Jullien's *L'Opéra Secret au XVIIIe Siècle*, Rouveyre, Paris, 1880. J.-B. Rey, after distinguishing himself as a conductor in Marseille, Bordeaux, etc., was assistant to Francoeur at the Opéra for five years and then, from 1781, a brilliant *premier chef d'orchestre* for thirty years.

25. Noverre: *Op. cit.*, Vol. II, p. 119.

26. For those who wish to learn all the facts connected with this ballet there is a delightful little book, *La Fille mal gardée*, edited by Ivor Guest, which appeared at the time of Frederick Ashton's new version for the Royal Ballet.

27. Goncourt: *Op. cit.*, p. 164.

28. Goncourt: *Op. cit.*, pp. 249–51.

29. Salvatore Viganò, 1769–1821, nephew of the composer Boccherini, created forty ballets, including *The Creatures of Prometheus*, Vienna, 1801 (for which Beethoven composed his only ballet score), *Otello* and *La Vestale*, Milan, 1818, *I Titani*, Milan, 1819, etc.

Louis Henry (1766–1836), who worked mainly in Milan and Naples, was the author of *Dircea*, in which Amalia Brugnoli gave one of the early displays of dancing on point. Although he staged several ballets in Paris in smaller theatres, he returned to the Opéra only once, shortly before his death, with *L'Ile des Pirates*, which was a failure.

Charles-Louis Didelot, 1767–1836. Although aerial effects were known from the time of Louis XIV, Didelot in *Flore et Zéphire*, London, 1796, was the first to fly his dancers on wires that were invisible. Dancer, choreographer, ballet master, teacher, and fanatical worker, he is also credited with inventing ballet tights, although this is disputed in favor of Maillot, who supplied hosiery to the Paris Opéra in the 1830s, or Jules Léotard, French acrobat and the original "man on the flying trapeze" in the fifties and sixties.

30. Jullien: *Op. cit.*, p. 78.

31. Mlle Clotilde, sometimes listed as Mlle Mafleuroy, was really named Clotilde-Augustine Mafleurai.

32. Although masks were no longer used at the Opéra after Max Gardel appeared without one in *Castor et Pollux*, January 21, 1772, they continued to be *de rigueur* at the Comédie-Italienne.

33. *Les Noces de Gamaches*, described as a *ballet-pantomime-folie*, at the Théâtre de la République, 28 Nivose, year IX. It is touching to find on the program as "villagers": Duport (aged 18); Philippe Taglioni (aged 23 and the future father of the great Marie Taglioni); his sister, Louise; and, in a solo role, Mlle Chameroy—she who died in childbirth the following year, and was refused burial at the Eglise Saint-Roch.

34. Noverre: *Op. cit.*, Vol. II, pp. 162–63.

35. Eusebio Luzzi, Giuseppe Trafieri, and Vincenzo Galeotti all used the story of Nina as libretti. In Copenhagen Galeotti's *Nina eller den Vanvittige af Kaerlighed*, 1802, was a favorite role of Anna Margrethe Schall.

36. Beaumont, Cyril: *Complete Book of Ballets*, Grosset & Dunlap, New York, n.d., p. 11.
37. Berlioz, Hector: *Memoirs of Hector Berlioz*, translated and edited by David Cairns, Alfred A. Knopf, New York, 1969, p. 83.
38. *Journal des Débats*, Paris, Dec. 14, 1815 (two days after the ballet was staged).
39. The Duke was also reported to have been briefly one of the lovers of Mlle Bigottini. Eight months after he was assassinated, Mlle Virginie had a second son by him, only a month after the Duchess also gave birth to a son. The posthumous heir, first known as the Duc de Bordeaux, later Comte de Chambord, reappears in ballet annals in connection with the American ballerina Augusta Maywood.
40. Oddly enough, the Grand Opera House in Lyon also has only eight muses.
41. Heine, Heinrich: *Lutezia* in *Vermischte Schriften*, 1854.
42. Ivor Guest notes one further appearance of Mlle Bigottini as Nina at Milon's benefit (April 18, 1827) in his book, *The Romantic Ballet in Paris*, Wesleyan University Press, Middletown, Conn., 1966, p. 54.
43. *Courrier des Théâtres*, April 8, 1827.
44. The review of Gautier in *Le Constitutionnel*, May 31, 1834. George Sand review quoted from André Maurois' *Lélia*, Jonathan Cape, London, 1953, p. 168.
45. Gautier, Théophile: *A History of Romanticism*, George D. Sproul, New York, 1902, pp. 156–57.
46. Bouteron, Marcel: *Danse et Musique Romantiques*, Le Goupy, Paris, 1927, p. 13.
47. [Vandam, Albert D.]: *An Englishman in Paris*, D. Appleton & Company, New York, n.d., p. 91.
48. Boigne, Charles de: *Petits Mémoires de l'Opéra*, Librairie Nouvelle, Paris, 1857, p. 7.
49. Maurois: *Op. cit.*, p. 105.
50. Levinson, André: *Marie Taglioni*, C. W. Beaumont, London, 1930, p. 15.
51. *Ibid.*, p. 14.
52. Vaillat, Léandre: *La Taglioni*, Albin Michel, Paris, 1942, p. 66.
53. Véron, Dr. Louis: *Mémoires d'un Bourgeois de Paris*, Librairie Nouvelle, Paris, 1856, Vol. III, p. 224.
54. Vaillat: *Op. cit.*, p. 82.
55. Although it was the custom elsewhere in Europe, it is believed that this was the first time that flowers were thrown on the stage of the Paris Opéra; they are also believed to have been offered by Duponchel. Today the custom is generally popular, and in Europe bouquets are often offered to male dancers.
56. *The Examiner*, London, June 6, 1830.
57. Véron: *Op. cit.*, pp. 162–63.
58. Jean-Madeleine Schneitzhoeffer, composer of *Proserpine* and *Le Séducteur au village*, 1818, *Zémir et Azor*, 1824, *Mars et Venus*, 1826, *La Tempête*, 1834.
Pierre Ciceri, designer at the Opéra from 1809; of his productions, too numerous to list, the most famous were *Robert le Diable* and *La Sylphide*.
Eugène Lami, painter and illustrator, celebrated in his day, designed for the Opéra occasionally. Ivor Guest throws doubt on his having designed the *tutu*.
59. Eugène Briffault in *Galerie des Artistes Dramatiques de Paris*, Article II, Marchant, Paris, 1841.

60. Not "*La Gitane* . . . as a set-off to the *Gipsy* created by Elssler," as André Levinson says in *Marie Taglioni*, p. 70. Taglioni's *Gitana* came first, in November 1838, and Elssler's *Gipsy* followed in January 1839.

61. In connection with Taglioni's eight appearances at La Scala, Milan, in May and June 1841, it is curious to find that L. Vaillat in *La Taglioni*, pp. 432, 433, and 444, has "borrowed," word for word and without any acknowledgment to the author, entire pages from a very long letter which appeared in *La Revue de Paris*, June 15, 1841, though oddly enough he attributes one of these paragraphs to Stendhal—poor Stendhal who at this time was at death's door at Civitavecchia.

62. [Vandam]: *Op. cit.*, pp. 106–107.
It is of interest to note that Mlle Taglioni's brother Paul choreographed and danced in a ballet entitled *La Prima Ballerina, ou l'Embuscade*, London, June 1849, using this highwayman episode as his libretto. Carolina Rosati was the ballerina.

63. Gautier in *La Presse*, June 13, 1844.

64. [Vandam]: *Op. cit.*, p. 99.

65. Second, Albéric: *Les Petits Mystères de l'Opéra*, Kugelmann & Bernard-Latte, Paris, 1844, p. 139.

66. *Pas de Quatre*: four performances, July 1845, and revived twice with Lucile Grahn's role taken by Carolina Rosati in 1847. For details of this historic event see Benjamin Lumley's *Reminiscences of the Opera*, Hurst & Blackett, London, 1864, pp. 114–18, and Ivor Guest's delightful account in *The Romantic Ballet in England*, Phoenix House, London, 1954, chapter XVI. The *Pas de Quatre* has been successfully revived with the original music by Keith Lester, 1936, and Anton Dolin, 1941, for various companies in Europe and the United States and is still popular.

67. Léandre Vaillat, in *La Taglioni*, p. 481, dates Marie Taglioni's last performances in July 1848, because of some press notice he found in her scrapbook, but these clippings undoubtedly refer to her niece, Marie Taglioni, the younger, who danced in London that year in ballets by her father and Perrot.

68. [Vandam]: *Op. cit.*, pp. 100–101 and 108.

69. Guest: *The Romantic Ballet in England*, pp. 49–50.

70. André Levinson, in his *Marie Taglioni*, p. 62, like so many other authors, states that Fanny Elssler was the god-daughter of Haydn, and *The Dance Encyclopedia* even says that he arranged for Fanny to study ballet. It must, however, be pointed out that Haydn died a year before Fanny was born.

71. Levinson: *Op. cit.*, p. 61.

72. Guest: *The Romantic Ballet in Paris*, p. 137.

73. Vaillat: *Op. cit.*, p. 75.

74. Dolores Serral, her popular partner Mariano Camprubi, Francisco Font, and Manuela gave the Parisians their first view of authentic Spanish dancing in 1834, at Opéra balls and briefly at the Opéra, and started a furor. Serral's *cachucha* and *bolero* were successfully imitated by the Noblet sisters (Mme Alexis Dupont and Lise), by Pauline Duvernay, and Lucile Grahn.
Briffault: *Loc. cit.*, Article V, 1841.

75. *La Presse*, October 2, 1837.

76. For further details of *La Gipsy* and *La Tarentule* see *The Romantic Ballet, as seen by Théophile Gautier*, translated and published by Cyril Beaumont, London, 1947; *The Complete Book of Ballets* by the same; and Ivor Guest's *The Romantic Ballet in Paris*.

77. Although Wikoff coyly refused to divulge his age even when he was in his seventies, it is known that he came of age between 1831 and 1834 and therefore was twenty-six to twenty-nine years old when he met Mlle Elssler in 1839.

78. Wikoff, Henry: *The Reminiscences of an Idler*, Fords, Howards & Hulbert, New York, 1880, pp. 515–16.

79. *Ibid.*, p. 566.

80. Delarue, Allison: *The Chevalier Henry Wikoff*, Princeton University Press, New Jersey, 1968, p. 29.

81. James Sylvain (sometimes Silvain), born James Sullivan, c. 1808, danced in London 1824–25, Paris 1826–33, in London again 1833–39, in the United States with Fanny Elssler 1840–42, and in London as Elssler's partner 1843; he died in 1856.
    Although the *Encyclopaedia Britannica*, *Grove's Dictionary*, etc., all say that Thérèse accompanied her sister, she stayed in Europe because she was terrified of the sea. Later, encouraged by Fanny's letters, she was about to make the voyage and again, at the last minute, lost her nerve.
    Charles, the coachman, fell in love with America; Mlle Elssler set him up in a livery stable and he remained there.

82. Crow, Duncan: *Henry Wikoff, The American Chevalier*, MacGibbon & Kee, London, 1963, p. 71.

83. Wemyss, Francis Courtney: *Twenty-Six Years of the Life of an Actor and Manager*, New York, 1847, p. 332.

84. Lifar, Serge: *A History of Russian Ballet*, Roy Publishers, New York, n.d., p. 89.

85. August Bournonville, 1805–79, one of the most important figures in ballet history; son of Antoine Bournonville, 1760–1843, who followed Galeotti as director of the Royal Danish Ballet. August studied with Vestris and Gardel, danced in Paris and London, before returning to Copenhagen in 1829, where he became director of the School and then ballet master and chief choreographer. Of his thirty-six ballets, many are still performed today.

86. Andersen, Hans Christian: *Digtsamling* ("Collected Poems"), Copenhagen, 1847.

87. *La Presse*, August 7, 1838.

88. *La Presse*, September 17, 1838.

89. Elena Andreianova, 1819–57, graduated from the Imperial School, 1837, was the first Russian Giselle, 1842; danced in Paris, 1845; Milan, 1846; London, 1852; retired, 1854.

90. Lifar: *Op. cit.*, p. 83.

91. *Ibid.*

92. Lucile Grahn, autograph letter dated Hamburg, September 1849. Author's collection.

93. The system of ranks, which stems from the French and is now quite international, does not prevail in Denmark where there are normally only three grades. Graduates from the School are taken into the company as "aspirants";

then, after a last examination, they become "ballet dancers" and finally "solo dancers."

94. *La Presse*, November 25, 1839.
95. Ballet school of M. and Mme Paul H. Hazard, at 96 South Fifth Street, Philadelphia, one of the first such schools in the United States. Paul Hazard and his wife had gained their experience at the Opéra de Paris, in Brussels, and in Germany, and were excellent teachers. Their pupils included Augusta Maywood and Mary Ann Lee.
96. Mlle Augusta, née Caroline Fuchs, b. Munich, 1806; d. New York, 1901. Her teacher, Albert, was in love with her while she was in love with his son Auguste. She was not popular at the Opéra, but was well liked in the United States. Her lover, Comte de Saint-James, married her and then tried to be her business manager during her American tour, with disastrous results.
97. Mary Ann Lee, 1823–99, a pupil of Hazard and James Sylvain, and, in Paris, 1844, of Jean Coralli. She danced only in the United States, and was seen in many of Taglioni's and Elssler's roles. She was America's first Giselle, but was also humorous enough to lend her talents to light entertainment, including a parody of the *Bayadère, The Maid of Cashmere* entitled *Buy It, Dear. 'Tis Made of Cashmere.*
98. *Philadelphia Inquirer*, December 10, 1852.
99. Augusta Maywood, autograph letter dated Vienna, March 31, 1855. Author's collection.
100. Gautier: "Mlle Elssler's smile . . ." in *Le Figaro*, October 19, 1837; and remarks on Carlotta Grisi in *La Presse*, March 2, 1840, and March 7, 1841.
101. Although Carlotta Grisi appeared at La Scala and at the Théâtre de la Renaissance as Mme Perrot, it has never been established that she was legally married to Jules Perrot.
102. Théophile Gautier remarks on *La Jolie Fille de Gand* in *La Presse*, July 2, 1842.
103. Gide, André: *Journal, 1889–1939*, La Pléiade, Paris, 1951, p. 511 (October 10, 1915). *Ibid.*, p. 714 (Feuillets, 1921).
104. Gautier: *The Romantic Ballet as seen by Théophile Gautier* (trans. Cyril Beaumont), p. 67.
105. Beaumont: *Op. cit.*, letter from Carlotta Grisi, p. 271.
106. Second: *Op. cit.*, p. 138.
107. Carlotta Grisi to Théophile Gautier, autograph letter dated November 22, 1864. Author's collection.
108. Levinson: *Op. cit.*, p. 79.
109. Gautier, Théophile: *Portraits Contemporains*, Charpentier, Paris, 1874, p. 375.
110. Since this extremely long letter concerns music as much as ballet and is signed "C.G.," we hazard a guess that the writer was Casimir Gide, the composer of *Le Diable boiteux, La Volière, La Tarentule*, etc.
111. Véron: *Op. cit.*, Vol. III, p. 222.
112. Katti Lanner, 1831–1908, was the daughter of the Austrian composer Joseph Lanner. She made her debut at the Kaernthner Thor while Elssler and Cerrito were there; in 1870 she appeared in *Giselle* in New York, and then settled in London, where she opened a ballet school, and also became a star, ballet mistress,

and choreographer at the Empire Theatre 1887–97. She was the connecting link in England between the Romantic ballet and the contemporary ballet, which Adeline Genée introduced.

Adeline Genée, 1878–1970, appeared in *Coppélia*, in 1896, in Munich, where she met Lucile Grahn. After dancing in Germany and at the Empire Theatre, London, and in Copenhagen, she traveled with her own company to the United States, Australia, and New Zealand, and then retired in 1914, in London. She became the founder-president of the Royal Academy of Dancing (1935–54), and was one of the greatest influences in promoting twentieth-century ballet in England.

113. Lifar: *Op. cit.*, p. 117.

114. De Boigne: *Op. cit.*, p. 345.

115. *Le Moniteur Universel*, November 1864.

This sad state of affairs also caused many twentieth-century dancers to Russianize their names in the belief that it would help them toward success, *i.e.*, Alice Marks, who became Alicia Markova; Patrick Healey-Kay, who was first Patrikeyev and later Anton Dolin; Hilda Munnings, famous as Lydia Sokolova; and many others.

116. Franz Hilferding, 1710–68, the galvanizing spirit of the eighteenth-century ballet in Vienna, as dancer, ballet master, and choreographer. Seconded by his disciple, Gaspare Angiolini, 1731–1803, he waged a war of prestige against Noverre, both of them claiming to have invented the *ballet d'action*. In Vienna, Angiolini was best known for his collaboration with Gluck; after Russia, he worked in Milan and again in Vienna.

Charles Le Picq, 1749–1806, favorite pupil of Noverre, appeared as a brilliant dancer in Stuttgart, Paris, and London. While in Russia with his wife Gertrude Le Picq, also a splendid dancer, he choreographed many ballets and also persuaded Alexander I to finance the most beautiful of all editions in the French language of Noverre's *Lettres sur la Danse*.

117. In St. Petersburg the Imperial Theatre was the Bolshoi, which means "big" in Russian. It opened on September 24, 1783; burned down, 1811; was rebuilt, 1812; closed, February 19, 1889. Its successor was the Maryinsky, built in 1860 and officially the Imperial Theatre from April 12, 1889. The Maryinsky was one of the most luxurious theatres in Europe. Under the Soviets its name was changed, in 1935, to the Kirov State Academic Theatre of Opera and Ballet.

Apart from the above, small theatres attached to the imperial palaces were used for gala occasions.

In Moscow the Bolshoi, also an Imperial Opera House, opened January 6, 1825. It burned down in 1853 and was rebuilt 1856 by Alverto Cavos, grandfather of Alexandre Benois.

118. Louis Antoine Duport, 1783–1853, the most celebrated dancer of his day. Rival of Auguste Vestris, who was twenty-three years older but persistently popular; their quarrel inspired Joseph Berchoux' book-length poem *La Danse ou les Dieux de l'Opéra*. After appearing in Russia nearly 150 times, Duport became director in Naples, where he met Barbaja, and, like him, became a director at the Kaernthner Thor, Vienna. He also choreographed several ballets.

119. ". . . like the Paris public," said Kschessinska, "who get impatient, stamp their

feet and shout in unison: *'Rideau! Rideau!'* " The spoiled Jockey Club members who dominated the audience were bored by opera and only arrived on time for the ballet which was always at the end of the program. Typical was their behavior at the première of *Tannhäuser* (March 13, 1861), when, in spite of the presence of the Emperor and Empress, they staged a near-riot because the ballet *divertissement* was insignificant besides being set in Act I. In Russia, on the other hand, the audience, mainly of court members, arrived very punctually, all the men remained standing until the Czar was seated and then, out of respect for him, stayed until he left.

120. Prior to the liberation of the serfs in 1806, many who were attached to large estates were trained as dancers and performed in ballets presented at private theatres. Some, such as those who belonged to Count Scheremetyev's company, were taught by masters as well known as Le Picq and became so proficient that they were purchased at the time of the liberation by the Imperial Theatres and continued as professional dancers.

121. Yrca Matthias, French dancer, born in Lyon, 1829; studied with Mazilier; first appeared in Moscow, 1847; married François Ravel and toured with his company in the United States, 1853–58.
Ekaterina Sankovskaia, 1816–78; entered the Moscow School in 1825, graduated 1836; danced *La Sylphide* in Moscow on the same day when Taglioni made her debut in the role in St. Petersburg. She was not pretty but was especially gifted as an actress and was much admired by Fanny Elssler. She also did choreography and taught, and she retired in 1854.
Praskovia Lebedeva, 1838–1917, graduated 1857, but made her debut two years earlier in *La Gitana*. In the Moscow tradition, she was an outstanding actress, admired by the visiting Carlo Blasis, and later was a success in St. Petersburg.
Anna Sobeshanskaia, 1842–1918, one of Moscow's outstanding dancers, who not only created the role of Kitri in *Don Quixote* but also appeared in the first version of *Swan Lake*, 1877, with Karpakova as Odile. A great future was predicted for her by Blasis. After retiring she became a teacher.

122. Contrary to André Levinson's opinion, this author has always considered Marie Taglioni to be as much an Italian ballerina as French. She was the product of three generations of Italian dancers, and she was taught by her father (himself Italian-trained) who utterly disapproved of the teaching she had received in France. In fact, when she appeared in Paris her style was the exact opposite of everything that was accepted there.

123. In addition to Beretta, Zucchi, Dell'Era, Bessone, Cornalba, Brianza, and Legnani, the dancers who came from La Scala included Maria Giuri, Adelina Rossi, Antonietta Bella, Giovannina Limido, and Enrichetta Grimaldi.

124. Paul Gerdt, 1844–1917, graduated from the School in 1864 and became one of Russia's greatest male dancers, appearing in 108 ballets. He was also one of the greatest teachers and was so handsome, tall, and blond, that many of his pupils were in love with him. He did not appear with Diaghilev's company in Paris although he was invited to do so, in spite of the fact that he was then fifty-six. His last appearance was as Gamache in *Don Quixote* in 1916 at the age of seventy-two.
Enrico Cecchetti, 1850–1928. His birth in a dressing room at the Tordinonia

Theatre, Rome, was symbolic: he devoted his whole life to the theatre and became the greatest and most beloved ballet master and teacher in the history of the dance. Studied with Lepri in Milan; danced in Milan and London, in St. Petersburg from 1887 to 1902, and was a guiding spirit of the Diaghilev Company. From 1923 until his death he was director of the School in Milan. teaching according to the now world-famous Cecchetti Method.

The role of the wicked fairy Carabosse, first performed by Cecchetti, is traditionally taken by a male dancer. Similarly, Frederick Ashton and Robert Helpmann took the roles of the Ugly Sisters in Ashton's *Cinderella*, London, 1948.

125. Mlle Legnani was the last of the so-called invasion of Italians, but when they had all left, Carlotta Zambelli arrived, 1901, for a series of seven guest appearances.

126. Fokine, Michel: *Memoirs of a Ballet Master*, Little, Brown & Company, Boston, 1961, p. 26.

127. Romanovsky-Krassinsky, Princess: *Souvenirs de la Kschessinska*, Plon, 1960, p. 81.

128. *Ibid.*, p. 78.

Bibliography

SEVENTEENTH AND EIGHTEENTH CENTURY

ANGIOLINI, GASPARE: *Dissertation sur les Ballets Pantomimes des Anciens*, Vienna, 1765.

ANON.: *Anecdotes Dramatiques*, 3 Vols., Paris, 1775.

ANON.: *Les Plaisirs de l'Ile Enchantée*, Imprimerie Royale, Paris, 1664.

ANON.: *Relation de la Feste de Versailles*, Imprimerie Royale, Paris, 1664.

ANON.: *Le Vol Plus Haut, ou l'Espion des Principaux Théâtres de la Capitale*, Paris, 1784.

ARGENS, MARQUIS D': *Mémoires*, Buisson, Paris, 1807.

ARGENSON, MARQUIS D': *Journal and Memoirs*, Caxton, London, 1901, 2 Vols.

BEAUJOYEULX, BALTASAR DE: *Balet Comique de la Royne*, Adrian le Roy, Robert Ballard, & Mamert Patisson, Paris, 1582.

BASCHET, ROGER: *Mademoiselle Dervieux, fille d'Opéra*, Flammarion, Paris, 1943.

BENSERADE, ISAAC DE: *Les Oeuvres de Monsieur de Bensserade*, 2 vols., Paris, 1698.

BONNET, JACQUES: *Histoire Générale de la Danse Sacrée et Prophane*, D'Houry fils, Paris, 1723.

CAHUSAC, LOUIS DE: *La Danse ancienne et moderne*, 3 Vols., Le Haye, Paris, 1754.

CAMPARDON, EMILE: *L'Académie Royale de Musique au XVIIIe Siècle*, 2 Vols., Berger-Levrault, Paris, 1884.

CAMPARDON, EMILE: *Les Comédiens du Roi de la Troupe Française*, Champion, Paris, 1879.

CAMPARDON, EMILE: *Les Comédiens du Roi de la Troupe Italienne*, 2 Vols., Berger-Levrault, Paris, 1880.

CAMPARDON, EMILE: *Documents Inédits sur J. B. Poquelin Molière*, Plon, Paris, 1871.

CAMPARDON, EMILE: *Les Spectacles de la Foire, depuis 1595 jusqu'à 1791*, 2 Vols., Berger-Levrault, Paris, 1877.

CAPON, GASTON: *Les Vestris*, Société du Mercure de France, Paris, 1908.

CAROSO, FABRITIO: *Nobilità di Dame (Il Ballarino)*, Venice, 1605.

CASANOVA DE SEINGELT, JACQUES: *Histoire de ma Vie*, 12 Vols., Plon, Paris, 1960.

CELLER, LUDOVIC: *Les Origines de l'Opéra et le Ballet de la Reine*, Didier, Paris, 1868.

COHEN, SELMA JEANNE; FLETCHER, IFAN KYRLE; LONSDALE, ROGER: *Famed for Dance: Essays on the Theory and Practice of Theoretical Dancing in England, 1660-1740*, The New York Public Library, New York, 1960.

COMPAN, CHARLES: *Dictionnaire de Danse*, 2 Vols., Cailleau, Paris, 1787.

COURVILLE, XAVIER DE: "Quinault, poète d'opéra" in *La Revue Musicale*, Numéro Spécial, Paris, January 1925.

DACIER, EMILE: *Les Dernières Années d'une Danseuse du XVIIIᵉ Siècle*, Société de l'Histoire de Paris, Paris, 1907.

DACIER, EMILE: *Mlle Sallé*, Plon, Paris, 1909.

DESPOIS, EUGÈNE: *Le Théâtre Français sous Louis XIV*, Hachette, Paris, 1874.

DESPRÉAUX, JEAN-ETIENNE: *Mes Passe-Temps*, Paris, 1806.

DESPRÈS DE BOISSY: *Lettres de M. Desp. de B—, Avocat au Parlement, sur les Spectacles*, Paris, 1771.

DOUGLAS, ROBERT B.: *Sophie Arnould*, Carrington, Paris, 1898.

DOUTREPONT, GEORGES: *Les Acteurs Masqués et Enfarinés du XVIᵉ au XVIIIᵉ Siècle en France*, Académie Royale de Belgique, Brussels, 1928.

DUFORT, GIAMBATISTA: *Trattato del Ballo Nobile*, Naples, 1728.

DUTHÉ, ROSALIE: *Souvenirs de Mlle Duthé de l'Opéra* (with introduction and notes by Paul Ginisty), Louis-Michaud, Paris, n.d.

FUNCK-BRENTANO, FRANZ: *Le Bastille des Comédiens, Le For l'Evêque*, Fontemoing, Paris, 1903.

GALLINI, GIOVANNI-ANDREA: *A Treatise on the Art of Dancing*, London, 1765.

GONCOURT, EDMOND DE: *La Guimard*, Flammarion-Fasquelle, Paris, 1893.

GONCOURT, EDMOND AND JULES DE: *Sophie Arnould*, Poulet-Malassis et de Broise, Paris, 1857.

GRIMM, BARON MELCHIOR VON: *Corréspondence Littéraire, Philosophique et Critique de Grimm et de Diderot*, 16 Vols., Furne, Paris, 1829.

JACQUOT, JEAN: *Les Fêtes de la Renaissance*, 2 Vols., Editions du Centre National de la Recherche Scientifique, Paris, 1956.

JULLIEN, ADOLPHE: *Amours d'Opéra au XVIIIᵉ Siècle*, Daragon, Paris, 1908.

JULLIEN, ADOLPHE: *La Comédie à la Cour*, Firmin-Didot, Paris, n.d.

JULLIEN, ADOLPHE: *La Cour et l'Opéra sous Louis XVI*, Didier, Paris, 1878.

JULLIEN, ADOLPHE: *L'Opéra Secret*, Rouveyre, Paris, 1880.

JULLIEN, ADOLPHE: *Un Potentat Musical, Papillon de la Ferté*, Détaille, Paris, 1876.

JULLIEN, ADOLPHE: *Les Spectateurs sur le Théâtre*, Détaille, Paris, 1875.

LA FERTÉ, PAPILLON DE: *Journal*, Ollendorff, Paris, 1887.

LA LAURENCIE, LIONEL DE: "L'Opéra français au XVIIe siècle: la musique" in *La Revue Musicale*, Numéro Spécial, Paris, January 1925.

LAUZE, F. DE: *Apologie de la Danse*, n.p., 1623.

LÉRIS, M. DE: *Dictionnaire Portatif Historique et Littéraire des Théâtres*, Jombert, Paris, 1763.

LETAINTURIER-FRADIN, GABRIEL: *La Camargo, 1710–1770*, Flammarion, Paris, 1908.

LETAINTURIER-FRADIN, GABRIEL: *La Maupin, 1670–1707*, Flammarion, Paris, 1904.

LEVINSON, ANDRÉ: "Les danseurs de Lully" in *La Revue Musicale*, Numéro Spécial, Paris, January 1925.

LIFAR, SERGE: *Auguste Vestris*, Nagel, Paris, 1950.

LYNHAM, DERYCK: *The Chevalier Noverre*, Sylvan Press, London, 1950.

MCGOWAN, MARGARET M.: *L'Art du Ballet de Cour en France, 1581–1643*, Centre National de la Recherche Scientifique, Paris, 1963.

MAGRI, GENNARO: *Trattato Teorico-Prattico di Ballo*, Orsino, Naples, 1779.

[MENESTRIER, L'ABBÉ C. F.]: *Des Ballets Anciens et Modernes selon les Règles du Théâtre*, Guignard, Paris, 1682.

[MENESTRIER, L'ABBÉ C. F.]: *Des Représentations en Musique Anciennes et Modernes*, Guignard, Paris, 1681.

MONNET, JEAN: *Mémoires de Jean Monnet, Directeur du Théâtre de la Foire* (with introduction and notes by Henri d'Alméras), Louis-Michaud, Paris, n.d.

MOORE, LILLIAN: *New York's First Ballet Season 1792*, The New York Public Library, New York, 1961.

NEGRI, CESARE: *Le Gratie d'Amore*, Milan, 1602.

NODOT: "Le Triomphe de Lully aux Champs-Elysées" in *La Revue Musicale*, Numéro Spécial, Paris, January 1925.

NOVERRE, CHARLES EDWIN: *The Life and Works of the Chevalier Noverre*, Jarrold and Sons, London, 1882.

NOVERRE, JEAN-GEORGES: *Lettres sur la Danse, et sur les Ballets*, Delaroche, Lyon, 1760.

NOVERRE, JEAN-GEORGES: *Lettres sur les Arts Imitateurs en Général et sur la Danse en Particulier*, Collin, Paris, 1807.

PAQUOT, MARCEL: *Les Etrangers dans les Divertissements de la Cour, de Beaujoyeulx à Molière (1581–1673)*, Brussels, 1932.

PARFAICT, FRANÇOIS AND CLAUDE: *Histoire du Théâtre François*, 15 Vols., Le Mercier-Saillant, Paris, 1745.

PARFAICT, FRANÇOIS AND CLAUDE: *Dictionnaire des Théâtres de Paris*, 7 Vols., Lambert, Paris, 1756.

POUGIN, ARTHUR: *Un Directeur d'Opéra au dix-huitième siècle*, Fischbacher, Paris, 1914.

PRUNIÈRES, HENRY: "L'Académie Royale de musique et de danse" in *La Revue Musicale*, Numéro Spécial, Paris, January 1925.

PRUNIÈRES, HENRY: *Le Ballet de Cour en France avant Benserade et Lully*, Henri Laurens, Paris, 1914.

PRUNIÈRES, HENRY: "Salvatore Viganò" in *La Revue Musicale*, Supplément, Paris, December 1921.

PRUNIÈRES, HENRY: *La Vie Illustre et Libertine de Jean-Baptiste Lully*, Plon, Paris, 1929.

RAMEAU, JEAN-PHILIPPE: *Le Maître à Danser*, Villette, Paris, 1725.

RITORNI, CARLO: *Vita ed Opere di Salvatore Viganò*, Milan, 1838.

SILIN, CHARLES I.: *Benserade and his Ballets de Cour*, Johns Hopkins Press, Baltimore, 1940.

SOLEIROL, H. A.: *Molière et sa Troupe*, Paris, 1858.

TESSIER, ANDRÉ: "Berain créateur du Pays d'Opéra" in *La Revue Musicale*, Numéro Spécial, Paris, January 1925.

[VALLIÈRE, LE DUC DE LA]: *Ballet, Opéra, et autres Ouvrages Lyriques*, Bauche, Paris, 1760.

VIÉVILLE, LECERF DE LA: "Vie de Lully" in *La Revue Musicale*, Numéro Spécial, Paris, January 1925.

WEAVER, JOHN: *Anatomical and Mechanical Lectures upon Dancing*, London, 1721.

WEAVER, JOHN: *An Essay towards an History of Dancing*, Jacob Tonson, London, 1712.

WEIGERT, ROGER-ARMAND: *Jean I Berain*, Les Editions d'Art et Histoire, Paris, 1937.

ROMANTIC AND POST-ROMANTIC PERIOD

ADAM, ADOLPHE: *Souvenirs d'un Musicien*, Lévy, Paris, 1857.

Album de l'Opéra, [Various Authors], Challamel, Paris, n.d.

ANON.: *Les Adieux à Mlle Taglioni*, Paris, 1837.

ANON.: *Les Belles Femmes de Paris*, Paris, 1839.

ANON.: *The Letters and Journal of Fanny Elssler*, New York, 1845.

ARAGO, JACQUES: *Mémoires d'un Petit Banc de l'Opéra*, Ebrard, Paris, 1844.

BARON, A.: *Lettres et Entretiens sur la Danse*, Dondey-Dupré, Paris, 1824.

BERLIOZ, HECTOR: *Evenings With the Orchestra*, translated and edited by Jacques Barzun, Alfred A. Knopf, New York, 1956.

BERLIOZ, HECTOR: *Memoirs*, translated and edited by David Cairns, Alfred A. Knopf, New York, 1969.

BINNEY, EDWIN, III: *Les Ballets de Théophile Gautier*, Librairie Nizet, Paris, 1965.

BLASIS, CARLO: *Notes Upon Dancing, Historical and Practical*, Delaporte, London, 1847.

BLASIS, CARLO: *The Code of Terpsichore*, London, 1830.

BLASIS, CARLO: *Traité Elémentaire, Théorique et Pratique de l'Art de la Danse*, Beati & Tenenti, Milan, 1820.

BLESSINGTON, LADY: *The Idler in France*, London, 1841.

BOIGNE, CHARLES DE: *Petits Mémoires de l'Opéra*, Librairie Nouvelle, Paris, 1857.

BOURNONVILLE, AUGUST: *Efterladte Skrifter*, Schous, Copenhagen, 1891.

BOURNONVILLE, AUGUST: *Lettres à la maison de son enfance*, Vol. 1, Munksgaard, Copenhagen, 1969.

BOURNONVILLE, AUGUST: *Mit Theaterliv*, Copenhagen, 1848, 1865, 1877.

BOURNONVILLE, CHARLOTTE: *Erindriger Fra Hjemmet og fra Scenen*, Gyldendal, Copenhagen, 1903.

BOUTERON, MARCEL: *Danse et Musique Romantiques*, Goupy, Paris, 1927.

BRUHN, ERIK AND MOORE, LILLIAN: *Bournonville and Ballet Technique*, Adam and Charles Black, London, 1961.

CASTIL-BLAZE: *L'Académie Impériale de Musique*, Paris, 1855.

CASTIL-BLAZE: *La Danse et les Ballets depuis Bacchus jusqu'à Mademoiselle Taglioni*, Poulin, Paris, 1832.

CROW, DUNCAN: *Henry Wikoff, The American Chevalier*, MacGibbon & Kee, London, 1963.

DELARUE, ALLISON: *The Chevalier Henry Wikoff*, Princeton University Press, Princeton, New Jersey, 1968.

EHRHARD, AUGUSTE: *Une Vie de Danseuse: Fanny Elssler*, Paris, 1909.

FELIX-BOUVIER: *Une Danseuse de l'Opéra: La Bigottini*, Paris, 1909.

FOURCAUD: *Léontine Beaugrand*, Ollendorff, Paris, 1881.

Galerie des Artistes Dramatique de Paris, [Various Authors], Marchant, Paris, 1841.

GAUTIER, T.; JANIN, J.; CHASLES, P.: *Les Beautés de l'Opéra*, Soulie, Paris, 1845.

GAUTIER, THÉOPHILE: *Théâtre, Mystère, Comédies et Ballets*, Charpentier, Paris, 1872.

GAUTIER, THÉOPHILE: *Portraits Contemporains*, Charpentier, Paris, 1874.

GAUTIER, THÉOPHILE: *Poésies, qui ne figueront pas dans ses oeuvres*, Paris, 1873.

GAUTIER, THÉOPHILE: *A History of Romanticism*, George D. Sproul, New York, 1902.

GAUTIER, THÉOPHILE: *Paris Besieged*, George D. Sproul, New York, 1902.

GAUTIER, THÉOPHILE: *The Romantic Ballet as seen by Théophile Gautier*, translated and published by Cyril Beaumont, London, 1947.

GUEST, IVOR: *Adeline Genée*, Adam and Charles Black, London, 1958.

GUEST, IVOR: *Fanny Cerrito*, Phoenix House, London, 1956.

GUEST, IVOR: *Fanny Elssler*, Adam and Charles Black, London, 1970.

GUEST, IVOR (editor): *La Fille mal gardée*, London, 1960.

GUEST, IVOR: *The Ballet of the Second Empire, 1858–1870*, Adam and Charles Black, London, 1953.

GUEST, IVOR: *The Empire Ballet*, Society for Theatre Research, London, 1962.

GUEST, IVOR: *The Romantic Ballet in England*, Phoenix House, London, 1954.

GUEST, IVOR: *The Romantic Ballet in Paris*, Wesleyan University Press, Middletown, Connecticut, 1966.

GUEST, IVOR: *Victorian Ballet-Girl*, Adam & Charles Black, London, 1957.

HEINE, HEINRICH: *Lutèce*, Paris, 1855.

HERVEY, CHARLES: *The Theatres of Paris*, John Mitchell, London, 1846.

LEATHERS, VICTOR: *British Entertainers in France*, University of Toronto Press, Canada, 1959.

LEVINSON, ANDRÉ: *Marie Taglioni*, Beaumont, London, 1930.

LEVINSON, ANDRÉ: "Théophile Gautier et le Ballet Romantique" in *La Revue Musicale*, Numéro Spécial, Paris, December 1921.

LIFAR, SERGE: *Carlotta Grisi*, Lehmann, London, 1947.

LIFAR, SERGE: *The Three Graces*, Cassell, London, 1959.

[LINDEN, ELISE]: *Fanny Elssler, Correspondence,* Ullstein, Berlin, 1921.

LUMLEY, BENJAMIN: *Reminiscences of the Opera,* Hurst & Blackett, London, 1864.

MAURICE, CHARLES: *Histoire Anecdotique du Théâtre,* 2 Vols., Plon, Paris, 1856.

MINNIGERODE, MEADE: *The Fabulous Forties,* Garden City Press, Garden City, New York, 1924.

MOGADOR, CÉLESTE: *Mémoires,* Locard-Davi and De Vresse, Paris, 1854.

MONALDI, GINO: *Le Regine della Danza,* Bocca, Turin, 1910.

MOORE, LILLIAN: "Mary Ann Lee, First American Giselle," in *Dance Index,* New York, Vol. II, No. 5, May 1943.

NEIIENDAM, ROBERT: *Lucile Grahn: en Skaebne i Dansen,* Copenhagen, 1963.

PIRCHAN, EMIL: *Fanny Elssler,* Wilhelm Frick, Vienna, 1940.

QUICHERAT, L.: *Adolphe Nourrit,* 3 Vols., Hachette, Paris, 1867.

ROQUEPLAN, NESTOR: *La Vie Parisienne,* Lévy, Paris, 1882.

ROQUEPLAN, NESTOR: *Les Coulisses de l'Opéra,* Paris, 1855.

SADLEIR, MICHAEL: *Blessington-D'Orsay,* Constable, London, 1933.

STERN, MADELEINE B.: *We the Women,* Schultz, New York, 1963, [chapter on Mary Ann Lee].

THÉLEUR, E. A.: *Letters on Dancing,* Sherwood, London, 1831.

→VAILLAT, LÉANDRE: *La Taglioni,* Michel, Paris, 1942.

→[VANDAM, ALBERT D.]: *An Englishman in Paris,* Appleton, New York, n.d.

VÉRON, DR. L.: *Mémoires d'un Bourgeois de Paris,* Librairie Nouvelle, 5 Vols., Paris, 1856.

WEMYSS, FRANCIS COURTNEY: *Twenty-Six Years of The Life of An Actor and Manager,* New York, 1847.

WIKOFF, HENRY: *The Reminiscences of an Idler,* Fords, Howard & Hubert, New York, 1880.

WINTER, MARIAN HANNAH: "Augusta Maywood," in *Dance Index,* New York, Vol. II, Nos. 1, 2, January-February 1943.

WINTER, MARIAN HANNAH: *Le Théâtre du Merveilleux,* Paris, 1962.

WYNDHAM, HORACE: *The Magnificent Montez,* London, 1935.

BALLET IN RUSSIA

BORISOGLEBSKY, M.: *Materials for a History of the Russian Ballet* (in Russian) 2 Vols., Leningrad, 1938.

BOWEN, CATHERINE DRINKER AND VON MECK, BARBARA: *Beloved Friend,* Random House, New York, 1937.

CELLI, VINCENZO: "Enrico Cecchetti," in *Dance Index,* New York, Vol. V, No. 7, July 1946.

CHUJOY, ANATOLE: "Russian Balletomania," in *Dance Index,* New York, Vol. VII, No. 3, March 1948.

CUSTINE, LE MARQUIS DE: *La Russie en 1839,* 4 Vols., Brussels, 1845.

FLORINSKY, MICHAEL T.: *Russia, A History and an Interpretation,* The Macmillan Company, New York, 1953.

FOKINE, MICHEL: *Memoirs of a Ballet Master,* translated by Vitale Fokine, Little, Brown, Boston, 1961.

FÜLÖP-MILLER, RENÉ AND GREGOR, JOSEPH: *Das russiche Theater*, Amalthea, Vienna, 1928.

KARSAVINA, TAMARA: *Theatre Street*, Constable, London, 1948.

LIFAR, SERGE: *A History of Russian Ballet*, Roy, New York, n.d.

MOOSER, R. ALOYS: *Opéras, Intermezzos, Ballets, Cantates, Oratorios, Joués en Russie durant le XVIIIᵉ Siècle*, Editions Bärenreiter, Basel, 1964.

ROMANOVSKY-KRASSINSKY, PRINCESS: *Souvenirs de la Kschessinska*, Plon, Paris, 1960.

ROSLAVLEVA, NATALIA: *Era of the Russian Ballet, 1770–1965*, Gollancz, London, 1966.

SLONIMSKY, YURY: "Jules Perrot," in *Dance Index*, New York, Vol. IV, No. 12, December 1945.

SLONIMSKY, YURY: "Marius Petipa," in *Dance Index*, New York, Vol. VI, No. 5, May-June 1947.

The Diaries of Tchaikovsky, translated and edited by Wladimir Lakond, W. W. Norton and Company, Inc., New York, 1945.

GENERAL REFERENCE

ACADÉMIE ROYALE DE MUSIQUE: *Chroniques.*

ANGELIS, ALBERTO DE: *Il Teatro Alibert o Delle Dame, 1717–1863*, Chicca, Tivoli, 1951.

ANON.: *L'Art du Ballet des Origines à Nos Jours*, Tambourinaire, Paris, 1952.

BARIL, JACQUES: *Dictionnaire de Danse*, Editions du Seuil, Paris, 1964.

BEAUMONT, CYRIL W.: *Complete Book of Ballets*, Grosset & Dunlap, New York, 1938.

BEETZ, DR. WILHELM: *Das Wiener Opernhaus*, Panorama, Zurich, 1949.

BERCZELI, ELISABETH AND HANKISS, ELEMÉR: *Bibliographie der in Ungarn Erschienen Theater Kalender*, Nationalbibliothek, Budapest, 1961.

BROWN, T. ALLSTON: *A History of the New York Stage*, Dodd, Mead, New York, 1903.

BUNN, ALFRED: *The Stage*, Bentley, London, 1840.

CAMBIASI, POMPEO: *La Scala 1778–1889*, Ricordi, Milan, 1888.

CAMETTI, ALBERTO: *Il Teatro di Tordinona poi di Apollo*, 2 Vols., Chicca, Tivoli, 1938.

D'ARONCO, GIANFRANCO: *Storia della Danza Popolare e d'Arte con Particolare Riferimiento all'Italia*, Olschki, Florence, 1962.

DESARBRES, NÉREÉ: *Deux Siècles à l'Opéra*, Dentu, Paris, 1868.

FOG, DAN: *The Royal Danish Ballet, 1760–1950, and August Bournonville*, Fog, Copenhagen, 1961.

Grove's Dictionary of Music and Musicians, 5 Vols., The Macmillan Company, New York, 1939.

GUEST, IVOR: *The Dancer's Heritage*, Adam and Charles Black, London, 1960.

IRELAND, JOSEPH N.: *Records of the New York Stage*, T. H. Morell, New York, 1866.

KAPP, DR. JULIUS: *185 Jahre Staatsoper*, Atlantic, Berlin, 1928.

KIRSTEIN, LINCOLN: *Dance*, G. P. Putnam's Sons, New York, 1935.

KOCHNO, BORIS: *Le Ballet*, Hachette, Paris, 1954.

KRAGH-JACOBSON, SVEND AND KROGH, TORBEN: *Den Kongelige Danske Ballet*, Copenhagen, 1953.

LOTHAR, RUDOLPH AND STERN, JULIUS: *50 Jahre Hoftheater, Geschichte beiden Weiner Hoftheater*, Expedition, Vienna, 1900.

MAGRIEL, PAUL: *A Bibliography of Dancing*, Blom, New York, 1967.

MILLE, AGNES DE: *The Book of the Dance*, Golden Press, New York, 1963.

MOORE, LILLIAN: *Images of the Dance, Historical Treasures of the Dance Collection 1581–1861*, The New York Public Library, New York, 1965.

ODELL, GEORGE C. D.: *Annals of the New York Stage*, Columbia University Press, New York, 1928.

PHELPS, H. P.: *Players of a Century*, McDonough, Albany, 1880.

POUGUIN, ARTHUR: *Acteurs et Actrices d'Autrefois*, Juven, Paris, n.d.

REYNA, FERDINANDO: *Des Origines du Ballet*, Tallone, Paris, 1955.

ROOTZÉN, KAJSA: *Den Svenska Baletten*, Wahlström and Widstrand, Stockholm, 1945.

ROYER, ALPHONSE: *Histoire de l'Opéra*, Bachelin-Deflorenne, Paris, 1875.

SMITH, WILLIAM C.: *The Italian Opera and Contemporary Ballet in London 1789–1820*, The Society for Theatre Research, London, 1955.

SORIA, HENRI DE: *Histoire Pittoresque de la Danse*, H. Noble, Paris, 1897.

STOREY, ALAN: *Arabesques*, Newman Wolsey, London, 1948.

Survey of London, edited by F. H. W. Sheppard, Vol. XXXV, The Athlene Press, London, 1970.

Teatro di San Carlo [Various Authors], Teatro di San Carlo, Naples, 1948.

The Dance Encyclopedia [edited by Anatole Chujoy and P. W. Manchester], Simon and Schuster, New York, 1967.

The London Stage: 11 Vols., Southern Illinois University Press, Carbondale, 1965.

VAILLAT, LÉANDRE: *Histoire de la Danse*, Plon, Paris, 1942.

VUILLERMOZ, G.: *Cent Ans d'Opéra à Lyon*, Bascou, Paris, n.d.

VUILLIER, GASTON: *La Danse*, Hachette, Paris, 1898.

X.Y.Z.: *Le Nouvel Opéra*, Lévy, Paris, 1875.

PERIODICALS AND NEWSPAPERS

AUSTRIA (Vienna) Allgemeine Wiener Musik-Zeitung; Blätter für Musik, Theater und Kunst; Monatsschrift für Theater und Musik; Neue Wiener Musik-Zeitung; Neue Wiener Theater-Signale; Oesterreichische Theater Zeitung; Wiener Allgemeine Theater Zeitung; Wiener Theater-Chronik; Der Zwischenakt.

ENGLAND (London) Le Courrier de l'Europe; Era; The Examiner; The Globe; The Morning Post; The Old Whig; The Satirist; The Theatrical Journal; The Theatre; The Times.

FRANCE (Paris) L'Annuaire des Lettres, des Arts et des Théâtres; L'Artiste; L'Audience; La Chronique Artistique et Littéraire; Les Chroniqueurs Parisiens; La Colonne; Le Constitutionnel; Le Corsair; Le Courrier Musical; Le Courrier de Paris; Courrier des Théâtres; L'Echo du Foyer; L'Echo Musical; L'Entr'acte; L'Europe Artiste; Le Figaro; La

France Littéraire; La France Musicale; Le Frondeur Musical; La Gazette du Progrès; La Gazette des Tribunaux; L'Illustration; Journal des Débats; Journal de Paris; Journal des Théâtres; Longchamps; Le Ménestrel; Le Monde Dramatique; Le Moniteur; Le Pont-Neuf; La Presse; La Revue des Deux Mondes; La Revue du XIX Siècle; La Revue Anecdotique; Revue et Gazette Musicale; Revue Franco-Italienne; Revue et Gazette des Théâtres; La Revue de Paris; Le Sabat Musical; Le Siècle; Tribune Dramatique; L'Univers Musical; La Verité pour Tous. (Lyon) L'Artiste en Province; Le Lyonnais. (Marseille) L'Asmodée Marseillais; Le Sud.

IRELAND (Dublin) Dublin Evening Mail; Dublin Evening Post; Freeman's Journal.

ITALY (Bologna) L'Harpa; Teatri, Arti e Letteratura. (Milan) Almanacco—Teatro alla Scala. (Naples) Omnibus. (Viterbo) Il Messagero; Viterbo Oggi. Turin: *Il Trovatore*. Argo; L'Arlecchino; La Gazzetta Musicale; I Teatri.

PORTUGAL (Lisbon) O Echo dos Theatros; O Espectador; O Raio Theatral; Revista Theatral; A Revista dos Theatros; Revista Universal Lisbonense.

SPAIN (Madrid) El Pasatiempo; Revista de Teatros.

UNITED STATES (Boston) The Boston Globe. (New York) Courrier des Etats-Unis; The Knickerbocker Magazine; The Morning Herald; The New York Clipper; The New York Courier and Enquirer; The New York Evening Post; The New York Mirror; Spirit of the Times. (Philadelphia) National Gazette and Literary Register; Philadelphia Inquirer; Poulson's American Daily Advertizer; Public Ledger; The Saturday Courrier. (Washington, D.C.) The Globe.

Index